AN INTRODUCTION TO
THE BIBLE

BY STANLEY COOK

AN INTRODUCTION TO

THE BIBLE

BY

STANLEY COOK

GREENWOOD PRESS, PUBLISHERS
WESTPORT, CONNECTICUT

Library of Congress Cataloging in Publication Data

Cook, Stanley Arthur, 1873-1949.
  An introduction to the Bible.

    Reprint of the 1945 ed. published by Penguin
Books, Harmondsworth, Eng., New York.
    Bibliography: p.
    Includes index.
    1. Bible--Introductions.   I. Title.
BS475.C653 1979   220.6   78-12762
ISBN 0-313-21028-4

First published 1945 by Penguin Books

Reprinted with the permission of Penguin Books, Ltd.

Reprinted in 1979 by Greenwood Press, Inc.,
51 Riverside Avenue, Westport, CT 06880

Printed in the United States of America

10 9 8 7 6 5 4 3 2 1

CONTENTS

PREFACE

THE Bible is the Sacred Book of Christianity. It grew up
in the course of some profound transitions in history and
religion, and its path in both ancient and medieval times
has been marked by suffering, persecution and martyrdom.
The unique part it has played in directing and framing
the thought of the West is often forgotten, and it remains
perhaps the most misunderstood of books of the world's
literature. To-day, biblical criticism, the comparative
study of religions, the recovery of much of the ancient
past, the increase of knowledge, and current conditions of
life and thought combine to make the Bible a book to be
read, not merely for its devotional value or for its literary
value, but as one that still has a meaning not less vital than
it has hitherto possessed.

In *The Rebirth of Christianity* (Pelican Books), to which the
present sketch is a companion volume, I was more concerned
with the restatement of our religion, and only a few pages
were devoted to the Bible. Here the endeavour is made to
give a very general introduction to the Bible including the
Apocrypha. A brief outline of the English Bible (ch. i.)
is followed by a digression on other sacred lore, indicating
some of the topics prominent in other great historical
religions and illustrating the background upon which the
Bible is now placed (ch. ii.), a short account of the growth
of the Bible, the canon, text and interpretation (ch. iii.),
leads to a rapid survey of the books of the Bible and
the Apocrypha (chh. iv. and v.). A fuller chapter deals
with the phraseology, and more particularly with the main
ideas which serve to interrelate the canonical, apocryphal
and apocalyptic writings (ch. vi.) A chapter, perhaps a
rather novel one to many readers, on Jerusalem and Mt.
Zion, strengthens this interrelation (ch. vii.). Both chapters
bring out the striking differences between the general unity

and continuity which appears on the surface and the traces of a religion and history which raise some fundamental biblical problems. These, however, could be only very briefly sketched (ch. viii.). Two concluding chapters offer remarks on our approach to the Bible, urging that with all our advances in scientific and other knowledge the Bible remains, as before, the Word of God. Chh. i–x., complete in their present form by January, 1944, are supplemented by an Epilogue on the bearing of the Bible upon the present situation.

In the desire to be as full as space permitted it has often been necessary to multiply the biblical references. Though important for the serious reader, they are apt to disturb those who prefer—at least to start with—a less broken text. Hence, where convenient, these have been placed by themselves independent of the footnotes, and a word of thanks is due to the printers for overcoming the technical and other difficulties involved.

The biblical references are made to the R.V., and an edition with marginal notes and references is strongly recommended. The usual abbreviations to the A.V., R.V., etc., and to the books of the Bible will be found in the Index. For the divine name Jehovah the form Yahweh has been preferred. In an objective statement such as is aimed at in these pages it seemed better to use what is probably the original form than one which strictly speaking is incorrect and among Christians has religious associations other than those at times met with in the O.T.

It remains for me to express my indebtedness to my friend, the Rev. W. F. Flemington, M.A., Tutor of Wesley House, Cambridge, for kindly reading chh. i–x. in typescript, and for making many suggestions. But for the various views and conclusions in this sketch I am solely responsible.

STANLEY COOK

CAMBRIDGE, *January* 1945.

CHAPTER I

THE ENGLISH BIBLE

THE Bible has been fittingly described as ' the most majestic thing in our literature and the most spiritually living thing we inherit '. The story of its growth, of its interpretation and of the way it became a popular possession is a stirring one: the path has been marked by conflict, persecution and martyrdom. But to-day it is perhaps one of the least understood and most misunderstood of books. It is a book of Eastern origin, the greatest of Eastern classics, representing long-past modes of life and thought very different from those of the West. None the less, it has established itself as one of the finest achievements in our language, entering into the hearts of our fathers, and in-fluencing their hopes, their actions and their writings more deeply than any other book. But the Bible comes from the East; even its name takes us there.

Round about the twelfth century B.C. an Egyptian envoy, Wen-Amon by name, visited the king of the Phoenician town of Byblus. At the advice of one of his prophets he was received by the king, who took occasion to admit very freely the superior culture of Egypt, a debt which archaeology and excavation have since abundantly illus-trated. Now, Byblus, to-day the small village of Gebal, was one of the oldest cities of Syria and Palestine. It had long been in close contact with Egypt and, as a trading centre, among the articles of import it included papyrus, a word possibly of Egyptian origin, whence through the Latin comes the word ' paper '. (We may recall that ' parchment ' is derived from Pergamum or Pergamos in Asia Minor, mentioned in Rev. i. 11.) From Byblus the Greeks called papyrus *bublos* or *biblos*; and from the plural of the diminutive *biblion* is derived our word Bible, properly ' (the) books '. In Latin the word was subse-quently treated as a feminine singular, and Old English spellings *bibul, bibil*, etc., date from the fourteenth century

A.D. If Eastern, Greek and Roman factors thus account for the name, so also do they combine to give the Bible the meaning it has for us. On the other hand, the Old and New ' Testaments ' owe their title to the Latin translation of the old and new ' covenants ' between God and his people (cf. 2 Cor. iii. 6, 14; Heb. ix. 15), and the rendering illustrates the subtle change that can ensue when significant terms and ideas are translated from one language into another.

Christianity in England dates properly from St. Augustine in 597 A.D., although at the Synod of Arles in A.D. 314 three English bishops had been present, while earlier, about A.D. 303, St. Alban was martyred at the place which bears his name. Latin long continued to be the official ecclesiastical language, but paraphrases of parts of the Bible in the native Anglo-Saxon language of the people appear to date from about 680. Of the various translations of parts of it, the most important are Caedmon's ' Song of Creation,' and the Fourth Gospel by the Venerable Bede (d. 735). Passing over the work of Alfred, one of the greatest of early English kings, and other paraphrasers and translators, we enter a new era with John Wycliffe and his followers, who, in an age of revived interest in religion, succeeded in spite of opposition and persecution in publishing the first copy of the whole Bible in English; it was translated from the Latin (1382–8). The invention of printing (1454) and access to MSS. in the original languages (Hebrew and Greek) mark the next stage in the history of the Bible, and the chief events are Tindale's translation from the original Hebrew and Greek (1525–34) and the ' Great Bible ' of Coverdale (1535–41), whose Psalter survives in the Prayer Book. The Bible was now to be read in the churches: ' one boke of the whole Bible of the largest volume in Englyshe '; and the Book ' whyche ys the verye lively worde of God ' was eagerly accepted by the people. So, in the sixteenth century the candle was lit which—to adapt the words of the martyr Latimer (1555)—by God's grace in England shall never be put out.

The modern stage of the Bible begins with the Authorized Version of 1611, made by leading scholars of the Reformed

Church. They went direct to the original languages, but freely utilized earlier English translations; nine-tenths of the A.V. New Testáment is Tindale's. They lived in an age of remarkable growth in English literature—the dramatists Marlowe and Shakespeare, the poet Spenser, and the ecclesiastic Richard Hooker, the author of what has been styled ' the first independent work in English prose of notable power and genius '. The A.V. has more than held its own, in spite of the R.V. (Revised Version), which, first undertaken in 1870, was published in 1881–5. The latter is based upon a superior knowledge of the original languages and access to far better MSS. Its translation of the Hebrew O.T. is a very considerable improvement upon the A.V., whereas the N.T., although to be preferred to the A.V., departed from the long-familiar wording in a way that, however justifiable in view of modern knowledge, aroused controversy among scholars and dis-satisfaction among ordinary readers. There is much to be said for both versions, and we may agree with Sir Frederic Kenyon when he sums up his estimate with the words: ' Both are now essential parts of our heritage; and the final verdict must be: the Revised for study, the Authorized for reading '. [1]

The A.V. was made in the age of the Renaissance and the Protestant Reformation. The Fall of Constantinople had opened up new stores of learning. The invention of print-ing, ocean voyages, the discovery of America, and the epoch-making announcement of Copernicus (A.D. 1530) that the earth and the planets revolve round the sun, are among the events that went to create a New World, a new know-ledge of the Universe, and a new acquaintance with the past. Interest in the O.T. was heightened by intercourse with the Jews and their traditions; and Jewish exegesis

---

[1] *Our Bible and the Ancient Manuscripts* (4th ed., 1939), p. 244. Kenyon also gives a list of the chief variations between the A.V. and R.V. of the N.T. (p. 239), and some notable variations from the readings adopted in the A.V. to be found in the best MSS. (pp. 17, 247 ff.). On the ' Variorum Bible ', see below, p. 44. Sir Arthur Quiller-Couch (*On the Art of Writing*, pp. 113 ff.) contrasts the intelligibility of Is. ix. 1–7 in the R.V. with the obscurity of the A.V., and admits after a prolonged comparison of the two versions in general his preference for the R.V.

has left abundant traces upon both the English A.V. and Luther's German translation. Moreover, the Spanish Armada had been defeated. Men felt their kinship with the Israel of old. The language of prophets and psalmists, even events in Israelite history, clothed feelings of vocation and destiny, and made the atmosphere of the O.T. familiar. The Bible influenced ideas of authority and rule, and of social and political relations; it inspired movements both reforming and rebellious. The simplicity of the A.V., its earnestness and dignity, its concrete and picturesque phraseology, made it appeal to the most untutored of men as to the skilled. It inspired Milton's *Paradise Lost* and Bunyan's *Pilgrim's Progress*, and the influence of even these can scarcely be calculated. There was a bond between those of old to whom we owe the Bible and those who in their turn became, like Israel, the ' People of the Book '.

The A.V. became part of English literature and left its imprint in a thousand ways upon English idiom and usage— *e.g.*, Tarry at Jericho till your beards grow, Adullamites, safe and sound, old wives' tales, pride goeth before a fall, and perhaps jerry-built houses (cf. the walls of Jericho, Josh. vi. 20). There grew up a profound affection for the Bible—but it was one that could also be purely sentimental, misguided and misleading. The great evangelist Spurgeon is reported to have said in one of his widely-read sermons: ' The Bible is in every house, but in many the dust on it is so thick that you might write on it *Damnation* '. And from America comes the story of the barrister who asserted ' Skin for skin, yea, all that a man hath will he give for his life ', observing with great unction that we have this utterance on the ' highest authority '. But it was pointed out the next day by a newspaper that as the words were spoken by Satan (Job ii. 4), ' we know now whom the barrister considered to be of the highest authority '. Bibliolatry and unreflecting reverence are not dead; and even in 1920 the first volume of the study of Acts in *The Beginnings of Christianity* by Foakes Jackson and Lake provoked a certain amount of criticism, mainly on account of what appeared to some the way a book of Holy Scripture was being approached in a thoroughly scientific spirit.

If the events of the fifteenth and sixteenth centuries shattered the medieval view of the world, to-day we live in another world, or rather, another world is opening out. If the religious revolution in Western Europe seems to have been catastrophic, the beginning of a fateful secularism, rather was it the adolescence of the West, an area whose history, compared with that of the ancient civilizations, is still relatively young. Whereas the Bible had been the authoritative basis of medieval culture, now the Bible and the lands amid which it grew up belong to the subject-matter of many branches of research. The study of the Bible involves some fourteen or more centuries of ancient history: it enters into studies of myth and legend, religion, custom and law, prehistoric man and ancient history, archae-ology and the monuments, anthropology and sociology, primitive and scientific ideas of the universe, men's thoughts about things, and the validity both of their ways of thinking and of our own. The Church can no longer be said to direct and control biblical teaching as once it did. Archaic phrases in the Bible, the strangeness of certain theological terms, the absence of that background of life and thought which would give context and meaning to any discussion of the Bible and Christianity—these are among the factors that sever laymen and scholars, and members of each of the two classes among themselves.

Accordingly, the Bible has a three-fold value, (1) as the basis of Christianity, (2) as literature of the noblest rank, and (3) as a most important source for diverse branches of ' secular ' research. It has had an enormous sale. It has been translated (whole or in part) into some 1000 languages and dialects, and the relevant literature is immense.[1] The Bible appeals to our private judgment, and it can be used—or misused—to prove too much. Everyone has sought his own ideas and found their confirmation: pacifism or mili-tarism, slavery or anti-slavery, teetotalism and prohibition or moderation, spiritism or the cruelty of the old witch-

[1] See *The Bible Throughout the World: A Survey of Scripture Translations*, by R. Kilgour (1939). In the British Museum *General Catalogue of Printed Books* (1936), out of thirty-six volumes for A–Chic, the Bible alone fills three, running into 2740 columns.

hunt, liberty or paternal rule, rebellion or submission to authority, ecclesiasticism or freedom of ministry. An untrained generation has sprung up, and fundamental questions—*e.g.*, of Inspiration and Revelation—demand a fresh answer. But excessive individualism breeds extreme subjectivity; the necessity of more unifying, harmonizing and integrating attitudes is keenly felt. The steps to the required objectivity are, however, in the making.

Critical or scientific research is giving the Bible a new meaning; the very ' criticism ' of the Bible which so often seems destructive is proving constructive. Every intelligent reader of the Bible is in some sense a ' critic ', and the rather misleading terms ' critic ' and ' criticism '—which have established themselves—are not to be understood in any derogatory sense, implying a captious or fault-finding spirit. ' All criticism ', it has been said, ' is really an application of the principles of common-sense by a person provided with the requisite knowledge of facts.' Sincerity, competence, a refusal to settle particular questions in isolation, and a patient seeking after the truth are the armoury of the discipline of Biblical Study.

These brief introductory paragraphs on the English Bible may be supplemented by a short account of other ' Bibles ' or Sacred Writings outside Christianity before we proceed to a further account of the growth of the Bible and of its interpretation.

CHAPTER II

OTHER BIBLES AND SACRED WRITINGS

THE Comparative Study of Religion has familiarized us with Bibles and sacred writings other than our own. In addition to the written material, we must include the un-written myths,[1] legends and sacred lore, as well as the cults and practices. All are authoritative, and usually have the value for their peoples that our Bible has for us. Much has been written on the subject,[2] and is readily accessible; it must suffice, therefore, (1) to specify some of the material, and (2) more especially to notice some of the facts to be borne in mind when we resume our account of our own Sacred Book.

1. Sacred Lore

Of the writings to be mentioned, the first place must be given to those of INDIA, whose religious history is con-tinuous, going back to the fifteenth century B.C. From this period dates the Rig-Veda (' pre-eminent knowledge '), with more than a thousand hymns in ten books. These are of different origin and the result of a lengthy develop-ment of religion. They are still an outstanding authority; indeed, they inspired the reforming nationalist movement, the Arya-Samaj (the ' Society of the Aryans '), founded in the last century with the slogan ' back to the Vedas '. The Rig-Veda contains hymns of praise to the leading deities and to nature-powers, who are treated as personal—e.g., the powerful and popular Agni (' fire ', cf. Latin Ignis), Mitra, the sun-god, guardian of treaties and of the domestic hearth,[3] and Indra, the beneficent national and fighting god. The most noteworthy is Varuna, the ethical sky-god, all-

---

[1] The term ' myth ' is used in these pages in no derogatory sense whatever.

[2] A. C. Bouquet, *Man and Deity* (1933) and *Comparative Religion* (Pelican Books, 1941), may be recommended. See further the Biblio-graphy on p. 217.

[3] He is the Mithras, the great rival of Christ in the early Christian centuries; see p. 150.

seeing, punisher of evil, the guardian of the order of the cosmos, nature and man.[1] In spite of the great antiquity of the Rig-Veda, the hymns represent the fruits of much early and deep reflection; but they also contain magical spells for protection against hostile powers, enemies and demons.

Later are the Brāhmaṇas, which illustrate the efficacy of the sacred word and ritual in the hands of the ' human gods ', the priests, and their control of nature and man by sacrificial rites, prayers, chants and charms. The Upanishads, from about the sixth century B.C., are more mystical. There are two leading ideas: (1) *Karma*, the inevitable result of man's good and bad deeds, and (2) reincarnation, an endless succession of rebirths such that a man's life depends on his previous existence on earth. This miserable round of births could, however, be avoided by realizing through renunciation and extreme asceticism the union of the ultimate Self in and behind every man (the Ātman) and the Brahmā, the ultimate Self or Essence of the Cosmos.

Next are two lengthy composite works dating from before the Christian era: (*a*) the Rāmāyana, which contains the story of the trials of Rāma and his faithful wife Sītā, and the victory of purity and fidelity over temptation and suffering. This, the most popular of all Indian tales, has been revised and supplemented to make it a veritable handbook of religion. (*b*) The Mahābharata, an immense work dealing with the more personal deities (Vishnu, Krishna, etc.), and especially noteworthy for a later addition, the Bhagavadgītā (the ' lord's song '). The latter is perhaps of about A.D. 100, and for its spiritual warmth and devotion to Krishna testifies—it has even been said—to a mind naturally Christian.

Indian religion as a whole includes the richest variety of belief, ranging from crude forms of animism and magic to the loving devotion (Bhakti) which plays a great part in personal religion, and to the profoundest meditation and speculation upon the mysteries of God, man and the

---

[1] Varuna, Mitra and Indra were known in North Syria about 1400 B.C., and to some extent probably also in Palestine. See the writer's *The ' Truth ' of the Bible*, pp. 62, 68.

universe. Its most characteristic feature is its other-worldness: the fleeting and illusory nature of this world, the overwhelming reality of the unseen power or principle behind it, and the longing for escape into a state which rises superior to man's fate in a land of extreme heat and of disastrous storms.

BUDDHISM, like Islam and Christianity, has a personal Founder, and more than any other religion is closely related to the last-mentioned. The Buddha or ' enlightened ' one (a title like Christ, ' anointed ' one) was Siddhārtha Gautama. He lived about 560–480 B.C., in an age of widespread religious activity of an individualist rather than a nationalist type. He renounced wife, child and all earthly ties in his search for deliverance from the world's sorrows and pains. Like Jesus he was tempted, and the traditions of his person and his miracles, and the vicissitudes of Buddhism in the East are of the greatest interest on account of the points of resemblance with the growth of Christianity in the West. Buddha was a remarkable teacher. The ' Blessed one ', as he was called, would have every disciple ' a lamp unto himself '. His teaching was of the simplest. He enunciated the Four Noble Truths or Certainties: suffering, its cause, the removal of the cause, and the method to be adopted. This was the Eightfold Noble Path: right belief, resolution, speech, conduct, means of livelihood, endeavour, reflection and concentration. Buddhism was both a monastic and a missionary religion, appealing not so much to the poor and simple as to individuals who sought escape from the iron law of cause and effect, of transmigration and rebirth. For the newborn inherits his fate from his predecessor, somewhat as the events of the ' New ' Year cannot escape the consequences of the events in the ' Old ' Year that ' dies '; and just as the Old Year has gone for ever, so the individual has gone, though his general character is transmitted to the one who is reborn. In other words, a man is the fruit of his former thoughts and deeds although he is not conscious of any continuity with his past.

The early Buddhist writings dealt with the rules of the Order, dialogues exemplifying Buddha's teaching, and stories of his previous births. The Canon was fixed about 250 B.C. It is about twice the length of our Bible, and consists of the 'Three Baskets' (the Tripitaka). There are also other works; and as Buddhism spread there grew up divisions and sects and a great variety of grades of belief and speculation. The original Hīnayana, or Little Vehicle, was primarily non-theistic and non-speculative, but as the religion spread among the masses, it became more 'catholic', more in touch with popular needs. This is the 'Mahāyana', or Great Vehicle; it has a heaven and hell, good and bad spirits, and a theology and philosophy to match. One of the most attractive features is the ideal of imitating Buddha in order to save men, of aiming, not at delivering oneself from rebirth, but at saving others. There are also merciful gods and goddesses (e.g., Amitābha, Kuan-yin) who do for toiling and suffering men what neither theology nor philosophy can achieve. Of Amitābha (or Amida) it has been said that he 'had no historical existence, but is a personification of the spirit of saving renunciation . . .' And as for Buddha, 'unless he had been man, we should never have had his system or his influence, unless he had been conceived as more than man, we should never have had his religion'.[1]

CHINA lays claim to the oldest continuous culture, one extending over forty centuries. Apart from the popular religion with all the animistic and superstitious beliefs and practices that are common everywhere, the cult of ancestors is its most characteristic feature. Confucius (551–478 B.C.) is the founder of the state-religion, or rather of the ethical and moral principles of social and political well-being which distinguish a country that is a living example of the familiar injunction: 'Honour thy father and mother that thy days may be long upon the land which the Lord thy God giveth thee' (Exod. xx. 12).

With Confucius are associated the five Canonical Books (King) and the four Classics (Shu), which for their antiquity and wisdom have since been authoritative, though they

---

[1] The quotations are respectively from Streeter, *The Buddha and the Christ* (1932), p. 91, and A. M. Fairbairn, *The Philosophy of the Christian Religion* (1902), p. 276.

are not regarded as inspired. The former contain annals, traditions, songs, rites and ceremonies; the latter, the teaching of Confucius and his great successors (notably Mencius). On the other hand, his older contemporary, Lao-tse, opened the way for supernaturalism, polytheism and polydemonism, mystical communion and an abstruse philosophy. Fundamental is the conception of Tao, or Way, the cosmic order to which heaven itself is subordinate. Man must live in harmony with it and conform to it, and by passive surrender to it attain peace. Herein it recalls, more than does Confucianism, the characteristics of Indian religion, and especially of Buddhism.

Buddhism, with its numerous sects, became the one great positive religion in China and Japan, for of JAPAN the only indigenous religion is Shinto ('the way of the gods') with its myths and legends, its fusion of conduct and ceremonial, and its characteristic Emperor-cult, the Mikado tracing his ancestry back to the Sun-goddess Ama-terasu.

More relevant for our purpose is ZOROASTRIANISM, the religion of ancient Persia. Spitāma Zarathushtra (Zoroaster) probably lived about 600 B.C. He was the reformer of a much older religion which had been in contact with both Mesopotamia and India, even as his religion influenced that of Palestine later when the Jews were part of the Persian Empire (after 539 B.C.). He was inspired by Ahura Mazdā (the ' Wise Lord '), the sole creator, the first and last, one who brooks no rival, who sees the secret deeds of man and knows all things. Ahura Mazdā is a distinctly ethical god, and his attributes are to be copied by men. There is conflict between Truth and Lie, and every man reaps the reward of his choice in the judgment after death.

As the religion spread it absorbed many older and popular features adapted to a peaceful agricultural people beset by hostile neighbours. Opposed to Ahura Mazdā is Ahriman, the creator of all that is evil; but men are fortified by belief in a coming kingdom and saviours (*saoshyants*) who shall bring in righteousness. This and the belief in numerous angels and protecting spirits are among the many interesting constituents of a religion that once played a great part in the history of religion, but is now represented only by the Parsees of Bombay. The sacred book of Zoroastrianism is the Avesta, compiled and canonized round about A.D. 300; but a portion of it (the Gāthās) may go back even to the founder. The later part, the Vendidād, contains myths and ritual, and laws and spells relating to ceremonial purification; it is more priestly than ethical.

ISLĀM (' submission ') is the third Semitic Monotheism, the other two being Judaism and Christianity. Like these, it is the Religion of a Book, and, like the latter and Buddhism, it owes itself to a single founder. It dates its era from A.D. 622, and, though essentially Arabian, manifests the influence of Jews and Christians. Its founder, Mohammed (A.D. 570–632), was born at Mecca, and, as his Qurān or Koran (' recitation ') well illustrates, he was a strange blend of extremes, and no deliberate or sustained thinker. The Koran is a collection of 114 Sūras or chapters of uneven length which were revealed on different occasions by Allah (Al-Ilah, ' the God '). ' There is no God but Allah, and Mohammed is his messenger (or apostle) '—this is its keynote; and Islām is a rigorous monotheism, a ' white-hot ' religion it has been styled. Allah is a majestic and transcendent sovereign, all-powerful, autocratic and absolute, but he is also compassionate and merciful, and needs no mediator. Islām acknowledges Judaism and Christianity; Adam, Noah, Abraham, Moses and Jesus (who is regarded as the only sinless man), were exalted intercessors, but Mohammed supersedes them all and is the final prophet. Islām is a simple religion with crude anthropic conceptions of Allah and with the plainest notions of future bliss and woe. It enjoins brotherhood and good deeds among true believers. It spread with remarkable rapidity; and while it has been most successful among the simpler folk of Africa and Asia, in its later theological and philosophical developments it, like Judaism and Christianity, was influenced by Greek thought.

Owing to the growth of divergent copies of the Koran, the text was fixed in A.D. 651 by preparing a revised version and burning all other existing MSS. Traditions concerning Mohammed multiplied at an amazing speed among conflicting parties, and in the latter part of the ninth century a ' genuine ' collection of some 70,000 of them was sifted out from 600,000 ! Of the various sects of Islām, mention should be made of the Wahhābīs, who demand a return to the original simplicity of Islām; and among noteworthy movements we may include the Bābīs and Bahā'īs, with their ideals of universal brotherhood and peace. The Bāb, martyred in 1850, claimed to be the Only God, the Lord of the Universe; and his successor, Baha Ullah, announced himself as 'Him whom God shall manifest '.

The history of Islām is of great interest for the biblical student, who will find much that is suggestive in its rise and vicissitudes, its relations to other religions, its militant spirit and insistent adherence to its sacred Book. But this is a subject outside the scope of these pages.

Turning aside to Asia Minor and GREECE, we are in an area that was part of the cultural complex of the Eastern Mediterranean down to about 1200 B.C., and five or six centuries later was again knit, this time more enduringly, with what we may call—to use a familiar phrase—the ' lands of the Bible '. Early myths, cults and religious ceremonies abounded, but there was no priesthood and no priestly literature. Homer's epic of the Trojan war, however, created literature and art and laid down the lines of the education of the young. The poems were venerated as true and sacred, and their many deities have human virtues and vices, the former to be imitated, the latter providing men with excuse and condonation for their own misdeeds.

A formal effort to explain, not the origin of deities, but the beginnings of things, was made by the poet Hesiod (eighth century). It is the prelude to the line of speculative writers who may be said to have laid the first foundations of science. They introduced a world of thought which is the glory of Ancient Greece and subsequently shaped the course of western theology and philosophy. The great tragedians Aeschylus, Sophocles and Euripides (fifth century B.C.) are marked by their fine humanist treatment of the problems of life and the unity of the rule of the gods and fate in the world. They paved the way, a century later, for the more philosophical treatment of man and the universe. Socrates, Plato and Aristotle are the three outstanding names, and to the marriage of Israel's monotheistic passion and the Greek humanist and reflective mind are due, first, the Bible, and, later, the treatment of the more intellectual questions that it brought to the growing Christian Church. This treatment still holds the field.

More important for us, through their close contact with Palestine, are EGYPT and ACCAD (*i.e.*, Babylonia and Assyria), where the religious beliefs and practices were firmly fixed by 2000 B.C. Although there is no ' Bible ', there are innumerable sacred writings (papyri, tablets, etc.), and they reveal the difference between Egyptian humanism, secularism and love of story-telling and Accadian intensity and sombreness. The two differ also as regards ideas of existence after death: Egypt being remarkable for its funereal texts, mummification and the care to provide for the dead, while Accad, with its gloomy and hopeless underworld, resembles the Israelite Sheol (see p. 99). Egypt especially is noteworthy for its reflection upon human vicissitudes, its proverbial philosophy (see p. 65), and its concern with social and family affairs. In both magic abounds, and in Egypt the numerous sacred animals and animal cults have struck observers from Roman times onwards.

In both countries the great cities with their deities played an important part; and their rivalries, and the measures taken to co-ordinate their pantheons, and the periods when one city enjoyed supremacy over others, have left their trace upon the religion. In both there are two types of religion: the more popular and the more political and nationalist, the religion of the ruling authorities, though the difference between them must not be pressed. Political expansion extended the status and sway of the rulers and their great deities; and from an early date we find cosmic powers whose attributes and functions were more universal than the deities and spirits whom the ordinary man venerated, feared or propitiated.

In EGYPT the great national all-seeing Sun-god was at the head. He knows heaven and earth, and in one most

interesting utterance he proclaims the complete equality
of all men: ' I have made every man like his brother, and
I have forbidden that they do evil; it was their hearts
which undid that which I had said '.   The Egyptian Book
of the Dead, which is sometimes spoken of as the Bible of
Egypt, is a collection of funereal passages or ' coffin
texts ', and was not finally fixed before the fourth century
B.C.   Here the dead man identifies himself with the great
gods; he knows their names, and in the judgment scene
before Osiris he enumerates, in what is often styled a
' Negative Confession ', the offences of which he has *not*
been guilty.   These include murder, robbery, immorality,
blasphemy, deceit, avarice, etc., and a spell is bound upon
his heart lest it should oppose him—it is a primitive way of
stilling the voice of conscience!   Short scrolls of papyrus
were also on sale with a space for the name of the deceased;
in this way the individual could hope to overcome the terrors
of death.   The Osiris religion became that of the people;
and the story of Osiris, his faithful wife Isis, and the filial
Horus who slew his father's enemies was widely popular.
Osiris had been murdered by Set, but was restored to life;
and, after successfully defending himself against the charges
brought by his enemies, became king of the dead.   Through
his death and resurrection a dead man by becoming an
Osiris could in turn survive death.   The representation of
Isis, who became Queen of Heaven (cf. p. 138), with the
young Horus on her knee served to familiarize the Christian
world with the figure of the Madonna and the child Jesus.

In both Egypt and Accad there are numerous sentiments
of the deepest devotion; the phraseology is often almost,
or even quite, identical with that in the Old Testament.
But Accadian and Hebrew belong to the same family of
(Semitic) languages, whereas Egyptian is quite distinct,
hence the Accadian parallels are usually the more striking.

In ACCAD, answering to the ' Negative Confession '
of Egypt, is the so-called ' Interrogative Confession '.   A
sufferer is asked: Has he estranged relations or friends,
offended or neglected the deities or his parents, used false
weights, removed a boundary, said ' yes ' for ' no ' or ' no '
for ' yes ', has he murdered or stolen? . . . Ritual and

ethical offences are intermingled. The laws, notably in the markedly secular Code of Hammurabi (perhaps twentieth century B.C.), represent an advanced social organization, they include jerry-building, breach of promise, over-charging for wine, witchcraft, etc., etc. (see p. 60). There are many Accadian ' penitential psalms ' expressing the fear of transgression, though it is the fear of offending the gods rather than of injuring one's fellow-men that is prominent. Men are obsessed by their belief in demons, evil spirits and somewhat arbitrary deities; and by the side of the many expressions of devotion and religious conviction must be placed the resort to incantation, charms and magical practices to ensure deliverance from evil.

The astral religion of Accad is especially noteworthy; the land is the father of astrology and of its successor, astronomy. The myths are famous. Of the adventures of the great tyrant Gilgamesh there are several versions. We read of the first man, Engidu, who loses his innocence and with it his mystic gifts, also of the early struggle with problems of life and death, and of the fruitless search for the tree of life. Ishtar, the goddess of love, motherhood and war, descends into the underworld to seek Tammuz, the god of vegetation, and mankind and nature are sterile until she returns. The saviour-god Marduk overcomes the dragon-monster Tiamat, the mother of chaos; the name reappears in the ' deep ' (*tehōm*) of Gen. i. 2, and other passages. The Accadian myth of the Deluge, the discovery of which in 1872 created widespread interest, is the source of the story in Gen. chh. vi–ix, where, however, it has been treated more ethically and has been made part of Israelite tradition.

Space forbids more than a brief reference to the recently discovered library of tablets (since 1929) from Ras Shamra on the Syrian coast, south of the Gulf of Alexandretta. They are in cuneiform (like Accadian), but in an archaic Hèbrew language. They contain, among much else, cult-myths and legends, some of them very elaborate, and they testify to a highly developed literary tradition round about 1400 B.C. They tell of the aged god El (cf. Gen. xvi. 13 mg.), his wife, the wise goddess Ashirat (cf. Exod. xxxiv. 13 mg.), his young warring son Baal (often in the O.T.), the struggle with Mot (' death '), and the slaying of the many-headed serpent Lotan—*i.e.*, Leviathan (cf. Isa. xxvii. 1, Ps. lxxiv. 14). The tablets are of extraordinary interest for the biblical student, and convincingly prove, what was already evident from the monuments and archaeology of Egypt and Accad, that the religion of Palestine was essentially one with the religions of the immediately neighbouring lands. But whereas these underwent relatively little real development, the religion of Palestine—of Israel—developed in a way that gave it a permanent value (see p. 149 f.).

2. *General Characteristics* [1]

Sacred writings, myths included, deal primarily with practical, social and economic affairs, with human life in all its interests. The stages from birth to death and after, the food supply, the fertility of man and nature, sickness, disasters and war, are therefore among the subjects of concern. There are, of course, different sorts of difficulties and problems for the desert-dwellers, pastoralists, agriculturists and townsmen, and for the tribe, the city, the state and their several interrelations. The supernatural or unseen plays the dominant part, and although there is everywhere much that we call secular, the first place is held by religious belief and ceremonial. We have the myths of origins; they explain and justify, they evoke the appropriate response and keep it fresh. We learn of the origins of tribes and peoples, their movements, their ancestors and the existing conditions.

The deities and other supernatural beings are feared, worshipped and propitiated, their help is implored, or their enmity warded off. Much is said of their attributes and functions, and of their relations among themselves, and between them and men. The traditions inform and instruct men as regards conduct, and satisfy their enquiries both as to themselves and the world in which they live. There is constant tension between the relatively local religion, whether urban, tribal or national, and other cities, tribes and nations. The human and the supernatural

[1] See also the writer's *Rebirth of Christianity*, ch. III.

are so interwoven that the deities are concerned in all human relationships—*e.g.*, alliances, wars and treaties—and in the history of the great religions the vicissitudes of the leading deities will often reflect in large measure social, political and national vicissitudes. A powerful ruler or people can extend the power and sway of religion, the more readily if the deity is a nature-god, notably the sun. In Henotheism one deity is supreme over the rest; but in strict Monotheism, which is rare, there is a one and only god. It is interesting to observe how a worshipper will address his god or goddess as solely supreme, though other deities may be recognized on other occasions. Efforts will be made to co-ordinate the deities and pantheons of different cities when the latter are brought into close relationship one with the other.

In the more developed societies there is considerable range and variety of belief and usage. The ruling, the priestly and the more responsible authorities have wider interests as distinct from the broad masses; and everywhere we can observe the contrast between the more dominant institutional religion and that of ordinary individuals. The individual, as such, is submerged in the larger social unit into which he is born; and the story of the growth of individual rights and responsibilities, of his privileges and limitations, though far from continuous, is of great importance. In Ancient Egypt it seemed incredible that the powerful and unique Pharaoh should really die; later, in the Feudal Age, the higher ranks surely outlived death; and finally, in the Osiris cult, the future of the ordinary man could be assured. In Egypt, too, more than elsewhere, there is from time to time so deep a concern for the oppressed and suffering that an eminent Egyptologist has described the course of Egyptian religion under the not unjustifiable title, the ' Dawn of Conscience '.

The powers and functions of the leading individuals are to be seen in the value attached to the priestly ritual, as in India (cf. p. 16), in the penitential psalms of Accadian kings, who were at once semi-divine beings and representatives of the people, and in their various claims in Accad and Egypt to establish righteousness and justice (cf. Hammurabi, p. 60). Upon them the welfare of the land might depend, even as regards the gifts of nature. Such men exercised considerable influence by extending both their realms and those of their deities. They were, in a sense, their own authority; and at their worst they were arbitrary, and a law unto themselves. But the same can be said of all outstanding authorities, or of founders of sects, new cults or religions; and it is always instructive to observe how far they succeed, the adjustments, compromises or reactions that follow, the speedy growth of tradition relating to their lives, and the extent to which they claim divinity or are regarded as divine. Through such vicissitudes new deities are introduced, or older ones gain a new prominence, or changes are made in the way in which they are regarded and must be worshipped.

In the history of religion there are periods of inertia and stagnation; or there is a revival, whether completely archaïzing, as in Accad and Egypt of the seventh and sixth centuries B.C., or conspicuously regenerative, as in Israel of about the sixth century (p. 160). But if religion undergoes change, more externally, by extending its field or by its claim to universality—as in the case of the common worship of a nature-god—it can also appeal to man's universal needs. The demand for a *personal* deity—that is, one immediately interested in and related to the individual—outweighs the recognition of *impersonal* deities or principles (*e.g.*, right and order, or the sun, as such); and modern writers err when they attend merely to the often crude or naïve anthropism which represents deities in even grossly human form, and neglect the psychological aspects and the human needs which lie behind the demand. Also, superstition and magical practices which this age rightly repudiates are indications, not necessarily of the childishness and stupidity of men, but of the failure of a more reasonable religion to influence their lives.

One very important reforming movement in Egypt round about the age of Moses may be briefly mentioned. It is that of Amenhotep IV or Ikhnaton (there are other spellings of the name) who lived about 1375 B.C. This youthful Pharaoh, a bust of whose sister-wife Nefertiti was once familiar in the neighbourhood of the British Museum, set up the cult of his sun-god Aton at the city of Akhetaton which he founded. It is the modern Tell el-Amarna, where numerous cuneiform tablets have been found (since 1896), the diplomatic correspondence between South-west Asia and Egypt. The idea of ' truth ' or ' order ' (*ma'at*) distinguishes his religion, and the symbol of Aton was the sun-disc, whose rays held out the sign of life and a hand to all men. It was a vivid symbol, and the hymns of his age and the ' truthful ' and naturalistic art of his day make Ikhnaton's reform one of extreme importance. It was opposed to the current religion of the sun-god Amon, and of short duration; and just as he had tried to obliterate the cult of his day, so in turn the signs of his cult were obliterated, and more successfully. Egypt subsequently became a sacerdotal state and sank into the background till the seventh century B.C. But Ikhnaton's reform belongs to an age of widespread interrelations, the prominence of the non-Oriental Hatti or Hittites of Asia Minor, the recognition of certain deities of Right or Order, and the prelude to the rise of Israel as a people (see p. 135).

Characteristic of the old religions is their polarity: the interaction of opposites, a tension of contrasts resulting in a certain dualism. Old myths of the conflict between Order and Chaos, or Light and Darkness, carried with them notions of right and wrong. They led on to the Zoroastrian antithesis of Truth and Lie and of Ahura Mazdā and Ahriman (p. 19), and to the familiar dualism of God and the Devil, and the ultimate overthrow of the old Dragon Satan (see pp. 79, 97). In more ' secular ' fashion the Chinese *Yang* and *Yin* are two categories comprising such opposites as heaven and earth, sun and moon, fire and cold, active and passive, strength and weakness, and male and female. But this polarity is treated in more philosophical manner in the Chinese *li* and *ch'i*, the intellectual and ethical principles in contrast to matter and the material. In this way we reach the contrast (in India) between soul or spirit and body or matter. Throughout, what is fundamental is the innate conviction that there is Right, Order, Law, a Way to be trodden. The earliest appearance of it is in the Egyptian *ma'at*, right as distinct from wrong, justice in contrast to injustice; and Ma'at is a goddess, and very appropriately the daughter of the all-seeing Sun-god. But whereas in the old religions of the Near (or Middle) East we find a clear recognition of this conflict, expressed in myth, in hymns, laws, social teaching and homely ' philosophy ', it is not treated in a reflective and philosophical manner. For this we have to look to Ancient India and, above all, to Greece.

In spite of the many differences in religion, human nature is essentially one. As opposed to the recognition that there is, and should be, Right and Order, is the feeling of frustration in the face of wrong and disorder. What we call ' Sin ' is due to the fundamental feeling that something has missed the mark—*e.g.*, actual deeds that are recognized as wrong, whether committed by oneself or with oneself as the victim. The many rites and ceremonies are concerned with this feeling, whether they are what we call ' religious ' or ' superstitious '. There is also the marked contrast of a sense of power and a sense of helplessness, of strength and of frailty; it goes to extremes when the Accadian poem declares that when all is well men speak of ascending to heaven, but when there is misfortune they descend to the underworld. The notion of man's almost boundless power appears in many so-called ' magical ' rites which seem to be intended to control nature or the gods; and the Egyptians even had a special term (*hīke*) for it. But man's helplessness is more particularly the subject of religion: his power is limited and conditional, although his weakness can be overcome.

What we may call the ' magical ' temper spells a feeling of power, self-sufficiency and—in early belief—a oneness with nature such that man can exploit or control it. But the ' mystical ' temper goes behind the visible world and is characteristically detached, quietist, and passive. There is a feeling of intimate relationship or community or unity with the essence of things, with the Order in the Universe (as in Taoism), or with its God. The feeling of frustration, helplessness and incompleteness in one's life, which in some quarters is very keenly experienced, is removed by trances, austerities and other methods of escape and detachment from the cares of this world, as notably in India (p. 16 f.). What some types of temperament gain by their personal religion or by this escape is, in others, acquired more reflectively and philosophically. Life's frustration is thus remedied by mysticism, by religion or by philosophy. In both mysticism and religion there is the characteristic experience that there is something more real than this world; and the necessity of adjusting the conflicting experiences—this world of daily life and a reality less temporary and less illusory—leads to various religious, theological and philosophical solutions. This incompleteness, which is felt *personally* by some, is felt *intellectually* by others, and the aim of philosophy is to find a place for all the fundamental modes of experience.

Myths will tell of the origin of things, although as a matter of fact we ourselves know nothing of actual origins. Reflection may suggest that the universe precedes the gods of the universe; but both mysticism and religion will transcend the world of daily life as known to us. Man's world surely antedates man himself, man is a late comer upon earth; but man is part of the world, and he should not leave out of account the fact that he is reflecting not merely on what he sees, but on his stock of knowledge of the world. In early Egypt it was recognized that mind or thought or word has the priority: it is mind or thought that has given man the world upon which he is now reflecting. Man, when he is feeling and thinking, finds incongruities and contrasts, and the thought which has gone to build up his notion of things is—surely—the divine creative power. So in Egypt the god Ptah is the ' heart and tongue of the gods '; and while in Egypt, too, there are divine personifications of Truth, Intelligence and Speech, centuries later we meet with the conception of a divine Wisdom, and, ultimately, the Christian Logos, which is not merely Word, or Reason, but Order. (See pp. 68, 129.)

The men of old are moving slowly towards the basic fact that it is the way men think about themselves, the world and its ultimate mysteries, and the source of these thoughts, that is the surest starting-point for renewed reflection. The perennial interest of the comparative study of all the world's religions lies in the fact that it throws light upon man's strivings to feel at home and secure in what so often seems to be an unfriendly or hostile universe. Speaking broadly, we may say that there are two main lines of approach: the one to secure freedom here and now from life's burdens, the other to enable men to face them; and excessive emphasis has sometimes been laid upon the one to the detriment of the other. In any case we have to recognize that man's consciousness goes beyond or behind the world of space-time: it is primarily a vivid experience, but it is also demanded by the persisting enquiry of the mind. Through a purely humanist and descriptive approach it is possible to compare religions and to consider the points of resemblance and difference among them. From the objective standpoint the religious differences are found to be intelligible; they are due to temperament, the current stage of life, personal disposition and thought. Everywhere there will be found striking resemblances and striking differences; but it is necessary to distinguish between those that are superficial and those that are essential. It is in the light of the world's religions that to-day the student should approach the Bible.

3. *The Bible*

Something has been said of the religions of the Ancient Near East. The Bible began to grow up at a relatively late date in the midst of lands of old-established culture whose Golden Age was past. The history of every religion has been very considerably influenced by the general temper of a people and its geographical and climatic conditions. Palestine was exposed to Egypt, Asia Minor and the Levant, and could never be cut off from external influences. Desert life gives full play to the imagination; India's climate has not encouraged the activity we find, *e.g.*, in Persia and Greece; physical conditions tended to develop a uniformity of culture along the rivers of Egypt and Accad; whereas the diversity of physical features in Greece fostered variety and originality. Sumerians in Accad, Hittites in

Asia Minor, and later the Persians—these have left their
mark upon the Semitic religions; and the difference between
Judaism and Christianity is due in several recognizable
respects to the fact that the latter manifests Greek influence
far more deeply than the former.

The remarkably lengthy history of religion in China and
India does not present the profound progressive development that we find in the Bible. The progressiveness of
religion depends on cultural continuity, a continuity of
tradition despite discontinuity and sweeping changes, a
persistence of essential features, though in new and more
pregnant forms. In the Bible we deal with a land and
people deeply affected by the desert on one hand and by
exposure to external influences on the other. It is a people
self-conscious, a people of extremes. Around them we
find undeniable examples of passionate religious devotion
and elevated ethical ideas. To the unthinking observer the
religion of the Old Testament might seem to be on the same
level as, and not superior to, these other religions; but the
course of history disproves this (p. 192).

Comparative religion and modern knowledge have seemed
to forbid us to speak of the Bible as the ‘ Word of God ’.
And even if we say that it *contains* the ‘ Word of God ’,
where shall it be found? To-day there are those who
reject the Apocrypha, others the Old Testament; some
will lay their foundation upon the Gospels to the exclusion
of Paul, and some even upon Paul rather than on the teach-
of Jesus. And yet others appear to be content with snippets
of the Bible, for example as regards social justice. Hence
it is not easy to say at the outset in what way the Bible *is*
or *contains* the Word of God; that is a question which is
left to the concluding pages of this book, and it depends
upon the meaning that God has for our life and thought.

To start with, we must first endeavour to understand the
Bible; to describe to the best of our ability what appears
to be most helpful for a comprehensive view of the Book,
not only on its religious and devotional side, but also
bearing in mind its unique place in the history of western
culture. Accordingly, approaching it from the human side,
we shall aim at being descriptive, remembering that, what-

ever we may think of the Bible, or of any part of it, or of any belief or sentiment in it, we are dealing with a Book that has stood the test of ages and has made history. We owe it to our forefathers no less than to the demands of progressive thought to-day that we should treat our subject sympathetically and critically.

CHAPTER III

THE GROWTH OF THE BIBLE AND ITS INTERPRETATION

THE Bible is the outcome of a lengthy development in the course of which documents have been compiled, edited, and their ultimate validity finally authorized by incorporating them in a Canon. Their authorship is often unknown, or attributed wrongly, but in all sincerity, to writers who, it is now clear, could not have written them—at least in their present form. The O.T. refers to such sources as the *Book of Jashar* (Josh. x. 13, 2 Sam. i. 18 ff.) and the *Book of the Wars of Yahweh* (Num. xxi. 14 f.).[1] As regards the latter, according to early belief the gods fought for and with their people; and the story of the defeat of Amalek (Exod. xvii. 14) and a Moabite inscription recounting Mesha's victory over Israel (about 850 B.C.) at the command of his god Chemosh find many parallels in Egypt and Accad (Babylonia and Assyria). Apart from various references to writing (*e.g.*, the *Song of Moses*, Deut. xxxi. 22), it is the compiler of *Chronicles* who is at pains to refer his readers to certain sources—*e.g.*, the accounts (lit. ' words ') of Samuel, Nathan and Gad, prophecies of Ahijah and of Isaiah, and extensive records of the kings of Judah and Israel. What is said elsewhere of the prophets Samuel (in 1 Sam.), Nathan (2 Sam. xii) and Gad (2 Sam. xxiv. 11 ff.) illustrates the sort of material that was available. Prophecies or oracles were transmitted orally or were put into writing (*e.g.*, Isa. xxx. 8, Hab. ii. 2); and we learn how the oracles of Jeremiah were put together by his scribe Baruch (Jer. xxxvi. 2, see ver. 32), though it is to be observed that in the Septuagint (see p. 38) the prophecies against foreign nations (Jer. xlvi.–li.) are inserted, but in another order, between xxv.

---

[1] The familiar spelling Jehovah is incorrect, and the consonants J-h-v-h (better Y-h-w-h) may, after Ex. iii. 14 (see R.V. mg.), be pronounced Yahweh.

13 and ver. 14. In general, modern critical analysis of the O.T. suggests the existence of a considerable body of written material, most of which, however, has been lost.

A definite stage in the growth of the O.T. is indicated by *Deuteronomy*, whose misleading title implying a Second Law is due to the Septuagint translation of the ' copy of the law ' in xvii. 18. Its discovery in the reign of Josiah is recounted in 2 Kings xxii. f.; and the term Tōrah or Law, applied to it in Deut. i. 5, etc., becomes later that of the whole Pentateuch, the promulgation of which is associated with Ezra (Neh. viii. 1). But difficult questions are here raised to which we shall return (pp. 50 f., 153). In any event, the *Hebrew* O.T. Canon, beginning with the Pentateuch, grew up gradually. It is threefold: (1) the Pentateuch (*Genesis* to *Deuteronomy*), (2) *Joshua* to *Kings* and *Isaiah* to *Malachi* (called respectively the Former and Later Prophets), and (3) the Writings, comprising the remainder (including also *Ruth*, *Lamentations* and *Daniel*). This Canon was fixed about A.D. 100, after doubts had been expressed in regard to *Chronicles*, *Canticles* (or *Song of Songs*), *Ecclesiastes*, and other books.

Certain writings accepted by the Church under the heading ' Apocrypha ' (*i.e.*, ' hidden ', from the ordinary reader) do not exist in Hebrew; but while they include 1 *Maccabees*, which is invaluable for the history of the second century B.C., and the much later 2 *Esdras* (or 4 *Ezra*) of the first century A.D., they exclude the *Psalms of Solomon* (illustrating Jewish Messianic ideas), the *Book of Jubilees*, the *Secrets of Enoch*, and other works which point to considerable literary activity round about the rise of Christianity. The Apocryphal and Apocalyptic literature (on the latter see p. 60) bridges the gulf between the O.T. and the N.T., and much of it was ignored, whether by Jews or Christians, or both, and fell into obscurity. The ' Apocrypha ', accepted by the Roman Council of Trent (1546) and also by the Vatican Council of 1870, was printed in Coverdale's Bible (1535) somewhat apologetically. It was rejected at the Reformation as not being in the Hebrew Canon, and also partly for certain doctrinal reasons. But by Article vi. the Church of England ' doth

read them for example of life and instruction of manners;
but yet doth it not apply them to establish any doctrine '.
It must be admitted that the book of *Judith* in the Apocrypha
is not less edifying than the Canonical *Esther* (p. 53), and
that the ' apocryphal ' book of *Wisdom* is delightful reading, and was valued by the Early Church (p. 67).

As regards the Greek N.T., there were evidently once
many accounts of Jesus and his works (Luke i. 1–4; cf.
John xxi. 25)—and perhaps of the forty days between his
Resurrection and Ascension (Acts i. 3). Comparison of
the three Gospels leads us to recognize certain sources
(see p. 70); and various sayings, whether exact or inexact,
were current, notably Acts xx. 35, ' It is more blessed to
give rather than to receive '. The famous Greek Codex
Bezae (fifth century A.D.) has an interesting insertion after
Luke vi. 4 (see p. 39); and various papyri, older and more
or less mutilated, contain others. Thus a papyrus of the
third century has, ' Jesus saith, Wherever there are two,
they are not without God, and wherever there is one alone,
I say, I am with him; raise the stone, and there shalt thou
find me; cleave the wood, and I am there '. Some papyri
are very fragmentary—*e.g.*, ' Jesus saith . . . The kingdom
[of heaven] is within you; whosoever shall know himself
shall find it; [strive therefore] to know yourselves, [and ye
shall know that] you are sons of the Father '. Here the
words in brackets are conjecturally restored. Still earlier,
fragments of papyrus in codex (*i.e.*, book) form contain
episodes in the life of Jesus in words not agreeing with,
but closely resembling, those in the four Gospels. In
general, as regards sources questions of analysis are involved; for example, are St. Paul's letters referred to in
1 Cor. v. 9 and 2 Cor. vii. 8–12 to be found in 2 Cor. vi.
14–vii. 1 and x–xiii respectively, and therefore were evidently once separate? (See p. 74 f.)

At one time or another certain books of the N.T. were
not accepted—*e.g.*, *Hebrews*, *James*, *Jude*, and especially
Revelation. The anti-Semite Marcion (about A.D. 140)
vehemently condemned the O.T. and much of the New
which he considered ' judaïzing '; he appears to have
been the first to force the Church to fix a Canon. Tindale

(like Luther) printed *Hebrews, James, Jude* and *Revelation* at the end of the N.T. as being of lesser value. On the other hand, in early Greek MSS. are to be found the *Epistle of Barnabas*, the *Shepherd of Hermas*, two *Epistles of Clement to the Corinthians*, and, in one case, the *Psalms of Solomon*. The N.T. Canon reached its final form during the fourth century A.D.

This must suffice for the present purpose. We see that (1) there are books in the Canon which have found a place, not without hesitation; (2) there are books now outside the Canon which (*a*), in the case of the Apocrypha, are accepted by the Roman Church, or (*b*), were known and used by early writers as though inspired and authoritative. But it does not follow that those regarded as Canonical are from the pen of the writers to whom they are ascribed, *e.g.*, the *Pentateuch* or Five Books of Moses, the book of *Isaiah*, the *Lamentations of Jeremiah*, the *Psalms of David*, the *Epistle of St. Paul to the Hebrews*, or the *Gospel according to St. John*. In these and other cases the task of criticism is to sift the traditions and estimate their value. But the Canons of the O.T. and N.T. were formed after discussion; and once fixed they were the rule to which Christianity (and, as regards the O.T., Judaism) adhered, the court of appeal in case of doubt.

We turn now from the Canon to the Text of the Bible. The O.T. is translated from Hebrew, a Semitic language very closely related to the ancient Accadian and the relatively modern Arabic. Egyptian and Accadian lore was not unknown in Palestine; an Egyptian original lies behind Ps. civ and Prov. xxii. 17–xxiii. 12. Accadian myths were familiar, and the Accadian language was known over a large area (including Palestine) in the Amarna Age—*i.e.*, roughly, the age of Moses (see p. 134). At the Phoenician site of Ras Shamra many tablets have been found of about the same age in a language almost identical with Hebrew, but written in cuneiform—not in syllables (as in Accadian) but in an alphabet of consonants only (see p. 24 f.). Our starting-point, however, is the O.T. in Hebrew. Some fragments of Aramaic, a later sister-language, appear in

parts of *Ezra* and *Daniel*,[1] and—still later—in the N.T.,
e.g., *Talitha cumi* (Mark v. 41), *Ephphatha* (vii. 34), cf. also
Mark xv. 22, 34. Aramaic became the language of
Palestine; and the words of Jesus, and probably some
original sources of the Gospels, were once extant in that
tongue. At all events the *thought* of the Gospels is often
Aramaic or Hebrew, though the N.T. itself is in Greek—
not the classical language, but the common idiom of the
time.

The Hebrew and Aramaic of the O.T. were written in
a script older than that used later in Hebrew MSS. and
Bibles. It was consonantal—shorthand may be compared;
hence the same consonants might be pronounced and
vocalized differently.[2] This accounts, for example, for
the difference between ' bed ' in Gen. xlvii. 31 and ' staff '
in Heb. xi. 21. In the Greek or Hellenistic period (third
century B.C.) the Pentateuch was translated into Greek for
Greek-speaking Jews in Egypt. It is known as the Septuagint. Greek translations of other books followed, and
were current both among Jews and in the early Christian
Church. In these numerous adjustments were made, and
particular usages of Classical Greek words were reshaped
theologically, with the result that this Greek ' Bible ' of
the Jews prepared the way for the transition from the Hebrew
and Jewish O.T. to the Greek and Christian N.T., wherein
many of the quotations from the O.T. are from the Septuagint and not the original Hebrew.[3]

The oldest extant Hebrew MSS. date around A.D. 900,
and differ among themselves so slightly that, as Spinoza
guessed (eighteenth century), they must be descended from
a single family or recension. But this identity and the
well-known meticulous care of Jewish copyists cannot be
earlier than about A.D. 100. There had previously been

[1] See R.V. mg. of Ezra iv. 8, vii. 12, Dan. ii. 4, also of Jer. x. 11, Gen.
xxxi. 47.
[2] Thus the consonants of the divine name (p. 34 n.) are given the
vowels of the more ordinary word ' lord ' *Ădōnăy*, whence the English
form Jehovah (from the fourteenth century).
[3] The divine name Yahweh (see p. 34) was translated ' Lord ', thus
giving Israelite religious ideas a less national and immensely wider
application.

many variations, as the LXX (Septuagint) clearly proves;
and as these caused disputes among the Jews and controversies between the Christians (who used the LXX) and
the Jews, the necessity of a single uniform text was felt.[1]
Moreover, the Hebrew and (later) Greek Canons differed
in their arrangement of certain books of the O.T. The
Hebrew ' Bible ' closes with *Chronicles*—that is, with the
destruction of Jerusalem, the Exile, and the hope of a rebuilt Temple (2 Chr. xxxvi. 23), whereas *Ezra-Nehemiah*,
which really follows on historically, ends with a hint of
the cleavage between the Jews and the Samaritans. On
the other hand, the Christian Canon placed *Malachi* at
the end of its O.T.; this formed a natural prelude to the
Gospels (cf. Luke i. 17 with Mal. iv. 6), and the wise
decision to include *Revelation* in the Canon made an
inspiring conclusion, in that its vision of a new heaven
and a new earth carries the reader back to the creation of
heaven and earth in Gen. i, and the coming of the Lord
Jesus points forward. In general, the study of the *letter*
of the O.T. takes us behind the fixed text (known as the
Massoretic Text) to a time when there were variations
and differences, some of them of very great importance.

The oldest extant Greek MSS. of outstanding importance
date from the fourth century A.D. The Sinaitic Codex
(acquired by the British Museum in 1933) includes the
' non-canonical ' *Epistle of Barnabas* and the *Shepherd of
Hermas*; and the rather later Alexandrine Codex (also in
the British Museum) includes the two epistles of Clement
of Rome, once regarded as almost inspired. Besides the
Vatican Codex (early fourth century), which is the most
valuable of all, mention should be made of the Codex
Bezae (fifth century, at Cambridge), which contains the
Gospels and Acts, but with remarkable variations and
additions. Thus, in place of Luke vi. 5 it has: ' on the
same day, seeing a man working on the Sabbath he (Jesus)
said unto him, Man, if thou knowest what thou doest,
blessed art thou, but if thou knowest not, thou art accursed

[1] Thus in Is. vii. 14 the Hebrew word ' young woman ' was wrongly
rendered ' virgin ' (quoted in Matt. i. 23) and used by Christians in their
disputes with the Jews.

and a transgressor of the law'. Earlier papyri have been found in Egypt, the most notable being in codex or book form: (*a*) a small fragment of the *Gospel of John* (said to be not later than A.D. 140), noteworthy evidence for the antiquity of that Gospel, and (*b*) the Pauline epistles, in a novel order, including *Hebrews*, but omitting the Pastoral Epistles (p. 76). In contrast to the uniformity of Hebrew MSS., the Greek translations of the Bible present innumerable variations, many of importance, raising very intricate questions of the history of the Greek version, its groups or 'families' of MSS., and their relative value. For example, we have to ask whether the Greek text of the N.T. which is used as the basis of the R.V. (or of the R.V. mg.) really represents throughout the best text. As for Latin versions, the oldest translations of the O.T. reflect a time before the Hebrew Massoretic text was definitely fixed; whereas the Vulgate, Jerome's translation of the Bible dating about A.D. 400, represents the current text and became the Bible of the Church until the Reformation, and of the Roman Church alone since that date. The oldest Syriac version, too, represents (in the case of the N.T.) in some respects a relatively earlier text.

In general, the Hebrew and Greek texts of the Bible and the versions present many difficult problems. The meaning of the Hebrew is often uncertain, and there are corruptions in the text which neither the versions nor modern research can satisfactorily correct. This is not surprising, for even in ancient contemporary inscriptions and papyri errors are sometimes found. But the difficulties do not affect the Bible as a whole; the English Bible remains trustworthy, though from time to time questions of the text arise which may be of considerable significance. These difficulties affect the original text, the translation and the interpretation, so that to understand the Bible adequately some guidance is necessary. In fact, a knowledge of Hebrew is quite as important for adequately understanding the O.T. as is that of Greek for the N.T.

It may be helpful now to notice some interesting vicissitudes in the growth of the Biblical text, and of the versions

or translations, as they exemplify the sort of thing that is
wont to happen.

(1) In spite of care, mistakes and corruptions creep into
MSS. and printed texts, and are apt to increase until steps
are taken to rectify them and restore what is supposed
to be the original. The history of the Latin Vulgate
affords many instances of this, though it will be claimed
that so long as it represents the sense of the Hebrew it
can be regarded as authentic. (2) There is a tendency to
remove or avoid difficulties in order to make the translation
more intelligible; Gen. iv. 8 (see R.V. mg.) is an example.
(3) Changes are made to accord with later spelling or usage
(as in the early editions of the A.V.). (4) By an oversight,
in one case in the A.V. 2 Chron. xxxii. 32 was repeatedly
overlooked; and in another some twenty words of Exod.
xiv. 10 were printed twice over. A printer's marginal note
that certain words were ' to remain ' (*i.e.*, that some
words were not to be removed) found their way into the
printed text of Gal. iv. 29 (A.V. of 1805); and the negative
' not ' was accidentally omitted in Exod. xx. 14 (A.V.
of 1631) and before ' inherit ' in 1 Cor. vi. 9 (A.V. of
1653).

(5) Provocative and controversial matter was sometimes
printed along with the Bible (in the margins, or in notes),
as in Tindale's Bible; but the Bishops' Bible of 1568 wisely
proposed ' to make no bitter notes upon any text, or yet
to set down any determination in places of controversy '.
There were also changes to avoid what seemed objectionable
or liable to be misunderstood, see, *e.g.*, Luke xxiii. 32,
A.V. ' two other, malefactors '—the comma is vital; R.V.
' two others, malefactors '; but some old MSS. omit
' other(s) ', and the Greek text of John xix. 18 omits ' malefactors '. (6) Doctrinal guidance was offered by the headlines and headings of chapters in the A.V.—*e.g.*, Isa. vii
(Christ promised for a sign), xxii (Christ's kingdom pre-
figured), see also on Isa. liii and the Song of Songs. These
are omitted by the R.V., which also prints prose passages
in paragraphs (verse-division as in the A.V. often obscures
the continuity). In the A.V. of Ps. ii. 12 (' kiss the Son ')
and Mal. iv. 2 (' the Sun of righteousness ') the capitals

indicate the supposed reference to Christ; but the R.V. rightly avoids this, though in the latter passage it still prints ' his wings ', for ' its ' (the Hebrew word is actually feminine). (7) New versions or translations have constantly to struggle for recognition, the older being treated as more authoritative. (8) Even a mere misprint in 1 Sam. xvii. 34 in an edition of the Hebrew O.T. (in 1525) was retained out of respect. Similarly in the M.T. (the Massoretic text) obvious errors have been allowed to remain. (9) Usher's chronology in the A.V. (from 1701), like the headlines, has sometimes been regarded as almost as sacred as the text; and even the vowel-points in the Hebrew O.T., though dating from about the sixth or seventh century A.D., were once deemed to be due to inspiration, like the earlier consonantal text itself.

Both the Canon and the Text of the Bible were fixed at a definite period and had a lengthy history behind them. Hence modern efforts to determine the best M.T. and the best LXX do not take us back far enough. Where the LXX (or any other old version) differs from the M.T. it is necessary to enquire whether it represents a better text, or is due to error or misunderstanding, or to some doctrinal or other cause. In both the M.T. and LXX there are occasions where the text or translation has been adjusted to safeguard the sanctity of God. Besides the ' canonical ' or accepted contents of the Bible, the general course of the historical framework proves on examination to have been standardized; it, too, is in a sense ' canonical ', and it is necessary to recover, if possible, the earlier stages (pp. 156 n. 2, 163).

Moreover, readers tend to approach the Bible with certain presuppositions, and these must be tested. The Bible grew up in an ancient land with ancient ways of thinking and writing. Hence it must not be judged by modern methods. For example, when modern critics conclude that our *Deuteronomy* did not exist before its ' discovery ' in Josiah's time (2 Kings xxii. f.), it does not follow that they regard it as a ' forgery ', as, for example, were the celebrated ' False Decretals ' of Isidore (ninth century A.D.). The names of Enoch, Moses, Solomon and Isaiah were attached to late pseudonymous writings or assumed by late unknown writers; but this was no more blameworthy than when, in modern times, passages in the Bible are given in all sincerity a meaning or interpretation which the original writers would at once repudiate— if they could.

As regards the use of the O.T. by Jesus, he undoubtedly treated it as authoritative for his hearers, and refutes his opponents from it.   He regarded himself as advancing beyond it and superseding it, and he found a new meaning in it—as the Church has done since.   There was in the O.T. what he considered no longer binding.   Thoughtful men of to-day agree that the use of the O.T. in the New neither attests its literal infallibility or literal inspiration, nor excludes or even discourages careful criticism.   The old divine Paley, in his celebrated *View of the Evidences of Christianity* (Part III, ch. 3; 1794), excellently lays down the leading principles, based on earlier writers.   Christianity, he says, must not be made answerable for the circumstantial truth of each separate passage in the O.T., the genuineness of every book, the information and fidelity of every writer in it: 'a reference in the N.T. to a passage in the Old does not so fix its authority'.   It cannot be too emphatically stated that many of the arguments still brought against biblical criticism, whether relying upon Our Lord's use of the Old Testament or upon the supposed witness of archaeology and the monuments to the traditional estimate of it, have been refuted in the past; and there is much to be found in writers of two or three generations ago who were fighting for the right to exercise criticism that is still worth recalling and restating.

A certain freedom of interpretation was admissible, and an allegorical treatment has often been used—and misused—to extract some symbolical meaning from narratives which could not be taken literally, or which in any case were supposed to have a deeper meaning than appears on the surface.   This practice, carried to excess by the Alexandrian Jew Philo (first century A.D.), has ever been popular, and later interpreters have ranged between the self-evident teaching conveyed in narrative or historical form and far-fetched and fanciful expositions—however devout and well-meant (see p. 182).

The aim to-day should be to endeavour to understand the thought of the ancient writers in relation to the times in which they lived, to treat the Bible historically, and to recognize that there will be identity as well as resemblance of thought, and variation and conflict of thought as well as continuity and development. Only in this way can we understand the Bible dynamically, treating it, not as a book on our bookshelves, but as enshrining the profoundest of developments in the past history of our race. So shall we not treat the Bible as an armoury of proof-texts, or solely as a record of successive individual and personal experiences of the past. If the Bible has been the book as taught solely by the Church, it is a reinterpretation of the Bible that modern conditions of life and thought are demanding.

Before considering the general thought and ideas of the Bible, it will be convenient to sketch in outline its contents. The R.V. will be followed, though English readers have access to other translations in commentaries and elsewhere. The Bible does not always interpret itself, and difficulties of translation depend, not only upon the genuineness and accuracy of the Hebrew and Greek *text*, but also upon determining the best *renderings*. It would be invidious to comment here upon current translations, and, until there is more agreement among scholars than at present, the old Variorum Bible of 1880 still deserves commendation. It prints the A.V. with Usher's chronology, chapter-headings and headlines, and marginal references, but it gives at the foot ' Various Renderings ' selected from the best commentators of its day and ' Various Readings ' of importance selected from the MSS., versions, etc., then accessible. Sir Frederic Kenyon in *Our Bible and the Ancient Manuscripts* (1939) well says, ' This is, I believe, the only critical edition of the Bible in English.' An entirely new edition is much to be desired.

CHAPTER IV

THE BOOKS OF THE BIBLE

(1) The Old Testament and Apocrypha

THE Bible is a library of ancient writings of the most diverse character, and utterly distinct from any other single collection by reason of the pervading unity and continuity of spirit that impress the ordinary reader. Its contents include myths (wherein the gods are concerned) and legends (where historical events and figures are treated more romantically); history and the religious or didactic treatment of history are blended. The prophets, their oracles and writings, and narratives relating to them make the Bible pre-eminent: the prophetical books of the O.T. are among the finest of world-literature. The poetry, which extends over secular, ritual and devotional subjects, has made it a treasure-house in all ages. Custom, ritual and laws combine simple and primitive ideas with elaborate arrangements for worship and daily life. The ' Wisdom ' literature is more humanist, but it is theistic—a blend of theistic and humanist common-sense. A strict classification is, however, impossible: prose, rhythmical prose and poetry overlap, and tradition (*i.e.*, what has been handed down), whether oral or in writing, has first to be analyzed and tested before we can use it as history. The contents of the Bible range over many centuries, some of marked and sweeping changes; the land and its writers are found to be influenced by intercourse with other lands and peoples; but a close examination of the biblical books makes the general unity and continuity only the more remarkable. It will be convenient in this chapter and the next to give a rapid outline of the contents before we turn to consider some of the characteristic ideas that unify the O.T. and the New (Chap. VI). Jerusalem and its holy Mount Zion will perhaps be the best binding link (Chap. VII), and it will remain to refer to some fundamental problems which arise as we proceed to go beneath the surface (Chap. VIII).

I. *Narratives*

The historical narratives are our source for all questions of the dates of the constituent parts of the Bible and their development. Historical writings of one sort or another go back to the records of the early kings of Egypt, Accad and the Hittites of Asia Minor; and in pre-Israelite Palestine itself among the Amarna Letters are some intelligent reports from local kings with phrases that sometimes have parallels in the Psalms and elsewhere (p. 134 f.). The antiquity of writing in and around Palestine and the existence of laws, psalms, proverbs, etc., before the Israelite period allow the possibility that there were in Palestine itself laws before Moses, psalms before David, and proverbs before Solomon. But the age of those that are preserved in the O.T. is a matter for enquiry. The retention of tradition in the East is not to be overlooked; but when we compare *Chronicles* with *Samuel-Kings*, or the *Book of Jubilees* (about 100 B.C.) with *Genesis-Exodus*, or the *Second Book of Maccabees* with the *First*, we see how earlier material can be presented in a distinctly later form. Elements of the myths found in the Ras Shamra tablets (p. 24 f.) long persisted, and they survive in a very late dress in the early Christian age. Hence when we examine our sources we must be prepared to find three classes of material: (1) the old, (2) the old in a later form, and (3) what belongs solely to the later age. Here, however, in these outlines questions of this nature cannot be discussed.

The East is famed for its expert story-tellers, its attractive imaginative creations, and its interest in the marvellous and supernatural. In the O.T. are some of the oldest known examples of well-constructed narrative. We may cite the story of Joseph (Gen. xxxvii, xxxix ff.) and shorter stories (*e.g.*, Jacob and Laban, Gen. xxvii–xxxiii); the account of David, Absalom and the rise of Solomon (2 Sam. ix–xx, 1 Kings i, ii), Abimelech (Judges ix), Jehu (2 Kings ix f.) and the book of Nehemiah. The simplicity of the narratives in *Matthew–Luke* may also be noted. Throughout the writers are of course bona-fide.

They give the answer to the question, What mean these stones (Josh. iv. 6, 21)? Note also the questions in Exod. xii. 26 and Deut. vi. 20. If the Israelite could give in a nutshell the outlines of his nomadic origin (Deut. xxvi. 3–10), it is on a very much larger scale that narratives describe the chief landmarks in Israel's early fortunes. Thus we have the selection of Israel from among all other peoples, the right of Israel to her land, the possession of Jerusalem and the foundation of the Temple, the superiority of Judah over the renegade Northern Kingdom, the continuity between pre-exilic and post-exilic Jerusalem, and its superiority over the mixed population of Samaria. We have, not the bare annals of history, but history written didactically and with a religious intention; and just as the writers did not, and indeed could not, propose to give a 'scientific' account of the universe (Gen. i f.), or of the origin of civilization (*e.g.*, Gen. iv. 20–22), but such knowledge as they had, so, too, we are not to expect modern rigorous methods when they deal with their past history.

For the history of Israel we have two distinct sources, and they are of prime importance for determining questions of the actual development of Israel's fortunes and thought.

(A) In *Genesis–Kings* we pass from the beginnings of the world and mankind to the Deluge as a punishment for man's evil. The Tower of Babel (Gen. xi), a failure in 'reconstruction', and the Dispersion of Mankind lead on to the divine selection of the 'patriarch' Abram (or Abraham), the great ancestor of Israel, and his settlement in Palestine. The 'patriarchal' history closes with the descent into Egypt of Jacob or Israel (Gen. xxxii. 28, xxxv. 10—the passages are conflicting). Israel and his *family* are individuals, but the 'exodus' of the *tribes* of Israel, the law-giving at Mount Sinai (or Horeb), and their settlement in the land promised to their ancestors (Exod. vi. 8, Deut. xxxiv. 4) describe the inauguration of Israel as a nation (*Exodus–Joshua*). A period of individual leaders ('judges') and the failure of the (northern) Saul to establish a united monarchy are followed by the stories of his successful rival (the Judaean) David and the occupation of Jerusalem, and of Solomon and the building of the Temple. But the

monarchy then split into two; and while the Judaean
kingdom enjoyed a continuous though chequered history,
the northern kingdom (Israel or Ephraim, later Samaria),
which had broken away at the death of Solomon, fell in
721 B.C. Judah, now the representative of the original
Israel, later suffered the same fate, and the fall of Jerusalem
and the Exile (586 B.C.) conclude the history, though there
is a hint that its last king, Jehoiachin, in exile, might be
favoured (2 Kings xxv. 27–30). The Exile is the great
break in Israelite history, and the precise difference between
pre-exilic and post-exilic conditions is one of the fundamental
problems that occupy O.T. scholars.

In this series we have the rise and fall of Israel as a nation.
The law-giving on Sinai (or Horeb) and other laws and
regulations make the Pentateuch (*Genesis–Deuteronomy*)
the charter of Israel, the Torah (law or direction) which was
shared also by the Samaritans. Now, *Deuteronomy* is of
special interest since, instead of the various sacred places
where sacrifices had been offered to Yahweh (Exod. xx. 24),
he would choose one tribe, one sacred site, a central
sanctuary, and place his Name there (Deut. xii. 1–12)—the
reference is here to Jerusalem (cf. 1 Kings iii. 2, v. 3, 5).
'Yahweh, our God, is one Yahweh [and therefore not
many], and thou shalt love Yahweh thy God with all thy
heart' (Deut. vi. 4 f.): a new stage is indicated (cf. Deut.
xii. 8, xxix. 4). Yahweh and Israel formally acknowledge
each other; Israel becomes the people of Yahweh (xxvi.
17 ff., xxvii. 9). The people are now responsible, and all
evil must be ruthlessly eradicated; but they must keep
Yahweh's law, and not take the relationship for granted,
for Yahweh is not one to be bribed (x. 17, xxix. 19). The
law of the covenant is not too difficult, but it must be observed and taught (xxx. 11 ff.). Yahweh is in their history,
for their good or for their hurt; and there are solemn
blessings and curses, the natural fruits of the people's
obedience or disobedience. We are introduced to a veritable
'philosophy of history' which evaluates men and explains
events according to their attitude to Yahweh's commands.
Thus, when we turn to the 'Deuteronomic' writings, the
account of the 'judges' connects the fortunes of Israel

with their loyalty to Yahweh (Judges ii. 11 ff., cf. iii. 7, 12, etc.). The kings of Judah and Israel are estimated by their attitude to idolatry and—in the case of (north) Israel—by their repudiation of Jerusalem; and to their apostasy the writer attributes the fall of the northern kingdom (2 Kings xvii. 6—41, xviii. 11 f.). This 'Deuteronomic' treatment of history is even intensified in *Chronicles* (see below).

But in the Pentateuch we have, what was more important, the inauguration of the sacrificial ritual and the priestly and Levitical organization (*Exodus–Numbers*). The Tabernacle is the forerunner of the Temple in Jerusalem. The pattern of it was given by Yahweh to Moses (Exod. xxv. 9), and with the sacred ark it accompanied the Israelites on their journey into the promised land and the city chosen by Yahweh. Moses is the leader of Israel, the uniquely inspired prophet (Num. xii. 7 f., Deut. xxxiv. 10); and his spokesman is the priestly Aaron, whose name closely resembles the Hebrew word for 'ark', *ăhărōn*. Aaron is the head of the priests and Levites who minister to Yahweh and mediate between him and the people; and a close analysis of the history of the priesthood and of the relation between *Deuteronomy* (which breathes a more democratic spirit) and the 'priestly' and ecclesiastical elements of the Pentateuch forms the basis of modern O.T. criticism.

We turn to the second source (B), *Chronicles–Ezra–Nehemiah*. Of these three, *Chronicles*, a strange and in some respects rather neglected book, opens with genealogies showing (1) the relation between Israel and other peoples, and (2) the subdivisions of Israel. The narrative starts with the death of Saul and David's accession and ends with the fall of Jerusalem, the Exile and the invitation of Cyrus the Persian to the exiled Jews to return and rebuild their Temple. It concentrates upon the Temple, built after the pattern David gave to Solomon (1 Chron. xxviii. 11, 19); and David is the founder of the temple-service and organizes the Levites, priests and singers. Of the histories of the two kingdoms in *Kings* it gives only the Judaean, practically ignoring the northern (Samaria). For the northern priests are unorthodox; they are not of the sons of Aaron

(2 Chron. xiii. 9 f.). Yahweh is not with Israel (*i.e.*, Ephraim, 2 Chron. xxv. 7, 10; cf. Isa. ix. 8-12). Judah is *the* Israel, and Yahweh fights against Israel's enemies (xx. 29), and no one can withstand the kingdom of Yahweh in the hands of the sons of David (xiii. 8). The twofold use of the term ' Israel ' (1) as distinct from Judah, and (2) as comprising or including the land or kingdom of Judah, should be noticed (see p. 157). Success and failure turn upon Judah's relation to Yahweh: return to him and he will give peace and rest (2 Chron. xv. 15, as in Judges iii. 11, viii. 28). The thread of history is that of *Samuel–Kings*, but it is an ecclesiastical one, and it gives a less trustworthy account of events. *Chronicles* illustrates the growth of tradition (*e.g.*, Asa, 2 Chron. xiv); and its interest in priests and Levites is well illustrated when we compare the two accounts of the Ark (2 Sam. vi and 1 Chron. xiii, xv). In general, it has two main trends, (*a*) the importance of David, the Davidic dynasty and the Temple—*i.e.*, the king and the sanctuary, and (*b*) the superior importance of the priestly organization (note Uzziah's sin, 2 Chron. xxvi. 16 ff.). On the one hand, prophets play a prominent part in national events (2 Chron. xv. 1-15, xx. 37, xxi. 12, xxv. 15), but on the other, the priests are indispensable for the ritual: Moses the prophet (Deut. xviii. 15, Hos. xii. 13) is overshadowed by Aaron the Levitical priest.

On internal grounds *Deuteronomy*, in its present form, is to be placed not earlier than the time of Josiah, in whose reign it was discovered (621 B.C.); whereas the priestly sections of the Pentateuch (and other passages) in their present form are certainly to be dated after the return from Exile, but not before the return of Nehemiah (p. 159). *Chronicles*, when compared with *Samuel–Kings*, illustrates the development. But we emphasize ' the present form ', because throughout we deal with compilations consisting of earlier and later passages. Particularly is this the case in the Pentateuch and *Joshua*, where clearly defined and more or less continuous series can be traced, and are known

---

[1] In 1 Chron. xxiii. 14 f. the sons of Moses are reckoned to the tribe of Levi, and his sons Gershom and Eliezer are clearly represented by the Levites Gershon and Eleazar.

among biblical scholars as J (or Yahwist) and E (or Elohist), from their typical use of these divine names (p. 153). But the many questions arising out of the literary analysis of the narratives do not concern us here. It is, none the less, important to remember that, however old the oldest parts may be, the Jewish historian Josephus in the first century A.D. testifies to the way in which the Jews of even his time would justify their pride in their past and refute the libellous stories put about by their enemies.

Ezra–Nehemiah is inseparable from *Chronicles*. Here Cyrus the Persian permits the Jews in exile to return and rebuild their temple (Ezra i. 1 ff., vi. 3 ff.). Their adversaries prevented them, but in the reign of Darius the work was resumed and completed (520–516 B.C.). This was due to the zeal of the prophets Zechariah and Haggai, who enthusiastically hail the returned Zerubbabel, who was probably of Davidic descent. But he mysteriously vanishes from history, and, nearly sixty years later, Ezra, a priestly scribe, well versed in the Law of Moses, returned and instituted a great religious reform, laying the religious foundations of a new community (Ezra vii–x). Twelve years elapse, and Nehemiah, probably also of Davidic descent, overwhelmed when he hears of the miserable state of Jerusalem, returned, and in spite of opposition from outside, rebuilt the walls, and made sundry temple, economic and social reforms. The book concludes with the solemn reading of the Law by Ezra and measures taken by Nehemiah to reorganize the community, to safeguard the Sabbath, and to expel a priest who had married the daughter of the Samaritan Sanballat (Neh. viii ff.). Contemporary Jewish papyri from Elephantine in Upper Egypt throw independent light upon the period. Persian patronage, serious internal rivalries in Palestine, and the transition from the monarchy to a pre-eminent priesthood are the outstanding features.

1 *Esdras* in the Apocrypha, though now incomplete, represents another recension or arrangement of events, by transferring the reading of the Law by Ezra (Neh. viii) to the end of *Ezra* (ch. x). Also Josephus treats Nehemiah independently of and after Ezra, and in fact late tradition increased the prominence of Ezra by ascribing to him the

dictation and publication of the books of the Hebrew Canon and of seventy others to be reserved only for the wise (2 Esdras xiv. 37 ff.). On the other hand, Nehemiah is said to have collected sacred writings about the kings and prophets, the work of David, etc. (2 Macc. ii. 13 f.); and Nehemiah, and not Ezra, is named in the list of famous men in BS (Ecclesiasticus), xliv. 13 (after about 130 B.C.). The apocryphal 1 *Esdras* appears in the best Greek MSS. and was familiar to early Christian writers; it is better known for the three orations on Wine, the King and (at greater length) Women, with an appendix on Truth ending with the well-known words ' Great is Truth and strong above all things ' (iii f.).

Of other narratives, (1) *Ruth*, which in the Hebrew Canon is placed in the third division (p. 35), is a charming and independent story, not in line with the literary style and structure of *Judges* and 1 *Samuel*, between which it is now placed. It explains the Moabite origin of David, and we contrast the attitude to Moab in Deut. xxiii. 3, and Ezra ix. 1. (2) The central figure of the ever-debated book of *Daniel* is an old and venerated name (Ezek. xiv. 14, xxviii. 3). It purports to refer to the sixth century, from Nebuchadrezzar [1] to Cyrus and Darius, but is of more than doubtful historical value. It contains the popular stories of the Three Youths in the fiery furnace (ch. iii), and the writing on the wall, with the plays upon the mysterious words which, in point of fact, are probably weights (v. 25, a mina, a mina, a shekel and half-minas). The Apocrypha adds *Susanna* (whence Shylock's ' a Daniel come to judgment '), *Bel and the Dragon*, and a lengthy interpolation, the *Song of the Three Holy Children*, from which has been taken the Benedicite (verses 35–66). Dan. vii–xii contains ' apocalyptic ' writings (p. 60), visions of the future. These reflect an age of persecution, now generally identified as that of Antiochus Epiphanes, when the Jews were in the gravest danger. An assured divine intervention takes the place of the noble faith expressed in iii. 17 f. The date will be about 166 B.C. We find our-

---

[1] This, and not Nebuchadnezzar, is the correct form of the name, as commonly in Jeremiah and Ezekiel.

selves in an age where 1 *Maccabees* (originally written in Hebrew) is a valuable historical source, 2 *Maccabees* being less trustworthy. Through the achievements of Judas Maccabeus and his successors there was a revival of Jewish religion and the rise of a series of powerful priest-kings (the Hasmonaeans). For the first time since the age of *Ezra–Nehemiah* light is thrown upon the internal and external conditions of the Jews, and not a few scholars think that to this Maccabaean period may be ascribed the writing, or revision, or collecting of some of the contents of the O.T.

(3) *Esther*, with additions in the Apocrypha, is ostensibly of the time of Ahasuerus (Xerxes, fifth century). It tells how the heroine became queen, foiled the plot of the infamous Haman, and saved the Jews from being massacred. These were permitted to defend themselves, which they did, ever after celebrating the slaughter of their enemies by the popular festival of Purim. It is a remarkably secular piece of writing, intensely nationalist; and the names of Esther and her cousin Mordecai inevitably recall those of the Accadian deities Ishtar and Marduk, while with those of Haman and queen Vashti the names of certain Elamite gods have been identified. More definitely religious motives, on the other hand, can be found in the apocryphal *Tobit* and *Judith*. (4) The former of these, with its emphasis on the care for the helpless and burial of the dead, is particularly interesting. Not to speak of the archangel Raphael, who protects Tobias, the violent demon Asmodeus (of Zoroastrianism), who destroys one after the other the seven husbands of Sarah, and the reference to Tobias's faithful dog, we hear of his kinsman Achiacharus, who, as is known from other sources, was the hero of a much-travelled tale (see p. 66). (5) *Judith*, like *Tobit*, was originally in Hebrew. It is a didactic work (with a fine prayer, ch. ix), and narrates how the heroine slew Holofernes, commander of the army attacking the Jews. The moral behaviour of Judith is naturally to be judged in the light of its age. The book is a romance; in fact, little was preserved in memory of the times after Ezra and Nehemiah. Apart from the triumphant recovery of the Jews in the Maccabaean age, the greatness

of Israel belonged to the past and the story of it shaped
their hopes for the future. Consequently we hear far more
of the preparation and early discipline of Israel than of the
part she played in later history.

II. *Prophecies*

The great prophets of Israel are the outstanding glory
of the O.T. and the secret of its inexhaustible and permanent
worth. Attention, it is true, has long been directed to
them as foretellers; but the character of their utterances,
the principles involved, and the psychology of prophecy
are now rightly regarded as more important. There were
prophets of all kinds: men eccentric, ecstatic and seemingly
mad,[a] aroused by dreams and visions, by wine or music;
living in groups ('sons of the prophets'), or lonely and
isolated by the nature of their message (like Jeremiah) or
their mission (like Elijah). They might be diviners and
wonder-workers, and thus earn a living[b]; though their
extortions would expose them to condemnation.[c] They
were a recognized class along with the priests, and
patronized by the Court[d]; but the prophets who stand
out for all time were not of them. Whether men of rural
origin (like Amos and Micah), or of high rank (Isaiah and
Zephaniah), they were of social and national importance,
supporting or opposing political movements—*e.g.*, Samuel,[e]
Elisha,[f] Jonah,[g] Isaiah, in the days of the Assyrian threat,
and Jeremiah, when Babylonia was the foe. Yahweh
was a god of war (see p. 93), and the prophets can be
fiercely uncompromising,[h] denouncing Israel's enemies,
who were also the enemies of Yahweh, and exulting over
their present or imminent fate.[i]

To these prophets was revealed the secret of Yahweh.[j]
They might look back upon an inaugural vision[k], or feel
themselves to be chosen from birth.[l] Yahweh gave them

[a] Jer. xxix. 26.　　　　　　　　[b] 1 Sam. ix. 7, Amos vii. 12.
[c] Mic. iii. 5, 11, Ezek. xxii. 25.　[d] Cf. 1 Kings xviii. 19, xxii. 6 ff.
[e] 1 Sam. ix. 16; contrast ch. x. 17 ff.　[f] 2 Kings ix.
[g] *Ib.* xiv. 25.　　　　　　　[h] 1 Sam. xv. 18 f., 2 Kings xiii. 14–19.
[i] Isa. xiii, Nah. ii.　　　　[j] Amos iii. 7.　　　[k] Isa. vi.
[l] Isa. xlix. 1, Jer. i. 4 ff; cf. Gal. i. 15.

strength,[a] and no man might keep silent,[b] or go contrary
to the message he had received.[c] Profoundly conscious
of the reality of Yahweh, they were keenly alive to the
welfare of their land and people—*his* land and *his* people.
They were the nation's watchmen.[d] They could take a wide
sweep of history, embracing Israel's neighbours near and
far; and they knew that Yahweh's concern was not
limited to Israel alone[e]; for he could use other nations
to punish and discipline her, or to deliver her. Yahweh's
supreme power in the world, and his nature, and all that
it meant for Israel lie at the root of their teaching.

They saw into the heart of things—social abuses, shallow-
ness, pride, luxury, heartlessness and cruelty; there was a
theistic foundation to their social ethical teaching. ' Religion ' there was, and in plenty, but it was unreal, superficial, like that of the ' hypocrites ' whom Jesus condemned.[f]
It was contrary to what they felt to be true. There was
ritual, but it was formal, without ethical emphasis. There
are many famous attacks upon the sacrificial system,
human sacrifice, sacred prostitution and the local shrines
or ' high-places '.[1] What *did* Yahweh require of men?[g]
And if we say that it was ' ethical monotheism ', we mean
that it was the whole-hearted recognition of a One and Only
God in the Universe and that his character was ethical:
we mean that this was ' pure religion and undefiled before
our God and Father '.[h] The ' Name ' of Yahweh, which
is often mentioned, connoted his nature and in his Name
the prophets spoke.[i]

At last the prophets came to realize the hopeless rotten-
ness of Israel; they condemn both the leaders and the led,
their complacency and blindness, even the religious guides
who cried ' peace ' (*i.e.*, ' all is well '), when there was no
' peace ',[j] and who forsook the living waters for broken
cisterns.[k] For there were ' false ' prophets,[l] men who went
with the tide[m]; or who by their personal character and the

[a] Jer. xv. 20, Ezek. iii. 8 f.   [b] Jer. xx. 9.
[e] Num. xxii. 18, xxiii. 12, 1 Kings xiii. 21 f., xxii. 14.
[d] Ezek. iii. 17, xxxiii. 7.   [e] Amos ix. 7.   [f] Matt. xxiii. 13.
[g] Mic. vi. 8.   [h] Jas. i. 27.   [i] Cf. Jer. xx. 9.   [j] Jer. vi. 14.
[k] Jer. ii. 13.   [l] Deut. xiii. 1–5.   [m] See 1 Kings xxii. 12 ff.
[1] See pp. 95 f., 162.

character of their utterances were felt to be false. But
the great prophets took a deeper and wider view; they had
insight into the conditions of the day, into the national
situation, and into what they were convinced was the secret
of Yahweh's dealings with men. They spoke in relation
to the circumstances of their age, and not for a future
beyond their ken, even though later generations might
find that their words were applicable to their own day, or
could be reshaped and interpreted afresh.

It is hardly possible here to do more than summarize
in a few sentences the great canonical prophets. Written
prophecy begins in the middle of the eighth century B.C.
with four leading figures. *Amos* emphasizes the ' righteousness ' of the God of the Universe, the coming ' Day of
Yahweh ', and the judgment, not merely on other countries,
but also on Israel, in spite of her unique relationship with
Yahweh. *Hosea* condemns the cults and abuses that destroy
the kinship between Yahweh and Israel; but at the same
time he emphasizes his love. *Micah* has at heart the cause
of the people against faithless and oppressive authorities.
Isaiah, the grandest of figures, also a ' theistic statesman ',
as he has been styled, speaks of the ' Holy One of Israel ',
and eloquently and forcefully stresses his holiness (p. 84).
Nearly a century passes, and although the Judaean king
Manasseh is condemned for his iniquities and their fateful
results (viz. the Exile), no prophecy survives.[1]

Of the three prophets next to be mentioned, *Nahum* is
distinctively nationalistic, seeing in Assyria's downfall an
example of Yahweh's supremacy and the promise of a
happier Israel. *Habakkuk*, though oppressed by the
sufferings of his day, is supported by his unshaken confidence
in Yahweh, who is supreme over the nations. As in
Nahum the iniquity of other peoples and not that of Israel
is the main theme. *Zephaniah* proclaims the contrast
between Israel's indifference to Yahweh and Yahweh's
consistent righteousness or loyalty; he sees approaching
doom, as do other prophets, but he is not alone in anticipat-

---

[1] Jer. xv. 4. The *Prayer of Manasses* in the Apocrypha is a late
composition on the efficacy of repentance (cf. 2 Chron. xxxiii. 11–13,
18 f.).

ing a grander future for Israel and her God. *Jeremiah* and *Ezekiel* are contrasting figures, the prophet-psalmist with his living religion and the more nationalistic prophet-priest; their keynote is respectively Yahweh's righteousness and his holiness. Theirs was a dying nation—it was a time of sweeping changes over a large area, but they had steadfast hopes for the future. Ezekiel has an impressive vision of the resurrection of Israel, and its new unity (ch. xxxvii), and of the return to Jerusalem of the God who had left it (cf. xxxix. 29, xlviii. 35). Both of them, living at a time of disintegration prior to the subsequent post-exilic reorganization, are noteworthy for their doctrine of individual, as distinct from collective responsibility (p. 111 f.).

We now reach Isa. xl–lxvi, the *Deutero-*, or *Second Isaiah*, chapters which, with parts of Isa. i–xxxv, are undoubtedly later than the Isaiah of history.[1] They presuppose the fall of Jerusalem, the distress of the exiled, and the desolation of their Holy City; they herald glad tidings of consolation, recovery and a world-mission for the now outcast Israel. Their universalism is in striking contrast to the nationalism of Ezekiel. They proclaim an absolute monotheism: a one and only eternal Creator God Yahweh is supreme, other gods are ' not gods ', images are simply ludicrous. There comes before us the ' Servant of Yahweh ', an enigmatic and much-discussed conception (p. 118), and in language of the loftiest spirituality. Isa. lii. 13–liii. 12 presents a still unsolved riddle, by reason of the undeniable likeness between this ' Suffering Servant ' and Jesus. This passage, which has many difficulties, *looks back* upon some event; the Servant ' grew up ', he bore our sorrows, and with his stripes we are healed. But the later chapters (lvi. ff.) strike a less exalted note; a new stage has been inaugurated, a community has been established, but its leaders are worthless, social conditions are bad, and there is idolatry. Moreover, instead of the Servant and Israel's mission to the

---

[1] Isa. xxxvi–xxxix corresponds to 2 Kings xviii. 13–xx. 19, with the omission of 2 Kings xviii. 14–16 and the addition of the Psalm of Hezekiah, Isa. xxxviii. 9–20.

nations, we hear of Yahweh's 'servants', their superiority over their enemies, and the glorification of Jerusalem (lxv. 13 f., lxvi. 14).

The *Second Isaiah* is to be supplemented by *Haggai*, *Zechariah* (chh. i–viii) and *Malachi*. In the two former we read of the indifference of the native Israelites. The Temple has not yet been built; Zerubbabel, the governor of Judah, is told of the coming overthrow of the powers of the world; he is to build the Temple of Yahweh, and happier days are in store for Judah and Jerusalem. Zerubbabel and the high-priest Joshua are to rule together harmoniously. But *Malachi* (the word really means ' my messenger ') condemns the neglect of the cult—the Temple has been rebuilt—and the indifference of the people, although Yahweh had recently shown his preference for Israel over his now desolate ' brother ' Edom. A notable passage (i. 11) tells of the wide recognition of Yahweh's Name among the Gentiles; iii. 16 speaks of Yahweh's ' book of remembrance ' (cf. Esther vi. 1) with the names of his worshippers; and the exhortation to remember the Law of Moses (iv. 4) leads to the foreshadowing of the coming of Elijah to reform Israel (cf. Mark ix. 11 f.). In *Malachi* we have left behind us the gospel of the *Second Isaiah* and appear to live, not in the time of Zerubbabel, but in the conditions illustrated in Isa. lvi–lxvi (hence called the *Third* or *Trito-Isaiah*) and in the work of Ezra and Nehemiah.

The prophetical books are compilations. An exception is *Jonah*, where a popular story is used in order to tell how the prophet, who at first was disobedient to Yahweh's command to condemn Nineveh for its wickedness, is subsequently reproved for his annoyance when, on its repentance, Yahweh spared the city that contained 120,000 young unable to distinguish between right and wrong ' and also much cattle '. As regards arrangement of prophecies, the inaugural vision of Isa. vi would be expected at the beginning of the book; and passages are often arranged according to association of ideas. Isa. ii. 2–4 and Mic. iv. 1–3 are duplicates and it is hard to say which is the older. Jer. xlviii f. contains the substance, when not the words, of Amos ii. 1–3, Isa. xv f., Zeph. ii. 8–10, and parts of *Obadiah* (the denunciation of Edom). In Jer. l. 41–46, passages elsewhere threatening Jerusalem (vi. 22–24) and Edom (xlix. 19–21) are applied to Babylon.

There are some instructive patterns: (1) Ideas of condemnation, punishment, repentance, consolation and recovery—as already in the ' Philosophy of History ' in Judges iii. 11 ff. (p. 48); (2) the Fall of Jerusalem, and its re-establishment; (3) the exile or scattering of tribes and people and their return. The actual sequence of Yahweh's departure from his people before the Exile and his subsequent return after the Exile (cf. Ezek. xi. 23, xliii. 4, Zech. i. 16, Jer. xii. 7) explains certain sudden transitions, due to later editors, as when an imminent doom is abruptly followed by words of promise, or by the punishment, not of Israel, but of her enemies.   In the *Second Isaiah* the tradition of the deliverance from Egypt and the Exodus is used to inspire hope—Israel will again be rescued; and in Hab. iii Yahweh's mighty deeds in the past are recalled as a guarantee of his present or approaching help.   Sometimes these deeds belong to myth; for there are many traces of religious ideas and beliefs very different from those that characterize what we may call the ' spirit of the Bible '.   Moreover, traditions of the past and current historical situations blend, and actual events are treated on a universal or cosmic scale, so that the fortunes of Israel are bound up with world-history and the universe (pp. 120, 142).

In *Joel* a disastrous plague of locusts becomes an invading army, but the Day of the Lord is at hand.   Israel's hostile neighbours will be punished, and the nations of the world who are threatening Jerusalem will be judged by Yahweh seated on Mt. Zion; Judah and Jerusalem will be purged, and future prosperity is assured, ' for Yahweh dwelleth in Zion '.   The ' Day of Yahweh ', which, as Amos warned (v. 18–20), would be, not one of glory for Israel, but a day of judgment, blossoms out into the Great Day when the Messianic king shall reign; cf. Isa. lxvi. 22, where the world will be superseded by a new heaven and earth as eternal as Israel.   Ultimately ' the Day ' is the impressive designation of the Jewish annual ' Day of Atonement ' for the sins of Israel.

Here we enter the sphere of 'Apocalyptic' (*i.e.*, revelation). Illustrated in Joel and Daniel, Ezek. xxxviii f., Isa. xxiv–xxvii and Zech. xii–xiv, it grows in various non-canonical writings, the most important of which, *Enoch*, was popular with Jews and Christians, and left its traces upon ideas of the ' Son of Man ' in the New Testament. This literature is characteristically pseudonymous, and dwells upon a future that shall compensate for the trials and miseries of the present. It culminates in *Revelation* (see p. 78).

The great prophets were confronted by what was virtually a nature-religion, one, however, not devoid of ethical ideas, and their achievement was to ethicize it, and to emphasize the fundamental principles of the relationship between God, the universe and man. The prophets of the O.T. in general find their successors at the birth and rise of Christianity; meanwhile their influence as seen in other departments of the O.T. literature must first be briefly noticed.

III. *Law*

Sacred and secular law in the O.T. has a lengthy history behind it. Efforts to regulate social and religious conduct, elaborate temple administration, and striking spiritual and ethical ideas can be found outside Israel. The famous Code of the Babylonian king Hammurabi, ' the Shepherd of the People ' as he was called, was at the command of his Sun-god, who ordained him ' to destroy evil and the wicked that the strong oppress not the weak ' (p. 24). The Code has several interesting points of contact with the O.T.—*e.g.*, the *lex talionis* (tooth for tooth, eye for eye, cf. Exod. xxi. 24), the case of the goring ox (cf. *ib.* verses 28 ff.), and a series of blessings for the obedient and curses for the disobedient (cf. Deut. xxviii). Laws and legal usages in Accad and elsewhere provide much illustrative material for the O.T.; and from all we know of ancient Palestine more legal material must once have been current than is actually preserved.

But in the O.T. Yahweh stands at the head, and the

Mosaic law is primary—even as the temple-service is traced back to David—and is the starting-point for all subsequent Jewish and Rabbinical law. Yahweh is the upholder of social and national welfare, and the temple-ritual ensures the indispensable ceremonial requirements. Sacrificial ritual is presupposed in parts of *Genesis* and in Exod. iii. 18, v. 3; and the late Book of Jubilees carries various priestly institutions back to pre-Mosaic times. *Tōrōth* ('directions') are given by Moses as occasion demands (cf. Exod. xviii. 16 ff.). They lay down principles, *e.g.*, the rule that non-combatants should share with combatants in the gains of war (Num. xxxi. 27)—elsewhere laid down by Joshua (xxii. 8) and David (1 Sam. xxx. 22–25)—embodies a true social ideal that is not vitiated by class or partisan interests.

The main divisions are five in number : (*a*) The markedly ethical Decalogue, in two recensions, Exod. xx. 1–17 and Deut. v. 6–21, with the interesting variation that the Sabbath was given as a day of rest: you were slaves once (Deut. v. 15), *or* because Yahweh rested on the seventh day (Exod. xx. 11, see Gen. ii. 2 f.). (*b*) The terms of Yahweh's Covenant with Israel, Exod. xxxiv. 10–26, where we should expect the Decalogue to be rewritten (ver. 1, 28 f.), but have instead various ritual and other commands (ver. 17 ff.); cf. the larger and more miscellaneous collection in Exod. xx. 22–xxiii. 19. (*c*) *Deuteronomy* includes numerous injunctions (chh. xii–xxvi) which repeat, expand or supplement the preceding. The book is a profoundly earnest endeavour to purge the religion of its idolatrous elements and to regulate national, social and family life. The people as a whole are responsible and must 'put away' (lit. 'burn out') all evil. Its interest is moral rather than ritual; it is humane and kindly; a mother-bird is to be spared (? 'the right of user'),[a] sanitation enforced,[b] the gleanings left,[c] the sexes must not interchange attire.[d] Ch. xxvii contains another formal series of laws (cf. xi. 29 ff., Josh. viii. 30 ff.); it is engraved, like the Decalogue, upon stone. The scene has been shifted to Mt. Ebal, but the Samaritans continued to

[a] xxii. 6 f.   [b] xxiii. 12 ff.   [c] xxiv. 19 f.   [d] xxii. 5.

locate it at their sacred Mt. Gerizim, and between these two mountains lay Shechem, the scene of a famous covenant between Yahweh and Israel (Josh. xxiv), and the site of a temple of a (non-Israelite) covenant-god (Judges ix. 4). But the commandment to worship only at a single sacred place (Deut. xii. 5) now points to the central sanctuary of Jerusalem in the place of all other shrines (see p. 62). It underlies the treatment of history in *Kings* (p. 49), and the subsequent increasing importance of the city (p. 140). The language of the book as a whole reminds one of *Jeremiah*, but its vehement nationalism and association with the unique claims of Jerusalem are scarcely in harmony with that prophet's spirit.

(*d*) A distinct and very miscellaneous, but notably ethical collection of laws is preserved in Lev. xvii–xxvi, perhaps the best representation of the ethics of Israel. It includes the second of the greatest commandments, ' thou shalt love thy neighbour as thyself ', and to this foundation-stone of social solidarity Jesus gave a universal application (Luke x. 26 ff.). The ' Code of Holiness ', as it is now styled, is characterized by the stress upon Yahweh's character and its demands: ' Ye shall be holy, for I Yahweh am holy ' (xix. 2, cf. 1 Pet. i. 15 f.). In thought and expression it closely resembles *Ezekiel*, whose ' blue-print ' for the future (chh. xl–xlviii) is remarkable as inaugurating a new stage in the history of the priesthood. (*e*) But this code in *Leviticus* is placed amid priestly and ceremonial laws comparable with those in Num. i–x and elsewhere. In fact the Pentateuch incorporates law and ritual for the Tabernacle which the Israelites are said to have brought into Palestine and for the Temple at Jerusalem. It centres upon the religious rites and institutions of Israel (cf. circumcision, Gen. xvii. 10–14), the history that was believed to lie behind and endorse the privileges enjoyed by Israel, and the means whereby the people of the Holy God Yahweh might by ritual and ethical ' cleanness ' retain his favour. It strangely mingles ritual and ethics, and in a primitive manner. The ' uncleanness ' of childbirth, skin diseases, certain animals, and mould or mildew on garments and houses—in fact, aught that was deemed to sever a man from Yahweh's holiness or to injure it was repudiated; the offence had contagious effects. But what was primarily non-moral did not exclude the recognition and growth of ideas of what this Holiness involved. The laws, indeed the whole Pentateuch itself, always aroused the enthusiastic devotion of the Jews (cf. Ps. xix. 7–14, cxix), but the complexity of their contents and the problems of their source and development have stimulated the most penetrating researches of modern scholars (see p. 153).

IV. *Poetry*

The lines between prose, rhymed prose and poetry cannot be rigidly drawn. By poetry we mean here, not so much a particular expression of feeling as its structure, the number of accented syllables, and the parallelism where one line is balanced by another,[a] or stands in contrast,[b] or expands it.[c] Actual rhyme is uncommon.[d] Poetry abounded at feasts, festivals and funerals. A popular vintage-song is probably quoted in Isa. lxv. 8 (cf. Ps. lvii title), and an address to a well appears in Num. xxi. 17 f. David's lament in 2 Sam. i is marked by the absence of any religious note; the song of Deborah in Judges v is of great historical value ; and the ' blessings ' of Jacob and Moses (Gen. xlix, Deut. xxxiii) illustrate what was thought of the destinies of the several tribes of Israel. Deut. xxxii presents a splendid and sustained survey of Israel's fortunes. In general, the O.T. testifies to a very extensive body of poetry, oral or written.

In the Hebrew Canon *Psalms* is divided into five books (commencing with i, xlii, lxxiii, xc and cvii). There are certain striking differences between them. In Pss. xlii–lxxxiii the divine name is Elōhīm (God) and not Yahweh; cviii is made up of lvii. 7–11 and lx. 5–12, and xl. 13–17 reappears in lxx. 1–5.[1] The musical directions, including Selah, are very obscure, and the ' historical ' superscriptions generally unsuitable (*e.g.* xxxiv, lii, lix); though David

---

[a] Ps. i. 5.   [b] Ps. i. 6.
[c] Ps. ii. 6.   [d] *E.g.*, Judges xvi. 24, 1 Sam. xviii. 7.
[1] The psalm in 1 Chron. xvi is made up from Ps. cv. 1–15, xcvi. 1–13 and cvi. 1, 47 f.

had a reputation for his music and poetry (Amos vi. 5;
2 Sam. xxiii. 1–7). Note the Psalm of David in lxxxvi after
the earlier conclusion in lxxii. 20. The subjects range
over national history (cv f., cxxxv), confession (xl),
victory (cxlix) and thanksgiving (xlvii f.), and individual
distress and gratitude (xviii, xxii, xci). They are for cult
and temple occasions, for pilgrims ascending to Jerusalem
(cxx–cxxxiv, cf. lxxxiv); and Pss. cxiii–cxviii now form
the *Hallēl* ('praise') sung at the three great Jewish feasts.
The association of the Psalms with the Temple is especially
noteworthy (cf. 2 Chron. xxiii. 18); since we can read them
along with the formal and often uninspiring ritual in the
Pentateuch and thus gain a sounder knowledge of post-
exilic life. However early some of them may be—and the
main ideas often cannot be dated—*Psalms* is the hymn-
book of the Second Temple (the one founded by Zerubbabel) and of the Jewish synagogues. Whether of foreign
origin (civ, see p. 135), or from songs to other gods than
Yahweh,[1] they are of inestimable value for individual or
communal worship, as also for the student of Biblical
thought. Metrical versions in English date from early
times, and through the centuries the Psalter has held sway
over the hearts of men.[2]

Lamentations consists of five independent poems, the
first four of which are acrostic. They express deep grief at
the fall of Jerusalem and the not unmerited misery of the
people, and appeal to Yahweh, who (as *e.g.* in Isa. lxiii.
10) had 'turned to be their enemy' (cf. Lam. v. 21). Tradition (in the LXX) ascribes the book to Jeremiah, but the
language and standpoint are against this. Even the
lament over Josiah attributed to him in 2 Chron. xxxv.
25 cannot be found in Jer. xxii. 15 f., and the *Epistle of
Jeremy* in the Apocrypha, though probably once in Hebrew,
is a rather prosaic and unoriginal condemnation of idolatry.

The inclusion in the Canon of the *Songs of Songs* may
cause surprise, until the A.V. headlines are found to point
to a *Christian* interpretation; and to this an allegorical

---

[1] *E.g.*, xix. 1–6, where, however, verses 7 ff. speak of the light, not
of the sun, but that shed by the Law.
[2] See especially *The Psalms in Human Life*, by Lord Ernle (R. E.
Prothero).

Jewish interpretation forms the prelude. These frankly sensual lyrics find parallels both in ancient Egyptian love-lyrics for ' brother ' and ' sister ' (cf. v. 1 f.), which are not without their charm, and in modern Palestinian wedding-songs. The book is a unity, and one or two late versions even attempted to assign parts with stage-directions. It has been suggested by some scholars that it belongs to a cult of a god, perhaps Tammuz; and of this cult, maintained at Jerusalem in Ezekiel's time (viii. 14), traces have also been found in the *Epistle of Jeremy*. The marriage-relation between Yahweh and Israel was a deep-seated conviction linking up, on the one hand, with fertility cults and, on the other, through the reforming activity of the prophets, with ethical estimates of the marriage-tie (Mal. ii. 14), and spiritual conceptions of the bond between God and man (see p. 89 f.).

V. *The Wisdom Literature*

Proverbs and popular edifying sayings, the fruits of observation, reflection and intellectual insight, have always been common in the East, from Ancient Egypt onwards. They are humanist and practical rather than religious, and individual rather than national; they are universal principles, timeless, international and part of world-literature. Besides some fables (Judges ix. 7 ff., 2 Kings xiv. 9) and the parables of Jesus—with parallels in Jewish or Rabbinical writings—and various isolated sayings (*e.g.*, 1 Sam. x. 12, 1 Kings xx. 11, Jer. xxxi. 29), we include in the Wisdom Literature Pss. xxvii, xlix, *Proverbs, Ecclesiastes, Job*, and in the Apocrypha *Ecclesiasticus* or BS (Ben Sira), the *Wisdom of Solomon*, and *Baruch* iii. 9–iv. 4.

Solomon is singled out for his wisdom,[a] but *Proverbs* and *Wisdom*, which bear his name, are now of the Greek age. Although isolated maxims can never be dated, the series in Prov. xxii. 17–xxiii. 12 is derived from an earlier Egyptian source—viz., the proverbs of Amen-em-ope.[1] Here and elsewhere the ethical tone is high; and, where God is

[a] 1 Kings iii. 28, iv. 29 ff., x. 6–9.
[1] Other traces of their influence in the O.T. are noted by Breasted, *The Dawn of Conscience* (1934), pp. 364 ff.

mentioned, it is the writer's God and not necessarily Israel's Yahweh. The standard of the wise life is judicious common-sense or God's will; and good and bad actions receive their due in this life. The 'fools' (in *Proverbs*) are immature or incorrigibly obstinate, and the object of contempt.[1] Ben Sira comments upon the temptations of the business man,[a] good and bad friends, 'new wine, new friend ',[b] the advantages of visiting the sick,[c] proper mourning, to avoid scandal,[d] behaviour at meals,[e] and the honourable vocation of the wise scholar[f]—though the craftsmen are indispensable.[g] The physician is to be honoured: the Lord created him, but before you visit him cleanse your heart and offer up sacrifices.[h] The praise of famous Israelites (BS xliv. ff.) is excellent, the opening passage is particularly well known. Behaviour towards women[i] and good and bad wives[j] are also among the subjects of BS; and the description of the ideal housewife in the acrostic passage Prov. xxxi. 10–21 is delightful. Good advice to young men is common in both Israel and Egypt; and the popular and wholly uncanonical, if not 'pagan', Romance of Aḥiḳar (Achiacharus), whom Tobit (i. 21) claims as his nephew, blends select tales with maxims— of a markedly secular character—for *his* nephew. BS decries any hollow doctrine of sacrificial atonement.[k] God is everywhere supreme Creator, men cannot ignore Him; and in his book the standpoint is definitely Jewish, Israel being God's favoured people. Egypt might be famed for its ancient culture (see p. 22 f.), but Ps. cv. 22 will have it that Joseph had taught its senators wisdom!

Ecclesiastes, or the Preacher, is of quite another stamp. An old sceptic, seeking for an answer to life's problems, finds them insoluble, and recommends a life of moderate enjoyment—'All is vanity'. His is a Stoic courage, without hope. But there is a Sovereign God, an arbitrary one; and

[a] xxvi. 29–xxvii. 3.   [b] ix. 10, xxxvii. 1–6.
[c] vii. 35.   [d] xxxviii. 17.
[e] xxxi. 12–xxxii. 13.   [f] xxxix. 1–11; cf. John vii. 49.
[g] xxxviii. 24–34.   [h] xxxviii. 1–15; cf. vii. 29–31.
[i] ix. 1–9; cf. xxxvi. 21–26; Prov. xviii. 22; Eccles. vii. 26, 28.
[j] xxvi. 1–18.   [k] vii. 8–10.
[1] 'Folly' is the term also applied to offences that are more specifically sexual (2 Sam. xiii. 12) or ritual (Josh. vii. 15).

He is responsible for his creatures. Passages which soften
or correct his pessimism appear to be later interpolations
(*e.g.*, ii. 26, vii. 2, xii. 1, 13); and the Jews—in order to give
the book a happy ending—repeated the last verse but one
(xii. 13) after its close, a characteristic procedure, illustrated
also at the end of *Malachi*. The obscure words of Agur in
Prov. xxx. 1–4 strike a similar agnostic note.

Job, one of the greatest of the world's writings, is an
arraignment of God's rule, a passionate discussion of the
justice, or rather the lack of it, in the world, by a man
undeservedly tormented and suffering. He and his friends
dispute, at no little length, the fairness of the 'Almighty '
(Shaddai, a favourite name in the book), but the problem
remains insoluble. None may question the righteousness
of the Creator. None the less, in a difficult passage (xix.
25), Job clings to the hope of ultimate vindication, and a
vision of God leaves him humbled (xlii. 5 f.). The drama of
Job, one of the three typically righteous men of old (Ezek.
xiv. 14), is set in a popular prose frame which describes how
the Satan (it is not yet a proper name) was permitted by God
to afflict him in body and estate, and how in the sequel the
once-prosperous man was restored to greater prosperity
and happiness. The speeches of the reverent but self-
confident Elihu (xxxii–xxxvii), who can only agree that
Job's misfortunes must be due to his sins, may be regarded
as an insertion, and the same may be said of the poem on
Wisdom (xxviii.). Unfortunately the book contains several
obscure passages, among the most notable being xiii. 15,
' though he slay me, yet will I wait for him ', though the
general sense is clear, see R.V. mg.

The *Wisdom of Solomon*, like BS, comes from Egypt, and
reflects the influence of Hellenistic (Greek) thought upon an
orthodox Jew. Highly esteemed by the early Christians,
who saw a prophecy of Christ in the sufferings of the
righteous man in ii. 12–20 (p. 119 ff.), it is, as it were, an
answer to *Ecclesiastes*. It is directed against the heathen and
their idolatry; and extravagantly exalts the privileged status
of Israel, justifying her religion against the anti-Jewish spirit
of the day. It throws light upon one phase of Jewish
thought in and about the first century B.C., and is particu-

larly interesting for its conception of ' Wisdom ' as an intermediary between God and Man. It is a stage towards the N.T.

In the Wisdom Literature ' Wisdom ' is both human and
divine. Man should seek wisdom; it is practical and
effective knowledge and understanding. It is a precious,
divine gift, and moral laws should be the guide of men.
The Wisdom of God is seen in Creation,[a] it preceded
Creation, and was created by Yahweh.[b] Wisdom comes to
be a personification, almost a person; it is the artificer of all
things. It is God's Holy Spirit, and it enters only into
those who are not enslaved by sin.[c] Earlier men had
certainly observed nature;[d] but Solomon owed to Wisdom
his ' scientific ' spirit and an almost encyclopaedic knowledge.[e] Wisdom is regarded as man's quest; but God's
wisdom is unattainable (Job xxviii. 28, contrasted with ver.
1–27). Wisdom is to be wooed. She is the Woman who
appeals to youth; contrast the seductive Strange Woman,
the harlot (Prov. i–ix); ' Say unto Wisdom, My sister ',[f] cf.
the use of ' sister ' in the Song of Songs (p. 65). Definitely
Jewish is the statement that Wisdom dwells in Jerusalem, in
the Temple; she is the Torah, the Law.[g] God gave her to
Israel; she is ' the book of the commandments of God and
the Law that endureth for ever ' (Baruch iii. 36–iv. 1), and a
Christian interpolator inserts the words, ' afterwards did she
appear upon earth, and was conversant with men ', a
reference to Christ. Thus Wisdom is man's prudence,
insight and intelligence, it is God's created creator; it is the
Law, and it is Israel's own possession. In the Alexandrian
Hellenistic Jew Philo its place is taken by the Logos; and
whereas the Wisdom Literature fell into the background of
Jewish thought, the essential conceptions of Wisdom and the
Logos took a new form and a new life at the rise of the
Jewish sect that became Christianity. To quote the opening
words of Seeley's once-famous Ecce Homo, ' the Christian
Church sprang from a movement which was not begun by
Christ '.

[a] Job xxviii. 1–27.   [b] Prov. viii. 22 ff.
[c] Wisdom i. 4, vii. 22, ix. 17.
[d] Cf. Isa. i. 3, Jer. viii. 7, Prov. xxx. 25 ff.
[e] Wisd. vii. 15 ff., viii. 1 ff.   [f] vii. 4.   [g] BS xxiv. 8 ff.

CHAPTER V

THE BOOKS OF THE BIBLE

(2) THE NEW TESTAMENT

I. *The Narratives*

TURNING from the Old Testament to the New, we leave the old Israel for the ' Israel of God '.[a] The O.T. is the sacred book of Jews and Christians; but the parting of the ways now lies before us: Jesus, the Christ ('anointed one'), the awaited Messiah, heralds the Kingdom of his Father, and a corporate band of followers, the ' Body of Christ ', animated by his Spirit, is in course of formation. The N.T. inherits the O.T., and although it has a Hebrew or Aramaic background, it differs from the Judaism of the Rabbis through the influence of Greek-speaking Jews and the Greek world (cf. p. 38). Once more there are prophets, and Jesus was a prophet.[b] Even 'false prophets' appear.[c] There are parables (as also in the Rabbinical writings), and visions (as in the O.T.); and Amos vii. 1–3 could be rewritten in the style of the N.T., even as Matt. xiii. 33, xiv. 27 could be reframed in that of the O.T. There are similar problems of composition, for example, the Sayings of Jesus, like the oracles of the earlier prophets,[d] are not consecutive—*e.g.*, the Sermon on the Mount and Matt. xxiii. 13–36. We are present at sweeping changes, as impressive in secular as in religious history. The Christians must contend with both Jewish and Gentile foes, and the destruction of Jerusalem by the Romans in A.D. 70 is a conspicuous landmark. Although the contents of the N.T. do not extend over a long period (a century or less), they reflect some unmistakable developments as regards the teaching *of* Jesus and *about* him, and the steps in the growth of the Church.

We start with the Narratives—the Four Gospels and the

[a] Gal. vi. 16; cf. 1 Pet. ii. 10.
[b] Luke i. 76, Matt. xxi. 11, John vii. 40; cf. Mark vi. 15.
[c] 2 Pet. ii. 1 f., I John iv. 1.　　　　[d] *E.g.*, Isa. v. 8–24.

Acts of the Apostles. The Gospels lead up to the Crucifixion of Jesus, his death for men's sins, and his Resurrection—this, the Passion-story, is fundamental.[1]   There is a
great deal of repetition, and about A.D. 170–180 there was
written a ' Harmony of the Gospels ' which became popular.
This, the Diatessaron of Tatian, had the Fourth Gospel as
its base,[2] thus recalling the modern view that the Pentateuch
is composed of various sources and has as its base a priestly
writing, which in this case gave it its present form.   But on
deeper examination of the contents the Fourth Gospel is
now seen to be distinct from the first three, and the latter
are called ' Synoptic ' on account of the extremely close
relation between them (e.g., Matt. ix. 14 ff. = Mark ii.
18 ff. = Luke v. 33 ff.).   Passages in *Mark* that do not
reappear in *Matthew* and *Luke* are peculiar to that gospel.
But *Matthew* and *Luke* have material in common which (a)
rewrite *Mark*, or (b) come from some other common
source.   The latter, following German scholars, is called Q
(*Quelle* = source); it supplements *Mark* (e.g., it contains
more about John the Baptist, Matt. iii. 7–10, Luke iii. 7–9),
and finely illustrates the ethical teaching of Jesus.   Q
strikes one as belonging to a manual of instruction.   It
presents Jesus himself, whereas *Mark* tells us about him.
Mark in itself is inadequate.   It ends abruptly (xvi. 9, R.V.
mg., see p. 168), and does not, like the other gospels, afford a
self-explanatory account of Jesus; though it might have
been used by teachers.   It was the least read and was rather
neglected.

Matthew, which has a strong Jewish tone, will group
together material according to subject-matter (e.g., v–vii).
Luke abbreviates *Mark* or omits (e.g., Mark vi. 45–viii. 26).
It rewrites *Mark*, it has the best Greek style, and its non-
Markan material (notably vi. 10–viii. 3, ix. 51–xviii. 14)
presents a fairly coherent narrative.   *Luke* has a strong human
note and the eighteen parables peculiar to it include some of

[1] Peter's confession at Caesarea Philippi, that Jesus was the Christ,
is the turning-point in the earlier narratives (Mark viii. 29, Matt. xvi.
16, Luke ix. 20).
[2] *E.g.*, John i. 32–34 is followed by Luke iv. 1a, Mark i. 12, Matt.
iv. 1b, Mark i. 13b, Matt. iv. 2a, Luke iv. 2b.

the most impressive. It is not so Jewish as *Mark*, and reads (particularly in its continuation in *Acts*) as a defence of Christianity, appealing to non-Jewish circles. *Luke*, like Josephus (there appears to be some relation between them), dedicates the book to a non-Jewish patron; and, while interested in social matters, lets it be seen that Christianity is not a political revolutionary religion, and that the Romans had shown it tolerance and fairness. His is a beautiful Gospel, reflecting the character of ' the beloved physician ' (Col. iv. 14). Like the Pentateuch, the Synoptic Gospels raise intricate problems of literary analysis, and of the development of the religion.

Later than these three, and independent, and of another stamp is the Fourth Gospel, which can be read along with the three *Epistles of John* and *Revelation*, all traditionally ascribed to John the son of Zebedee (Mark i. 19 f.). Though relatively late, the Fourth Gospel was extant in some form before the middle of the second century A.D. (p. 40). It has distinctive features—*e.g.*, the prominence of the ministry of Jesus in Jerusalem, and not (as in the Synoptists) in Galilee; the cleansing of the Temple is placed early (ii. 14 ff., contrast Mark xi. 15 ff.), and the Last Supper is not, as in Mark xiv. 12, a Passover Meal. It is an interpretation rather than a simple narrative, emphasizing the spiritual rather than the bodily life of Jesus; it has discourses and controversies rather than parables. God is Spirit, and this Spirit is here and now. Not the Kingdom that is to come, but the present life, is its key-note; Life, Light and Spirit are the leading concepts. Though it is mystical, it has its feet on earth and treats Jesus realistically, dwelling on the human nature of the divine Jesus who is subordinate to his Father.[1] From the first, Jesus is the Light of the world, the Messiah, the Son of God. The Jewish Law is of the past (i. 17); the Logos has become flesh and has dwelt among men (i. 14). The rhythmical Prologue on the Eternal Logos (i. 1–18) develops earlier conceptions of the creative Word;[a] for Logos is more than

[a] *E.g.*, Ps. xxxiii. 6, 9; cf. Heb. xi. 3.
[1] The ' anti-Christs ' denied the human nature of Christ: Jesus was not Christ, nor was he of God (1 John ii. 18, 22, iv. 3, 2 John 7).

' word ', it is ' reason '. The earlier conception of ' Wisdom ', too, has contributed to it (p. 68). Hence the Prologue is of great philosophical value, and the whole Gospel, with its absolute simplicity, its realistic mysticism and its philosophical and metaphysical teaching, stands pre-eminent. Chh. xiv–xvii and the verse now familiar in so many languages (iii. 16, cf. xiii. 1) have, not least of its contents, made it the most beloved of all the books of the N.T.

Luke, who shows himself a consummate artist in the Gospel, gives in *Acts* the account of the spread of the new religion from the Resurrection (? A.D. 33) onwards, ' beginning from Jerusalem ' (Luke xxiv. 47). The book indicates how Christianity was being preached. It tells of the rise of the Church at Jerusalem under James the brother of Jesus,[a] and of the first martyr, Stephen, after his statement of the case for Christianity (ch. vii). Philip preaches among the Samaritans, and Paul (Saul) from being a violent leader of the persecutors is converted and becomes as vehemently Christian. Peter, a more liberal-minded man than James, wins the right to admit Gentiles to the Christian community (note x. 34 f.), but the question of the conditions of membership becomes acute. The question of ' clean ' and ' unclean ' food—*i.e.*, of common meals with the uncircumcised —is settled, but that of circumcising Gentile Christians becomes more acute as Paul goes his journeys and makes numerous converts. The very important Apostolic Council (ch. xv) brought the challenge into the open; but it was not conclusively settled, and Paul, who is the central figure of the rest of the book, continues his missionary journeys with results that can be gathered from his Epistles. Indeed, of this difficult and much-discussed but extremely valuable book, which is indispensable for the chronology of the rise of Christianity, it is enough to say that the new faith is seen spreading through Palestine, Syria, Asia Minor—Egypt is ignored—and thence to Europe until it reaches Rome. The distinction between the Jewish-Christians and Christians (whether Jews or Gentiles) is growing more clear, with the result that the Destruction of Jerusalem A.D. 70 did not have

[a] Mark vi. 3; cf. 1 Cor. xv. 7, Gal. ii. 9.

the same consequences for the Jews as for the Christians. Almost the last words of the book speak of the rejection of God's salvation by the Jews (xxviii. 23 ff.).   *Acts* as a whole reflects changing circumstances and a developing terminology; the Greek MSS. of the ' Western ' type contain many noteworthy variations, a selection of which is given by Kenyon, *Our Bible and the Ancient MSS.*, pp. 252 ff.

II. *Paul*

Of the mission-work of the Apostles, other than Paul, and of the founding of many of the churches (notably at Rome and Alexandria) little or nothing is known.   But of Paul, the greatest of teachers of Christianity, we have a considerable series of writings.   Both the order of his Epistles and the authenticity of some of them are disputed; but modern students who come to them from other fields are impressed by his freshness and vitality.   He was a Jew of Tarsus, and therefore even more removed than the Galilaean disciples of Jesus from the centre of Judaism. He writes, or dictates, like an impassioned speaker, without formal coherence.   Emotional and controversial, mingling authority with humility, he varies his emphasis according to his readers and the needs of the occasion (1 Cor. ix. 20 ff.). He was open to the charge of inconsistency, especially in the matter of circumcision.   He was also liable to misinterpretation (2 Pet. iii. 16, cf. *James*, p. 77).   He took a keen personal interest in individual and social problems, inculcating submission to authority; but he could also intervene on behalf of a converted slave (*Philemon*).

Paul took his stand upon the Crucifixion and the Resurrection.   In 1 Cor. xv he sets forth his ' gospel '.   The risen Christ had revealed Himself to him at his conversion, and he looked for the Second Coming.   His personal experience formed the basis of his theology and laid the foundation of Christian theology.   His letters indicate how Christianity was to be taught; and he had to fight and defend his position against Jews, Jewish-Christians, Christians and Gentiles.   Newly-made converts, especially Jews, could not shake off their past.   Churches were lukewarm, without unity or loyalty,. and in need of discipline.   His doctrine of the ' Body of Christ '—a lasting contribution to Christianity—involved ethical requirements;[1] and since membership was for Jew and Gentile alike, the significance of Christ for men and for the world must be made clear.

Christianity was not yet standardized. There were rival parties (1 Cor. i. 12 f.) and conflicting trends of thought. He must exhort the persecuted and reprove the waverers; but for the ' weak ' he had understanding (1 Cor. viii. 11 f., ix. 22). There was spiritual enthusiasm which needed careful checking. There were false doctrines and false teachers and prophets. He shared the current beliefs in the reality of angels, spirits and celestial powers; but would allow nothing to come between men and ' the love of God that is in Christ Jesus our Lord ' (Rom. viii. 38 f.). Christian knowledge was a spiritual enlightenment; but it could be intellectualized (as in Gnosticism), and this he condemned. If other apostles corresponded with their churches or their followers, it is Paul, and Paul above all, whom the Early Church theologians venerated, and it is only in modern times that some have ventured on the opinion that he perverted the simple gospel of Jesus, and that others have believed that without him it would have died out. We turn to a brief survey of his Epistles, taking them in what is probably their chronological order.

In 1 and 2 *Thessalonians* Paul addresses a Church in which he takes pride; he clears himself of charges, and prepares it for the Second Coming, which is not necessarily immediate (1 Thess. iv. 13–17, 2 Thess. ii. 1–12). The ' man of sin ' (a false Messiah or Antichrist) will arise and must be destroyed by the Lord Jesus. In *Galatians*, a tempestuously human epistle of autobiographical value, to be read with Acts xv, xxi, Paul justifies himself against Judaïzing opponents. The circumcision of Gentile converts is the issue, for Christ has freed men from the Law. It had been a guardian or tutor (A.V. schoolmaster, Gal. iii. 24 f.), but it had served its purpose; henceforth there could be neither Jew nor Greek—all are one in Christ Jesus.

1 and 2 *Corinthians* refer to two other letters, one before and the other after the first epistle (1 Cor. v. 9, 2 Cor. vii.

---

[1] See *The Rebirth of Christianity*, pp. 24 ff., and index.

8–12). They illustrate the situation in a church disturbed by questions of belief and conduct, split by factions, and for a time disloyal. 2 Cor. x. 1–xiii. 10, the most personal of Paul's extant writings, is a vehement letter in striking contrast to the affectionate tone of what precedes. Both epistles are of leading theological importance, especially 1 Cor. xv, on the resurrection of the dead, unique testimony to early Christian belief. The ' praise of charity ' (1 Cor. xiii) is of outstanding beauty, and has been well described as ' a lyrical interpretation of the Sermon on the Mount— the Beatitudes set to music '. That our treasure is in ' earthen vessels ', that the greatness of power is of God and not of ourselves (2 Cor. iv. 7) is in the spirit of Judges vii. 2.

The epistle to the *Romans*, the greatest of all Paul's writings, is of the highest doctrinal value. It is addressed to Jews and Gentile Christians, and has in view the questions that could be raised from the Jewish side. Besides dealing with doctrines of justification and salvation, it is a powerful exposition of the election and rejection of Israel, and unfolds a veritable Christian philosophy of history. Though its phraseology reminds us of *Wisdom*, there is an unbridgeable gulf between Paul's attitude to Israel and that of the Jewish writer; only as regards God and pagan idolatry is there agreement in spirit. The many references to this epistle in the following pages will illustrate its importance.

Philippians protests against Jewish or Jewish-Christian intrigues. The noble rhythmical passage, ii. 5–16, on the self-emptying of Christ and his exaltation (the *Kenotic* doctrine), is directed against misleading (Gnostic) speculations, and forms a basis of the later doctrine of the Incarnation. *Colossians*, in an impressive passage (i. 15–ii. 15), sets forth the cosmic significance of Christ, a noteworthy development of 1 Cor. viii. 6, and (iii f.) opposes an esoteric Jewish-Gnostic type of philosophy, confronting its ritualist and ascetic teaching with a sketch of Christian ethics. As for *Ephesians*, its authenticity has been questioned. It is closely related to *Colossians* and 1 *Peter*. It reads as a theological tract, perhaps a circular letter, as an introduction to Paul's epistles or, preferably, as a later condensation of his teaching. Ch. i. 3–14 is a fine rhythmical statement of the finality of Christ and, through Him, of the Christians chosen from the first before the foundation of the world. Both *Colossians* and *Ephesians* have a marked philosophical and metaphysical interpretation of Christ, and may therefore be among the latest of the epistles.

Hebrews, only traditionally attributed to Paul, is directed against the weaklings who had not realized that Christianity superseded Judaism, with its Tabernacle and Temple, its priestly ritualism and sacrificial system. The unforgettable opening words are the key to the Epistle. Christ is supreme over Moses and over angels; his willing sacrifice is final, the Old Covenant is superseded by the New. The faith which had inspired Israel in her past history should encourage Christians, who, through Jesus, the Mediator of a New Covenant, have no unapproachable Mt. Sinai (a reference to Exod. xix. 12 f.), but are come unto Mt. Zion and the city of the living God, the heavenly Jerusalem, and to God the Judge of all (ch. xi f., cf. Gal. iv. 26). An ultimate Greek (Platonic) influence by way of Alexandrian Judaism (p. 67) can be traced in the contrast between this transitory world and the reality of the heavenly realm. We are seeing how all that was implied in Christian experience was being thought out and set down in writing.

III. *Other Writings*

Pauline, rather than by Paul, are the three personal ' Pastoral Epistles ' to Timothy and Titus. They contain practical admonitions regarding Church life, commend ' sound doctrine ', and warn against false teachers who, like some of the prophets of old, made money out of their calling (1 Tim. vi. 3 ff., Titus i. 10 ff.; cf. Mic. iii. 11). 2 *Timothy*, which seems to be the earliest, urges endurance amid suffering and stresses current controversies. In 1 Tim. iii. 16 the R.V. mg. points out that the true reading is ' He who was manifested ', etc.—the words are rhythmical. 2 Tim. ii. 11–13 appears to be from a hymn, and iv. 1–8 does seem to read like the Apostle's finale. *Titus* is a simpler epistle: ' sound doctrine ' for Christians in a quarrelsome world and exposed to false teaching.

Of the ' General or Catholic Epistles ', *James* (hardly by

the head of the Church at Jerusalem) has been considered to be one of the earliest or of the latest. Jacob (the form James comes through the late Latin Jacomus, cf. the Italian Giacomo) writes to the ' twelve tribes of Israel ' scattered abroad. He is strongly Jewish, and reminds us of both the O.T. and the Wisdom literature; definitely Christian ideas are scanty. Like a prophet of old, he proclaims unselfishness, brotherliness and social righteousness (cf. *e.g.*, Amos v. 12 ff.). He is practical rather than doctrinal, for if faith does not lead to good works it is dead (i. 22, ii. 26); some aspects of Paul's teaching or of those who misunderstood him appear to be in his mind.

1 *Peter* is a warmly-written and practical letter to Gentile Christians encouraging patience and hope to withstand persecution. It has many interesting features, *e.g.*, the meaning of service (ii. 18–25) and the preaching to the dead (iii. 18 f., cf. iv. 6). On the other hand, 2 *Peter* is a ' tract for the times ', using Peter's name and incorporating some of *Jude*. It attacks the current immorality and the ' false prophets '. The Day of the Lord will assuredly come, and suddenly; and after a universal conflagration there will be a new heaven and earth, the abode of righteousness (see p. 121 f.). *Jude* (scarcely the Judas of Acts i. 13) denounces the seducers who are undermining Christian teaching: the ' liberty which we have in Christ ' (Gal. ii. 4) was abused. He encourages his readers to contend for the faith which had previously been given once and for all to the saints, ' the apostles of our Lord Jesus Christ ' (vv. 3, 17). In this short book reference is made to the myth of the fallen angels (cf. 2 Pet. ii. 4), also to Michael, the Archangel (as in the apocryphal *Assumption of Moses*), and to the prophecy of Enoch, thus testifying to the popularity of writings or traditions which gradually disappeared (see p. 35).

The ' Johannine Epistles ' are traditionally ascribed, together with the Fourth Gospel (p. 71) and *Revelation*, to John the son of Zebedee, and assumed to be written at Ephesus, where he became head of the churches of Asia Minor. All show, however, a unity of environment rather than of authorship. 1 *John* is an authoritative and ' catholic ' tract against false teaching and the ' docetic ' Christology which would deny the bodily appearance of God as Christ on earth (iv. 2) and sever spirit and matter, whereas the true division is between good and evil. Not every ' spirit ' is to be believed, and in this un- or anti-Christian world many antichrists have arisen (cf. 2 John 7). The true fellowship of the ' children ' of God is with God and with one another. The central theme of this beautiful Epistle is Love: to know what God is like we must look at Christ. In v. 6–8 the R.V. and the American Standard Version rightly omit a later addition which mentions three other heavenly witnesses and identifies them with the Father, the Word and the Holy Spirit. 2 *John* is for the ' Elect Lady ' and her ' children '—*i.e.*, the Church and its members (cf. Israel and the Israelites in *Hosea*, see p. 89). It is on the lines of the preceding. 3 *John* is a private letter to a convert, commending ' my children ' walking in the truth. It comes as from an ecclesiastical dictator, and rebukes an insubordinate and disloyal church-leader.

The last of the varied contents of the N.T. is *Revelation*. It has been as mystifying and fascinating as *Daniel*, and was long in gaining general acceptance. It is ' apocalyptic ' (p. 60), and, like other literature of that class, appears under a great name; later on an apocalypse was even attributed to Peter. It is extremely ' Hebraic ' rather than ' Israelite ', and has echoes of Accadian and other myths. But it is the Christian climax, and fittingly closes the Bible. Like *Daniel*, it deals with (*a*) a particular situation, and (*b*) visions of the future communicated to the seer by one ' like the Son of Man ' (cf. Dan. vii. 13, see p. 121). It represents grave conditions, persecution is rampant, the martyrs are many, and the cult of Caesar is being forced upon Christians. Rome is the ' Babylon ' (xiv. 8), the tyrant and shedder of blood, the great Harlot; and the number of the beast 666 (xiii. 18, in some MSS. 616), for which the most fantastic identifications have been found (including Luther and Napoleon), probably refers to Nero Caesar, though *Revelation* itself is of a later date, that of Domitian (A.D. 93–96).

The book falls into two unequal divisions: (*a*) Letters to seven churches in Asia Minor, or rather to the ' angels ' of which they are the embodiments (chh. i–iii). They condemn lukewarmness, compromise and apostasy; Jewish calumnies are rife. They refer to the false teaching of ' Balaam ', the prototype of idolatry (Num. xxxi. 16; contrast the earlier estimate in Num. xxii–xxiv), and of Jezebel (1 Kings xxi. 25); and the ' synagogue of Satan ' consists of men who say they are Jews but lie. (*b*) The very elaborate series of visions (chh. iv ff.) cannot be easily summarized; they continue to perplex commentators. God is on his throne in heaven, and with Him is the Lamb (Christ)—a reference to the Passover victim and to Isa. liii. 7—or the Lion (of the tribe of Judah, cf. Gen. xlix. 9). The Lamb opens a book, and the Four Horses of the Apocalypse issue with plagues and woes for the wicked, and redemption for the faithful. Babylon (Rome) is overthrown, and after the downfall of Satan Christ reigns for 1000 years. There is then a new heaven and earth, and God and the Lamb occupy the throne.

Finally, a heavenly Jerusalem descends upon earth. Its gates are named after the twelve tribes of Israel, and its foundations after the twelve Apostles of the Lamb (cf. Eph. ii. 20). The city is measured, as in Ezekiel's vision (Ezek. xlviii); and the foundations laid with precious stones (cf. Is. liv. 11 f., Tobit xiii. 16 ff.). The Lord God and the Lamb are the temple (see John iv. 21) and the source of light (cf. Is. lx. 19). There is another Paradise, with the Tree of Life, as in that before the Fall (cf. Gen. ii. 9). The visions of the imminent future imparted to the seer from the God of the spirits of the holy prophets cease. Christ has summed up all that has gone before, and perhaps no other book in the N.T. is so penetrated with the imagery of the O.T. and its leading ideas. So the N.T. ends: The Church has conquered Rome; Christianity has overcome the world (cf. 1 Cor. xv. 24–27).

To conclude this and the preceding chapter: we pass from an old religion and its vicissitudes to the rise and early steps of a new one. Both are distinguished by the prophetic spirit, attacking and reforming the life and thought of the day. In both we find three stages: (1) the current conditions, (2) the new spiritual and ethical impulse, and (3) its subsequent application with loss of freshness, deteriora-

tion of ethical standards, and the difficulties arising from
varieties of temperament and training, conflict of opinions
and party divisions.   The O.T. extends over a much longer
period than the N.T.; but there are similar sorts of vicissitudes and similar problems of literary analysis and date.
Where there were bands of prophets (1 Sam. x. 5, 2 Kings
ii. 3), disciples (Isa. viii. 16), and prophets true and false,
and discrimination was necessary (cf. 1 Cor. xiv. 29, 1 John
iv. 1), it is not surprising that in contrast to real and vital
differences of thought, there might also be identity of spirit
without precise identity of emphasis.   Hence it is not surprising (*a*) that in *Isaiah*, *Jeremiah* and other prophets there
are passages which closely approximate the prophets'
thought, but can scarcely be from their mouths, they are
Isaianic, Jeremian, etc., and (*b*) that in the N.T. we may
find what is Pauline, Petrine or Johannine rather than the
words of the apostles themselves.

Throughout, questions of canonicity and authenticity crop
up, and it is impossible to confine oneself solely to what is
' canonical ' or ignore any questions of the authenticity of
the latter that may be raised.   The O.T. naturally leads on
to the N.T.; and the latter cannot be truly understood if we
neglect the former.   The N.T. is permeated with the O.T.
and the apocryphal and apocalyptical literature : the Gospels
and the Messiah, Paul and the Law, *Hebrews* and the
priesthood, *Revelation* and the visions of old.   In no other
collection of writings is there any similar continuity and
development by the side of discontinuity and sweeping
changes in history and in religion.   This must be borne
in mind when we proceed to consider some of the ideas in
the Bible (Chap. VI).   These can be said to centre ultimately upon Jerusalem and Mt. Zion (Chap. VII), and they
introduce us to certain fundamental problems of the O.T.
and N.T. which sooner or later confront the careful reader
(Chap. VIII).

CHAPTER VI

THE LANGUAGE AND IDEAS OF THE BIBLE

I. *Phraseology*

To understand the spirit of the Bible it is necessary to get behind the letter and grasp the leading ideas that pervade it. At the outset the English reader is confronted by a number of archaisms which are often still retained in the R.V., for example, ' dreadful ' (terrible, Gen. xxviii. 17), ' tale ' (number, Exod. v. 8), ' cunning ' (skilled, Exod. xxvi. 1), ' usury ' (interest, Exod. xxii. 25). ' Eared ' is replaced by ' plowed ' in Deut. xxi. 4; but ' prevent '—*i.e.*, be beforehand—is retained in Ps. lix. 10, cxix. 147 f., although in Ps. xvii. 13 the Hebrew word is rendered by A.V. ' disappoint ', R.V. ' confront ', and more suitably by the R.V. mg. ' forestall '.[1] The conviction that God takes the first step, so to speak, is obviously a very important one; cf., *e.g.*, Ps. lxxix. 8, ' let thy tender mercies speedily prevent us, for we are brought very low '; see also Ps. xxi. 3.

As regards translation, there is an important distinction between ' captivity ' (loss of freedom) and ' exile ' (without necessary loss of freedom). The latter is used of the Jews dispersed from their native land after the fall of the northern and southern kingdoms; this is the Dispersion or Diaspora (1 Pet. i. 1). In the English A.V. ' strange ' is an archaic use for ' foreign ', but the ' stranger ' should not be confused with the ' sojourner ' who is one that lives under the protection of another; this difference is recognized by the R.V. (*e.g.*, in Exod. ii. 22), but not in Lev. xxiv. 22, etc. In Isa. xi. 6, the corresponding Hebrew verb means that the wild beasts shall dwell under the protection of the kid and the lamb. Fuller information on such points as these will be found in the lists of renderings preferred by the American

[1] In Matt. xvii. 25, where Jesus ' prevented ' Peter, R.V. renders ' spake first to him '.

Committee of the R.V. and printed in our Bibles, and in the usual commentaries (especially by S. R. Driver).[1]

A knowledge of Hebrew usage is constantly indispensable. In Ps. ii. 7 ' begotten ' means rather ' adopted as a son ', and the ' sons ' of the prophets,[a] gods,[b] death,[c] or peace [d] had the characteristics of their respective classes. ' Son of man ' means properly a human being (cf. Num. xxiii. 19), but it has a specific use in *Ezekiel*, where the contrast between man and God is balanced by the close relationship between them. Hebrew thought is practical. Love, knowledge and covetousness (as in the Decalogue) imply the effective practical consequences—*e.g.*, Yahweh ' loved ' Jacob and ' hated ' Esau, as was shown by his actions (Mal. i. 2 f.). A ' covenant ' implies the consequent protection or immunity (as in Jer. xxxiii. 20), and to ' judge ' is also to execute judgment; note Deborah as ' judge ' in Judges iv. 4 ff. stirring up Barak, and the ' judges ' raised up to deliver Israel (ii. 18). ' Salvation ' implies deliverance or victory; it is material and actual, and not solely deliverance from spiritual sin. ' Peace ', too, is more than pacificism; it is— if the colloquialism be forgiven—the state of being O.K.; more formally it is the state of total harmony and its effects. Parallelism is extremely common, as in Ps. ii, or Hos. v. 3, 5 (Israel = Ephraim); and the ' ass even a colt the foal of an ass ' means a single animal and not two (Matt. xxi. 7, contrast John xii. 14 f.).

Noteworthy also is the blending of cause and effect, or of prelude and sequel; thus the same words express toil and wages, acting wisely and the consequent success, iniquity and its retribution, blood-shed and blood-guilt. Men are said to make idols *that* they may be cut off (Hos. viii. 4)— the result for the deed, just as we say that children are mischievous ' in order to annoy ' their elders. Does a man sin against God *in order that* He may be justified (Ps. li. 4, see Rom. iii. 4)? This is to confuse the sequel with the sinner's purpose; and it opens up the immense problem of original

[a] 1 Kings xx. 35.					[b] Job i. 6, Ps. xxix. 1 mg.
[c] 1 Sam. xxvi. 16 mg.				[d] Luke x. 6.
[1] As regards the N.T., note, *e.g.*, that the Prodigal Son did not ' gather together ' but ' realized ' his share (Luke xv. 13).

intention and final end. We in turn often naturally look back and say that So-and-so was ' destined ' or was ' fated ' to produce such-and-such a result; we see the end in the beginning or assume a beginning appropriate to the end. The Hebrew usage bears upon the N.T. phrase ' that the Scriptures might be fulfilled ' (Matt. i. 22, etc.). On the one hand, ' fulfilment ' involves the idea of completing, supplementing or developing to the full; and on the other, ' that it might be fulfilled ' can mean ' by way of (or in effect) fulfilling '.[1] How the *spirit* of the O.T. is ' filled out ' in the N.T., we can see; but the fulfilment of the *letter* and its details is another matter, and to expect it and find it —as early Christians delighted to do—is to run the risk of obscuring the life-giving spirit. And it is not in theology alone, but also in history and in science, that the problem of design and purpose—the problem of teleology—is apt to be perplexing.

What is suggestive or illustrative or demonstrative is not necessarily proof. In the N.T. as also in Rabbinical writings passages from the O.T. are taken from their original context and used to establish an argument.[2] In the O.T. Hannah's joy (1 Sam. ii. 1–10) is expressed in a song that is not in place (apart from ver. 5); whereas the *Magnificat*, which is partly modelled upon it, is more in harmony with its context.[a] Jonah's song in the whale's belly is one of thanksgiving (ii. 2 ff.); and the passages in Ezr. iv. 6–23 which *illustrate* the hostility against the Jews, belong to a subsequent period. Similarity and identity were confused: the weak heart *is* water,[b] Jehu *is* Zimri.[c] The essence and the embodiment (or material form) are one, as when an idol does not merely represent or embody, but *is* the god itself, or when blood *is* the soul or essence of life.

Events were not mere happenings; to the prophets they were also the manifestation of principles—Yahweh's

---

[a] Luke i. 46 ff.   [b] Josh. vii. 5.   [c] 2 Kings ix. 31.

[1] In John xii. 38 the words are ' that it might be fulfilled '; but in Rom. xi. 8 ff. the quotation is introduced with the words, ' as it is written '. (In verse 11 ' that they might fall ' is rather ' so as to fall ', *i.e.*, thereby the Gentiles and not the Jews were saved.)

[2] Cf. the use of Deut. xxv. 4 in 1 Cor. ix. 9, 1 Tim. v. 18; see also Rom. iii. 10 ff., 1 Cor. x. 1–11, 2 Cor. vi. 16–18, Gal. iv. 21 ff.

principles. Conversely, the story of events could be re-written or reshaped in order to convey principles and fundamental ideas. There was an intense realism. Bless-ings and cursings were almost material, they were pervasive like a contagious disease, and once uttered might be irrevocable (cf. Gen. xxvii. 35 f., and the story of Balaam, Num. xxii ff.). Righteousness and holiness are not so much abstract nouns as states of being right and holy, their pervasiveness and their consequences.[1] The former applied particularly to right conduct and relationship, the latter to the wide gulf between the sacred and the secular or profane, and neither had necessarily a solely ethical meaning. Job's character (i. 1) was not so much absolute ethical sinless-ness as a complete and single-minded integrity.

Ideas which we treat as abstract are personified (*e.g.*, Wickedness, Zech. v. 8). Symbolical language is common; but the symbolical acts of the prophets make actual and real their message.[a] Job xvi. 12–14 vividly describes God's fierce attack upon him; but Jacob's conflict with God in Gen. xxxii. 22–30 is no less vivid, and is narrated in a form wholly in accord with popular thought. The *Name* be-tokens the nature and personality of its bearer, and change of name indicates some significant change of status or for-tune. To blot out the name or to preserve it meant extinc-tion or survival (even after death, Deut. xxv. 6); and to *know* the name implied a special relationship and intimacy, with a claim to another's help or protection. Yahweh knows Moses by name,[b] and declares his own name.[c] So, the name signifies the whole personality,[d] and is used in working wonders[e] or in baptism.[f] (See p. 91.)

There is a vital distinction between words as such and what they stand for. Lip-religion is condemned[g] and ritual that is mere ritual is futile.[h] One's 'heart' must be in one's worship; the whole self is involved. The bodily

---

[a] *E.g.*, Jer. xix. 1, 10 f. (cf. Ezek. xxxvii. 16 ff.).
[b] Exod. xxxiii. 12; cf. Isa. xliii. 1, Gen. xxxii. 29, Judges xiii. 17 f.
[c] Exod. xxxiv. 5 ff.; cf. vi. 2 f.   [d] Acts i. 15 mg., Rev. iii. 4 f.
[e] Mark ix. 38   [f] Matt. xxviii. 19, 1 Cor. i. 13 ff.
[g] Mark vii. 6.   [h] Amos v. 21 ff., Isa. i. 11 ff.
[1] See pp. 62 f., 140. Cf. Isa. lxv. 5 (where we should read ' come not near else I sanctify thee '), Ezek. xliv. 19, Exod. xxix. 37.

parts have psychical functions; the whole body is one, and the ' spirit ' or ' soul ' is not a distinct entity (see p. 176). There are, in fact, two modes of thought: one could think either from the more ' human ' point of view or from the more ' spiritual '; men did actually disappear at death *or* there might be some continuance; Yahweh is invisible and remote *or* he is effectively here and among his people.   God sends his own Son in the likeness of ' flesh ';[a] but that He was human, though not merely human, was the insistent conviction of the Church.   The literal and the symbolical intermingle, as in *Joel*, or in Ezekiel's description of the apostasy or whoredom of the people (chh. xvi, xxiii); and it is often clear that we must not too literally take, or assume that early readers took, the vivid and impressive pictures of the prelude to the reign of the Messiah or the end of the world (p. 122).   But the Bible extends over many centuries of the ebb and flow of fortunes, times of profoundest faith and of scepticism, of moral decline and rebirth, of a despiritualized worldliness and respiritualized belief, and unless this is remembered the Bible runs the risk of remaining a closed book.

II. *Israel and her God*

Israel was an ' elect ' people, selected by Yahweh, and his ' peculiar ' (*i.e.*, his own personal) people and treasure.[b] And the Christians, the new ' Israel of God ',[c] claimed to inherit her privileges.[d]   The conviction that she was ' chosen ' from the days of her patriarchal ancestors always prevailed—Abraham,[e] Jacob or Israel;[f] it embraced the whole people.[g]   Other gods belonged to other peoples and were not to be worshipped;[h] indeed, Yahweh was king above all gods.[i]   No other people was like Israel:[j] the bond between her and Yahweh was unique.   The choice of this insignificant people was not due to her merits, but to his

[a] Rom. viii. 3.   [b] Exod. xix. 5, Deut. xiv. 2
[c] Gal. vi. 16.   [d] 1 Pet. ii. 5–10.
[e] Gen. xii. 1, Neh. ix. 7 f., Luke i. 72 f., Acts iii. 25.
[f] Gen. xxviii. 3 f., Isa. xli. 8.
[g] Exod. vi. 6–8, Ps. cv f.; cf. Acts xiii. 17 ff.
[h] Deut. iv. 19, xxix. 18, Mic. iv. 5
[i] Ps. xcv. 5, xcvi. 4 f.   [j] Deut. iv. 33 ff.

love;[a] it was an everlasting love,[b] that could grieve over her sins and sufferings.[c] Similarly in the N.T. the choice is made, not by men, but by God,[d] and Yahweh's 'Name' (p. 84) has been placed upon or called over Israel, thus establishing a relationship with protection and claims.[1]

There was a covenant between Yahweh and Israel: I, your God, and ye, my people:[e] it is the keynote of the Bible.[f] His covenant is with the world, man and nature,[g] with David,[h] and the priesthood.[i] Israel may be faithless, but Yahweh is 'righteous', i.e., loyal;[j] and in spite of his threats and punishment of her,[k] the covenant is renewed and stands firm.[l] Along with Ezekiel's promise of a new heart and spirit (Ezek. xi. 19 f.) a new and direct covenant with individual Israelites is announced by a contemporary prophet (Jer. xxxi. 31 ff., cf. p. 111 f.); even as a new covenant superseding the old one is inaugurated by the sacrificial death of Jesus who is the mediator between God and man.[2] Covenants were ratified by a sacrificial rite,[m] by throwing (not 'sprinkling' as in E.V.) blood upon a sacred object (the altar) and the contracting parties,[n] or by a common meal before the god.[o] The addition of salt was believed to make a covenant permanent; compare Yahweh's covenant of salt with David (2 Chr. xiii. 5), and the words of Jesus to his disciples in their dispute: 'Have salt in yourselves, and be at peace one with another' (Mark ix. 50). The rite of circumcision, which was originally a puberty rite before admission to the privileges of a tribe or group, was later performed in infancy;[p] the uncircumcised had no part in Yahweh's covenant.[q] The question of its necessity was the cause of serious controversy at the rise of Christianity (pp. 72 and

[a] Deut. iv. 37, vii. 7.   [b] Jer. xxxi. 3.
[c] Isa. lxiii. 9, Hos. xi.   [d] John xv. 16; cf. Gal. iv. 9.
[e] Deut. xxvi. 17 f.   [f] See Rev. xxi. 3.
[g] Jer. xxxiii. 20; cf. Gen. viii. 21 f., Hos. ii. 18, 21 ff.
[h] 2 Sam. vii.   [i] Jer. xxxiii. 17 ff.   [j] Zeph. iii. 5.
[k] Ezek. xvi. 60, 62.   [l] Jer. xxxi. 1–4.   [m] Cf. Jer. xxxiv. 18 f.
[n] Exod. xxiv. 8.   [o] Exod. xviii. 12, xxiv. 11; cf. Gen. xxxi. 54.
[p] Gen. xvii.   [q] Ib. ver. 13 f.; cf. Exod. xii. 48.

[1] Cf. Acts ix. 15, xv. 14, 17; 'called by' his Name, in Deut. xxviii. 10 and elsewhere, is inexact; cf. 1 Kings viii. 43 mg.

[2] 1 Cor. xi. 25, Heb. vii. 25, viii. 6. By a play upon words the 'covenant' is a 'will', the force of which depends upon the death of the testator (Heb. ix. 17 ff.).

126), but the prophets had long before taught that the 'circumcision' of the heart (*i.e.*, the mind and spirit) was more essential for the covenant relation between God and man.[a] Israel, as a kingdom of priests,[b] was to be also a covenant-people [c] to establish, as later did Christ, harmony between God and man.

Israel was holy to Yahweh, the Holy One of Israel, and therefore under his special protection.[d] He was in her midst, his Temple was in Jerusalem, and Israel was confident that no harm could befall her : it is a conviction which led to a careless confidence and was condemned by the prophets (p. 139). But Israel, in turn, must be 'holy', and the 'Law of Holiness' in Lev. xix–xxvi (p. 62) has specific ritual and ethical requirements. Yet in his chastening love Yahweh could discipline her;[e] and though he gives her into the hands of her enemies, and she even goes into exile, his wrath is not for ever.[f] 'Jealous' when his rights (or righteousness) are infringed by false cults,[g] he can be filled with 'zeal'—it is the same term—and, angered at the excesses of her victors, restore her to favour and deliver her.[h] Though he leaves Jerusalem to her fate and Israel goes into exile, he returns again.[i] It is this deep-rooted faith in God's covenant that moves Paul (Rom. xi) to end his condemnation of his people on the note of hope, quite in the style of the old prophets (*e.g.*, Amos ix. 11–15). Yahweh, as his name is explained, 'will be just what he will be ',[1] and the conviction that he was not arbitrary and changeable like men,[j] but holy and righteous in his rule in and over the world, whatever Israel—or a Job (p. 67)—might feel, lies at the basis of Israelite thought. The right relationship with a holy and righteous God, and all that this entails, is the fundamental truth that we owe to the Bible.

[a] Deut. xxx. 6, Jer. iv. 4, vi. 10, Lev. xxvi. 41; cf. Rom. ii. 29.
[b] Exod. xix. 6; cf. Isa. lxi. 6, 1 Pet. ii. 5, 9.
[c] Isa. xlii. 6, xlix. 8.   [d] Jer. ii. 3.
[e] Deut. viii. 4; cf. Heb. xii. 5 ff.   [f] Isa. li. 16.
[g] Exod. xx. 5, Deut. xxxii. 16, Num. xxv. 11.
[h] Isa. ix. 7, liv. 7 f., Ezek. xxxvi. 4–7.
[i] Zech. i. 15 f.
[j] Num. xxiii. 19, Mal. iii. 6; cf. Rom. xi. 29, James i. 17.
   [1] Exod. iii. 14 mg.; the rendering 'I am that I am' is incorrect and has vitiated theology.

The preceding is a simplification of the facts, for in the course of history Israel suffered many changes of fortune, and these naturally affected her beliefs. None the less, in a time of great distress and evil we meet with the idea of a ' remnant ', the nucleus of a future reorganization (p. 116). Even when her people were in exile or scattered abroad the close relationship between Yahweh, Israel and Palestine, though impaired, was not broken.[a] Moreover, this relationship affected ideas of that subsisting between Israel herself and Yahweh, on the one side, and between either and non-Israelite nations, on the other. There is a particularism or exclusivism, and Israel would abuse her privileged position; but there is also a fine universalism which looks beyond the borders of Israel, for Yahweh cared for other peoples besides Israel,[b] and Israel had a mission to the Gentiles.[c] There is a combination of both when Yahweh is the God of the world and nations do homage to Israel his ' peculiar ' treasure at his holy city of Jerusalem (p. 142).

The *solidarity* of Israel is a very important and pregnant conception, inasmuch as it paved the way for the later conception of the ' Body of Christ ' (p. 126). All Israel is one ' flesh '.[d] All have one father; hence brotherliness is enjoined;[e] and in one of the finest of ethical passages Job speaks of his regard for his servants, for all have been fashioned in the womb by God (xxxi. 15). For Paul the law of love is the fulfilment of law, or the Law, the Torah (Rom. xiii. 8–10). Solidarity was maintained by a not too close intermarriage (there are various marriage bars);[f] and by avoiding close contact or alliance with other peoples and their cults,[g] cf. Solomon's wives,[h] and Ahab and Jezebel.[i] Marriage with outsiders was denounced;[j] but with the exclusion of Moabites and Ammonites from the community in Deut. xxiii. 3, and Neh. xiii. 1–3, contrast the

[a] Cf. 1 Kings viii. 46–53.   [b] Amos ix. 7, Jer. xlviii. 47, xlix. 6, 11.
[c] Isa. xlii. 6, xlix. 6.
[d] Isa. lviii. 7; cf. Acts xvii. 26, Rom. xi. 14.
[e] Mal. ii. 10; cf. Eph. iv. 6.
[f] Deut. xxii. 30, xxvii. 20–23; Lev. xviii, xx.
[g] Isa. ii. 6, xxxi. 1–3.   [h] 1 Kings xi. 1 ff.
[i] 1 Kings xvi. 31 f.   [j] Ezra ix. 12; cf. Neh. xiii. 23 ff.

explicit record in *Ruth* that David himself had a Moabite ancestress (p. 52).

There was a feeling of corporateness and unity in space and in time: Yahweh's promises to the ancestors extended to their descendants; and for him to ' remember ' Abraham, Isaac and Jacob, or David, was to protect all Israel.[a] This was firmly believed; although the disintegrated conditions in the time of Jeremiah and Ezekiel and during the Exile must have broken the thread of the history, until there was a reorganization under Ezra and Nehemiah and a fresh solidarity.

The solidarity was understood realistically and physically before it was more ' spiritually ' interpreted. Israel is Yahweh's firstborn,[b] Judah is a ' backsliding daughter ',[c] Yahweh is the husband of Israel,[d] and the Israelites are his children: ' my children whom thou didst bare unto me ' (Ezek. xvi. 20, Hos. ii. 1 ff.) The belief reappears in the *Second Isaiah*, where Yahweh again takes the ' deserted ' one whom he had divorced, the barren one who was now to bear many children (Isa. l. 1, liv. 1, 5). Yahweh is again her husband; hence she is called Beulah, ' married ' (lxii. 4 f.); and Paul, citing Isa. liv. 1, speaks of the Heavenly Jerusalem as the ' mother ' of Christians (Gal. iv. 26 f.), even as Zion was the mother of nations.[e] Indeed, Yahweh, Israel's ' Redeemer ',[f] is the *gō'ēl*, a term for a man's near kinsman, who avenges his death, or vindicates his rights, or redeems his property, or who, by marrying his widow, if childless, secures the continuance of his family (Deut. xxv. 5 ff.).

The marriage symbolism is carried over into the N.T. in the ' elect lady and her children ' (2 John i. 4, see p. 78), in the intimate union between Christ and the Church[g] and in the ' bride ' whom the Lamb will take to himself.[h] For the Christian community is most closely united with Christ. He is the Vine, and his followers are the branches (John xv. 1 f.); He is the life-giving Spirit, and through Him they

---

[a] Exod. xxxii. 13, Ps. cxxxii, Rom. xi. 28, Heb. vi. 13 ff., Luke i. 72.
[b] Exod. iv. 22.   [c] Jer. xxxi. 9.   [d] Cf. Jer. iii. 14, xxxi. 32.
[e] Ps. lxxxvii. 5; cf. Isa. lxvi. 11.   [f] Isa. liv. 5; cf. Job. xix. 25 mg.
[g] Cf. 1 Cor. iv. 15, 2 Cor. xi. 2, Eph. v. 25.
[h] Rev. xix. 7 ff., xxi. 2, 9, xxii. 17.

bear fruit; Christians are sons of God and joint-heirs with Christ (Rom. viii. 16 f.), who is the firstborn of God and their ' brother '.[a] The husband loves his wife, and Christ loves his Church; its members are members of his body and members of one another.[b] He is in them and they in Him; they are the Body of Christ and the Temple of God,[c] even as the Word or Logos ' tabernacled ' among men.[d] He is the source of the corporate spiritual life, the *esprit de corps*, one might almost say.[1]

But here we reach a deeper spiritualizing of a much earlier conception. The ' marriage ' of Yahweh and Israel meant that apostasy and false worship were adultery, whence the common phrase of ' going a-whoring ' after other gods.[e] Sexual imagery was common among the sensuous and sensual Orientals, and the prophets condemn the sexual rites and ceremonial prostitution which expressed union with the god and also—as the gods were givers of fertility—were believed to promote the increase of nature and man. Physical union with the god or goddess could be actualized by intercourse with ' sacred ' men and women dedicated to the service.[2] But although crude ideas of the marriage-relationship with a deity involved impure cults, they also encouraged a more ethical conception of the marriage-covenant.[f] Indeed, the very intensity of the ethical and spiritual treatment of marriage indicates how realistic had been the earlier ideas before the great prophets purged the old religion of the land. This vivid but originally crude conviction of the unity of men and their deities lies behind the obscure statement in Gen. iv. 1, that Eve ' got ' a man with (the co-operation of) Yahweh, who indeed could prevent or promote child-birth;[g] while many centuries later the Talmud asserts that ' there are three partners in every human

---

[a] Rom. viii. 29, Heb. ii. 11; cf. Matt. xii. 50, xxv. 40.
[b] Eph. iv f.
[c] 1 Cor. iii. 16 f., vi. 19 f., xii. 27; cf. Rom. xii. 5.
[d] John i. 14 mg.
[e] Exod. xxxiv. 15 f., Deut. xxxi. 16; cf. Mark viii. 8.
[f] Mal. ii. 14, Prov. ii. 17.
[g] Gen. xvi. 2, xx. 18, xxix. 31, 1 Sam. i. 5 f.
[1] See below p. 176 and *Rebirth of Christianity*, pp. 24 f., 68.
[2] Deut. xxiii. 17 f., Jer. ii. 20, Hos. iv. 13 f.; cf. Gen. xxxviii. 15, 21 f. and mg.

birth: God, father and mother'. That unseen or super-natural beings play an indispensable part in the fertility of man and nature has been a very common and widespread conviction.

This intimate relation between Israel and Yahweh expresses itself also in a boldness and freedom of speech characteristic both of Israel and of the Jews. It sometimes approximates to a 'magical' control of the Deity. Yahweh *must* deliver Israel for the sake of his reputation;[a] hence when, as in *Ezekiel* (*e.g.*, xx. 9), he acts for his ' Name ', everything depended upon what the Name involved and what Yahweh was supposed to require or tolerate. Gideon boldly puts Yahweh to the test (Judges vi. 36–40);[b] but it is precisely this testing or tempting that is elsewhere condemned (Deut. vi. 16). Throughout there runs the paradox: the intense nearness of Yahweh or his ' immanence ' in Israel and his supreme remoteness or ' transcendence '. The strongest anthropic language is used of Yahweh. Popular narratives tell of his descent to verify for himself the con-ditions in Sodom and Gomorrah (Gen. xviii. 21),[c] and with his strange conflict with Jacob (Gen. xxxii. 24 ff., cf. Hos. xii. 4) compare the vivid description of his war against Edom (Isa. lxiii. 1–6) and his attacks upon Moses (Exod. iv. 24) and Job (xvi. 12–14).

The idols and other objects condemned by the prophets were believed to represent or to embody supernatural powers; and when Hezekiah entered the Temple with the threatening letter from Assyria and 'spread it before Yahweh ' (2 Kings xix. 14 f.) we should observe that Yahweh was enthroned upon the cherubim, the guardians of the sacred ark, which was as powerful as Yahweh himself.[d] In fact the common phrase ' to appear before Yahweh ' is in the Hebrew the slightest adjustment, from motives of reverence, of ' to see the face of Yahweh '. Even to see the king's face was a privilege;[e] and the phrase is used in the Amarna Tablets by Palestinian kings who hope to

---

[a] Exod. xxxii. 12, Num. xiv. 13 ff., Deut. xxxii. 27, Josh. vii. 9.
[b] Cf. Gen. xv. 8 ff., Exod. iv. 1 ff.
[c] Cf. Gen. xi. 5.
[d] Num. x. 35 ff., 1 Sam. v. 8 ff., vi. 9, 1 Kings vi. 23 ff.
[e] 2 Kings xxv. 19, Esther i. 14.

visit the Pharaoh, whom they regard and address as a veritable god (see p. 134 f.).

There is some likeness between God and man: man was made in the image of God, and the child in the image of his father.[a] But man cannot see God and live,[b] and it is expressly stated that the seventy elders who saw Yahweh on his holy mountain were not harmed (Exod. xxiv. 11). God is unsearchable, unattainable;[c] but Job is convinced of his reality, and argues with him boldly (p. 67). Nowhere as in the *Second Isaiah* is there the complete assurance of Yahweh's concern for Israel; but, with all his knowledge of Yahweh's nature, the prophet confesses that Yahweh's thoughts are not man's thoughts and that his purposes transcend those of men (Isa. lv. 8 f.). Israel's best writers are conscious of man's insignificance before a Supreme Power; they are convinced of man's exceeding greatness by reason of the knowledge which this relationship with Yahweh has given them (cf. Ps. viii. 4 ff.).[1] On the one hand, the post-exilic priestly ritual regulates the relations between Israel and Yahweh and safeguards his holiness; while, on the other, the post-exilic collection of Psalms breathes a spirit of personal devotion and intimately unites the Israelite with his God. In the solidarity of this relationship between Israel and Yahweh by the side of the consciousness of Yahweh's transcendence we have the step towards the N.T. conception of Christ, the Firstborn of the Father, the vivifying Spirit of the Body of Christ, at once the ' brother ' of Christians and subordinate to the Father, although possessing all His fullness.

III. *Yahweh in Heaven and on Earth*

Yahweh is kíng and reigns [d] in heaven (or the sky), where seated on his throne he holds court;[e] note the ' us ' in Gen. i. 26, iii. 22 and ver. 5 mg., also xi. 7. There are ' sons of gods ' (divine beings) or of the Most High,[f] his ' holy ones '.[g]

[a] Gen. i. 26 f., v. 1, vi. 3, ix. 6, James iii. 9.
[b] Exod. xxxiii. 20, Rev. i. 17.   [c] Job xi. 7; cf. Ps. cxxxix. 1–18.
[d] Ps. xcvi. 10.   [e] 1 Kings xxii. 19.
[f] Job. i. 6, Ps. lxxxii. 6.   [g] Job v. 1.
[1] But note the warning, Amos iii. 2.

Yahweh is a God of War;[a] he is the Lord of Hosts,[b] the armies whose captain confronted Joshua before his attack upon Jericho (Josh. v. 13 ff.). They are often mentioned.[c] They are stars or winds,[d] they are messengers or angels; they carry out his commands on earth, they protect the godly,[e] they pursue and destroy their enemies,[f] and among their number is ' the Satan ' who opposes and accuses Job (i f.). Yahweh is on the side of Israel against her foes.[g] Israel's foes are Yahweh's, and *vice versa*; cf. Gideon in Judges vii. 18 and David in 1 Sam. xvii. 26, 45, xviii. 17, xxx. 26. At the overthrow of Sisera Israel fights to help Yahweh, and the stars in their courses fought from heaven (Judges. v. 20, 23); or Yahweh himself can intervene as a veritable storm-god, like the earlier gods of storm and war in Palestine and neighbouring lands (Joshua x. 11, 1 Sam. vii. 10).[h] He will call for the sword against the nations,[i] and devote men to destruction.[1] Israel's fierceness against her foes—Yahweh's foes—shows itself in Pss. lviii f., lxix, cxxxix, 19 ff., and later literature; and Yahweh's warlike character corresponds to that of the ancient Palestinian god Hadad (p. 135). This wrathful and avenging God represents only one aspect of Israel's religious psychology; but it is in harmony with the passion and intense emotion that characterize her throughout the O.T. and later writings (see p. 131 f.).

But Yahweh's angels are not necessarily trustworthy.[j] Tradition told of the expulsion of rebellious ' sons of God ' (Gen. vi. 2) from heaven; and at the Final Judgment all his celestial enemies will be destroyed.[k] The celestial powers of wickedness against which men have to fight[l] and the great war in heaven (p. 97) were tremendous realities to the thought of the time. But Yahweh is supreme over man and nature,

---

[a] Exod. xv. 3. [b] Jer. xlvi. 18.
[c] Neh. ix. 6, Ps. xxix. 1, lxxxix. 6 f., ciii. 20 f., cxlviii. 2, Matt. xxvi. 53, Luke ii. 13.
[d] Ps. civ. 4, cxlviii. 8. [e] Ps. xci. 11; cf. xxxiv. 7.
[f] Ps. xxxv. 5 f., 2 Kings xix. 35. [g] Ps. cxxiv. 1.
[h] Cf. 2 Sam. xxii. 14 f., Job xxxviii. 23.
[i] Jer. xxv. 29. [j] Job iv. 18, xv. 15. [k] Isa. xxiv. 21. [l] Eph. vi. 12.
[1] Notably the native Canaanites (Deut. vii. 2; cf. Josh. vi. 17, 21), Amalek (Exod. xvii. 15 f., 1 Sam. xv. 3, 18, 22) and Midian (Num. xxxi. 7, 17). Cf. also the spirit of 1 Kings xx. 42, 2 Kings xiii. 17–19.

over powers above and powers below. He rules history; he controls Israel and other nations;[a] he grants fertility or sends sterility, drought and desolation; he is Creator of All,[b] and judge of the whole earth.[c]

Yahweh, the God of the Universe, is also distinctively the God of Israel, and Israel and her land are his ' inheritance '.[d] And as both people and land are holy, other lands are ritually ' unclean ',[e] and food eaten in them is ' unclean '.[f] Israel's Promised Land was ' unclean ' before she occupied it;[g] and the invaders must first be circumcised,[h] for the uncircumcised profane it.[1] Even the tribes beyond the Jordan were in an ' unclean ' land, in contrast to that wherein Yahweh's tabernacle dwelt (Joshua xxii. 19). Bloodshed and evil ' pollute ' (or profane) Yahweh's land, i.e., deprive it of its holiness;[i] and he himself ' polluted ' it when he handed land and people over to Babylon and cast them away from his presence.[j] David must worship another god, if he is driven away from Yahweh's ' inheritance ' (1 Sam. xxvi. 19). Conversely, Solomon's foreign wives have their own shrines or altars in Jerusalem (1 Kings xi. 8), and Naaman must take with him some Israelite soil in order to worship Yahweh fitly in Damascus (2 Kings v. 17). Each land has its own god; even gods of the mountain are stronger than those of the plains,[k] and Ahaz thought that the gods of his victorious enemies were stronger than his own.[l] Yahweh fights for Israel as does Chemosh, the Moabite god, for Moabites (Judges xi. 24). The inscription of Mesha king of Moab, who is mentioned in 2 Kings iii. 4 (about 850 B.C.), relates that the god was angry with his land,[m] and Israel ' afflicted '[n] Moab; then the god ' saved '

---

[a] Amos ix. 7, Mic. iv. 3, Jer. xlv. 4.   [b] Isa. xl. 28; cf. Col. i. 16.
[c] Gen. xviii. 25.   [d] Deut. ix. 26, 29; cf. Eph. i. 11.
[e] Amos vii. 17.   [f] Hos. ix. 3, Ezek. iv. 13, Dan. i. 8.
[g] Ezra ix. 11.   [h] Josh. v. 2 ff.   [i] Jer. ii. 7.
[j] Isa. xlvii. 6, 2 Kings xxiv. 20.
[k] 1 Kings xx. 23.   [l] 2 Chron. xxviii. 23.
[m] 2 Kings xvii. 18; cf. Num. xxi. 29.   [n] Cf. Gen. xv. 13.
[1] Ezek. xliv. 7–9. By a curious analogy fruit trees for the first three years were regarded as ' uncircumcised '; but in the fourth year their fruit was ' holy ' to Yahweh, and in the fifth the fruit might be eaten (Lev. xix. 23 ff.).

him,[a] and Mesha succeeded in regaining his lost cities and built a ' high place ' to Chemosh. The language is practically identical with Hebrew, and the style of the inscription is entirely that of the O.T. Similarity of phrase and thought prevailed over Palestine and its immediate neighbours.

Although Yahweh was the God of Israel, there were many local shrines or ' high places ': ' as many gods as cities ', says Jeremiah (ii. 28). There were the baals, and Baal was a name of the old god Hadad, the god of war and storm. There were also female deities, and tree and pillar cults. All the local cults long persisted, for these deities were givers of all that men needed. The great prophets denounced the cults and their immoral rites. Hosea seems to have been the first to repudiate the very name ' ba'al ', but with little success, at least as regards Jerusalem.[1] The name ' baal ' connoted that inveterate marriage-relationship referred to above, and because of its idolatrous associations Hosea (ii. 16) replaces the designation ' my baal ' by ' my man (or husband) '. *Deuteronomy*, ' discovered ' in the time of Josiah, is a landmark, definitely dissociating Israel from idolatry; yet since the ' baal '-idea recurs in the *Second Isaiah* (p. 57), the term had apparently been purged of its earlier connotation. Three phases can be discerned: (*a*) Israel must not confuse the baals with Yahweh, who alone is the giver of all increase (*Hosea*),[2] (*b*) the one central sanctuary at Jerusalem is to replace the local shrines (pp. 48, 62); and (*c*) the latter survive, but have evidently been purged and can be associated with the worship of Yahweh.[b] Both the *place* of Yahweh in the religion and his *character* underwent changes, though it is not easy to trace them so completely as one could wish.

At every place where Yahweh was commemorated he

---

[a] Judges vii. 2.   [b] 2 Kings xvii. 27 f., 32, 41, 2 Chron. xxxiii. 17.

[1] 2 Kings xxiii. In Zeph. i. 4 the LXX speaks of the ' name ' and not ' remnant ' of Baal; cf. also Jer. xii. 16.

[2] In the time of Elijah and the great conflict between Yahweh and Baal (ninth century, 1 Kings xviii), Ahab's sons Ahaziah and Jehoram have names compounded with Yahweh. Elijah himself repairs the altar to Yahweh at the local shrine on Carmel (1 Kings xviii. 30; cf. xix. 10); and Gideon is called Jerubbaal when he overthrows the cult of Baal at Ophrah, where he built an altar to Yahweh (Judges vi. 24, 26).

would come and bless his worshippers.[1] David celebrates an annual sacrifice at Bethlehem,[a] and Absalom could make a vow at Hebron near Mamre.[b] Samuel's sacrifice at the high-place was evidently ' orthodox ';[c] and surely Bethel, Gilgal, Mizpah and Ramah, which he regularly visited,[d] would scarcely merit the blame of a Hosea[e] or Amos.[f] Jacob finds Yahweh at Bethel, and discovers that it is a holy place;[g] but Bethel was also the name of a god, precisely like Chemosh,[h] and the place is contemptuously called Beth-Aven, *i.e.*, ' house of vainness ', instead of Bethel, ' house of God '.[i] At Gibeon near Jerusalem was the great high-place with the tabernacle of Yahweh, before the temple was built at Jerusalem.[j] Shechem, later the religious centre of the Samaritans, was especially famous.[k] So also was Shiloh; but its cult is condemned.[l] It must be remembered that these references date from different sources and periods, and to disentangle them is the task of biblical criticism.

Yahweh is varyingly a local god, a national god, or one more universal. Although he is closely associated with Bethel, he can protect Jacob in Syria;[m] and in a vision at the sacred site of Beersheba he undertakes to be with him in Egypt.[n] Jerusalem was sacred above all, though its cult is vehemently condemned by Jeremiah and Ezekiel (p. 139), and Yahweh was to be approached there at his Temple. None the less, he does not dwell in a temple made with hands.[o] He fills heaven and earth; even the ' heaven of heavens ', the highest heaven, cannot contain him.[p] But his Name is set in the Temple, men can come to his altar, and he will hear them,[q] and there the Israelite can see Yah-

[a] 1 Sam. xx. 6.   [b] 2 Sam. xv. 7 f., 12; cf. Gen. xiii. 18.
[c] 1 Sam. ix. 12 f.   [d] 1 Sam. vii. 6, 9, 12, 16 f., xi. 15.
[e] iv. 15, v. 1.   [f] iii. 14, iv. 4, v. 5.
[g] Gen. xxviii. 10 ff.; cf. Hos. xii. 4.   [h] Jer. xlviii. 13.
[i] Hos. iv. 15; cf. Amos v. 5 mg.
[j] 1 Kings iii. 4 f., 1 Chron. xvi. 39 f.
[k] Gen. xii. 6, Josh. xxiv. 26.   [l] 1 Sam. ii. 22, 27 ff.
[m] Gen. xxxi. 4, 13.   [n] xlvi. 1 ff.
[o] 1 Kings viii. 27, 31; cf. Acts vii. 48 ff.
[p] 1 Kings viii. 27, 2 Chron. ii. 6, Jer. xxiii. 24, Isa. lxvi. 1.
[q] 1 Kings viii. 31 f., ix. 3.
[1] Exod. xx. 24; cf. xvii. 15, Josh. viii. 30, Judges ii. 5, 1 Sam. xiv. 35, xvi. 2, etc.

weh's power and glory.[a]   Men afar off can pray towards Jerusalem with outstretched hands, and have their windows opened towards the holy city.[b]   Moreover, the Ark was a powerful symbol of his presence, and is addressed as Yahweh.[c]   His presence (literally ' face ') accompanies Israel,[d] as also does, in another passage, his Angel in whom is his Name.[e]   In this manner, although he is effectively with Israel, his real supremacy and transcendence are preserved.

Angels (or messengers) are the effective manifestations of Yahweh, whether they appear on earth[f] or call from heaven.[g]   In the story of Gideon the angel of Yahweh is only subsequently recognized as Yahweh, and he fears death (Judges vi. 11–24), for no man can see God and live.[h] Similar to the story of Gideon is that of Manoah and his wife (Judges xiii), which illustrates (a) the significance attached to a sacred name (verse 18), (b) the good sense of a pious but rational woman (verse 23) and (c) the doctrine that sacrifices must be made, not to a representative of Yahweh, but to Yahweh himself (verse 16).   Angels and other ' powers in the heavens ' are more common in the later writings and in the N.T.[i]   There are celestial guardian-angels who intercede for men, just as, much earlier in Accad, men could have their own protective deities.[j]   In Daniel's visions (ch. x ff.) there are ' princes ' who safeguard the destinies of nations.   In Isa. lxiii. 1–6 Yahweh directly intervenes on behalf of his people (cf. lix. 16–18), but in Daniel's vision Michael, one of the ' princes ', is the patron of Israel (Dan. x. 13, 21).   In the apocalyptic *Assumption of Moses* Michael avenges Israel on her enemies at the end of the world; and in Rev. xii. 7 he and the great red Dragon, the Devil Satan, contend with their angelic hosts, and the ' deceiver of the whole world ' is cast down from heaven to earth.   The relation between the subordinate beings and Yahweh on the one side, and man on the other, is too

[a] Ps. lxiii. 2.
[b] 1 Kings viii. 29, 31, Dan. vi. 10.
[c] Num. x. 35 f., xiv. 14, 1 Sam. iv. 7.   [d] Exod. xxxiii. 14 ff.
[e] Exod. xxiii. 20 f.   [f] Gen. xvi. 7, Exod. xiv. 19.
[g] Gen. xxi. 17, xxii. 11.   [h] Deut. v. 26; cf. Gen. xxxii. 30.
[i] Mark xiii. 25, Col. i. 16, etc.
[j] Zech. i. 12, Tob. xii. 12, 15, Matt. xviii. 10.

fluctuating to be described clearly. Sometimes these beings represent Yahweh himself or they are his effective messengers, and at other times they are closely associated with men. In Rev. i–iii the ' angels of the Churches ' are not so much patrons or guardians as personifications of the spirit that animates or is manifested in each. This was a very important conception, especially in earlier times.

It is not easy to trace in detail the complete historical development of the beliefs in Yahweh and the intermediaries between him and man.[1] The worship of Yahweh superseded that of the earlier great gods of Palestine (p. 135). He is above in heaven, but is effective on earth. The monotheistic ideal reached its finest expression in the *Second Isaiah*, but it was with difficulty maintained. As Yahweh was sole God, it could be said that he had given other nations their own gods,[a] nay, that all other gods were ' worthless ', mere nonentities.[b] There were many local sacred sites and local beings; they are at one time condemned on account of the nature of their cults, and/or because they weakened the religious and national superiority of the Temple at Jerusalem. But as more ethical and spiritual conceptions of Yahweh were developed, the local shrines appear to have been cleansed; and the fact remains that local cults are still common in Palestine under Islam.

Looking back on §§II and III, we can see two main lines of thought, the one emphasizing the solidarity of Israel and her God Yahweh, while in the other it is the kingship of Yahweh, his remoteness, and the need for intermediaries that are more prominent. Yahweh is in heaven or the sky; but he is effectively on earth among men. As elsewhere in the history of the world's religions, men are struggling with the paradoxical conviction of God's immediacy and the

[a] Deut. iv. 19, xxix. 26.   [b] Isa. ii. 8, Ps. xcvi. 5 mg.
[1] When it is said that the Law was given, not by Yahweh, but by angels (Acts vii. 38, 53), this is in harmony with the later desire to preserve the transcendence of God. Paul, however, argues that the Law is therefore inferior to Christ (Gal. iii. 19).

gulf between Him and man, his intimate concern with man's needs and welfare and his distant supremacy and 'otherness'. The fundamental paradox has taken many forms, but the lines of thought that are to be found in the O.T. lead on to the two later and specifically Christian conceptions of (a) the Israel of God, the Christian community or Church, the Body of Christ, embodying the spirit of its Founder, and (b) the Kingdom of Heaven, the Divine Sovereignty and its sway.

IV. *Life and Death*

The difficulty of tracing clearly the details of the belief in a life after death is not less than that we have already had when considering the beliefs in the relationship between God and man. Ideas of heaven as a place of future bliss and of hell as a place of torment are not primitive; and we have to think of these, not necessarily as definite localities above and underneath the earth, but as primarily due to states of feeling or mind. Heaven and hell are indeed localized above and below, but definite experiences and convictions account for the beliefs in the first instance and for their persistent revival. It was believed that the celestial realm was Yahweh's.[a] The earth he had given to the sons of men, and beneath was the ' grave ' or ' pit ', the abode of the dead which, as the Revisers' Preface to the O.T. points out, is better called by the original Hebrew term Shĕōl. To this Sheol there are parallels in Accadian and Greek (viz., Hades).

Enoch ' walked with God ' and ' was no more ', for God took him (Gen. v. 21–24), and Elijah was taken up in a chariot of fire (2 Kings ii. 11). But they are exceptional. Sheol was the natural abode of the dead, a gloomy dusty place with barred gates. Here lie the mighty with their swords under their heads,[b] and greet with astonishment the powerful tyrant who would have set his throne in the highest heaven like the Most High Himself.[c] Small and great alike are there, and the servant is free from the taskmaster; they know not what happens on earth and might

[a] Ps. cxv. 15 f.   [b] Ezek. xxxii. 27.   [c] Isa. xiv. 16 ff.

as well not have been born.[a]   The living and not the dead
can praise Yahweh;[b] these are no longer remembered by
him.[c] Sheol is a place without hope,[d] and no man can
deliver himself from this everlasting home or place.[e] Yet
Sheol is not hidden from God,[f] his hand could reach there;[g]
he could redeem a man from the power of Sheol and receive
him to glory. In Ps. xlix. 14 f. a distinction between the
good and the bad is to be seen; it was the relationship with
Yahweh that was essential, and at a later date Sheol has
three divisions, two for the wicked and one for the spirits of
the righteous.[h]

The belief in Sheol and the contrast between it and the
Christian hope of immortality have profoundly influenced
theology; but this belief was not, however, the only one
current. Jacob grieving for Joseph will, it is true, go down
into Sheol, but on his peaceful death-bed he expects to
' sleep with his fathers ' in their grave.[i] Abraham goes to
his ' fathers ',[j] or, like Moses and Aaron, to his ' people '.[k]
Men were buried in the family grave,[l] or in their own house.[m]
To be unburied was an evil fate,[n] and Tobit was always
careful to bury a dead countryman.[o] There were ceremonies at the graves,[p] and men sat there, presumably to
consult the dead,[q] or would resort to necromancers and
others.[r] Men could live on in their children, or if childless
could have their ' name ' kept alive by a monument,[s] or by
the custom of the ' levirate ';[t] some sort of memorial was
essential.[u] Saul at Endor can consult the dead Samuel,
who was buried at Ramah (1 Sam. xxviii. 3 ff.); apparently

---

[a] Job iii. 11–19, xiv. 21; cf. Wisdom ii. 2.
[b] Ps. vi. 5, xxx. 9, cxv. 17.   [c] Ps. lxxxviii. 5.
[d] Isa. xxxviii. 18.   [e] Eccles. xii. 5, Tob. iii. 6.
[f] Job xxvi. 6, Prov. xv. 11.   [g] Amos ix. 2, Ps. cxxxix. 8.
[h] 1 Enoch xxii. 9–13.   [i] Gen. xxxvii. 35, xlvii. 30.
[j] Gen. xv. 15.
[k] Gen. xxv. 8, Num. xxvii. 13, Deut. xxxii. 50; cf. xxxi. 16.
[l] 2 Sam. xvii. 23, xix. 37.
[m] 1 Sam. xxv. 1; cf. 1 Kings ii. 34.
[n] 1 Kings xiii. 22, 2 Kings ix. 10, Jer. xxv. 33.
[o] i. 17, ii. 7 ff.
[p] Tobit iv. 17; contrast BS xxx. 18.   [q] Isa. lxv. 4.
[r] Lev. xix. 31, xx. 6, 27, Isa. viii. 19, xxix. 4, 1 Chron. x. 13 f.
[s] 2 Sam. xviii. 18, Isa. lvi. 5.
[t] Gen. xxxviii, Ruth iv.   [u] BS xliv. 8 f.

in some way the dead are not confined to their place of burial. Great figures like Abraham and Israel (Jacob) could be mindful of their descendants[a] (Isa. li. 2; note the complaint in Isa. lxiii. 16); and Rachel could weep for her exiled children.[b] In the late *Fourth Book of Maccabees* (dated roughly 50 B.C.–A.D. 50) the faithful sons of Abraham hope to be gathered together unto their ancestors,[c] and this is presupposed in the Parable of the Rich Man and Lazarus; it is a belief which Jesus could regard as active and intelligible.[1] When Moses, whose relationship with Yahweh was unique,[d] offers to be blotted out of Yahweh's book (Exod. xxxii. 32), it is surely unlikely that merely physical death or confinement in Sheol is meant. Moreover, Yahweh has his book containing the names of those that feared him.[e] Once it is said that the souls of all men are bound up in Yahweh's bundle of life (or, of the living), and he will sling out those of David's enemies (1 Sam. xxv. 29). But precisely what all the funeral customs and beliefs meant it is impossible to say: relationship with Yahweh and/or with one's kith and kin are the main ideas.

Again, if the wicked go to Sheol, what of the upright whose soul will be redeemed?[f] And when the Psalmist looks forward to 'awaking' (Ps. xvii. 15), we are uncertain whether he means after his night's sleep or after death (Isa. xxvi. 19). Babylon is threatened with a lasting sleep (Jer. li. 39, 57). Did David expect to meet his babe in Sheol (2 Sam. xii. 23)? David, like other kings, and like Jacob and Moses, 'slept with his fathers',[g] and the royal burial-place, like the palace, adjoined the temple—the same word is used for both in Hebrew. But Ezekiel among other changes will not tolerate what he considers to be a profanation (xliii. 7–9).

In point of fact there is archaeological evidence for an early belief in Palestine in an existence after death. Food,

[a] Luke xvi. 19–31; cf. Matt. xxii. 32.   [b] Jer. xxxi. 15.
[c] v. 37, xiii. 17, xviii. 23.   [d] Num. xii. 7.
[e] Mal. iii. 16; cf. Ezek. xiii. 9, Dan. xii. 1, 1 Enoch ciii. 2, civ. 1, Luke x. 20, Phil. iv. 3, Rev. xx. 12.
[f] Ps. xlix. 14 f.   [g] 1 Kings ii. 10, xi. 43, etc.
[1] Note Luke xx. 35 ff.; the dead who are worthy of resurrection are 'equal unto the angels, and are sons of God'.

utensils, jewellery, mirrors and toys are among the objects
that are found buried with the dead; and the remains of
infants have been found under the corners of rooms.
Lamps are often found; and while those in Christian times
bear such inscriptions as ' the Lord (or the Christ) is my
light ', the king of old could be called the ' light' of Israel [1]
and light was a symbol of life. Moreover, the presence of
Egyptians in Palestine would familiarize Israel with ideas
of another life; and the care taken to avoid spilling blood—
the life, or the vehicle of life (Lev. xvii. 11)—or to leave it
exposed,[a] like the care to bury the dead, when taken with the
evidence already mentioned, makes it clear that the belief in
some sort of survival after death was far from uncommon.[2]
No doubt it was largely wrapped up with beliefs in the
solidarity of Israel and her relations with Yahweh, but with
usages which the more spiritual minds repudiated; although
it could be made more ' orthodox ' if the dead Israelite went
to his fathers, like Lazarus in Abraham's bosom (Luke
xvi. 22). It is noteworthy that an eighth-century inscription from North Syria registers the belief that a king
may ceremonially associate the name of his dead father with
that of Hadad and wish that his father's ' soul ' may eat and
drink with that god. Such a god (once familiar in Palestine),
the god of a people closely related to Israel, would naturally
be rejected by the great prophets, loyal worshippers of
Yahweh; but an echo of a very similar sort of belief recurs
when Moses, Aaron and others behold Yahweh on his holy
mountain and eat and drink with him.[3]

The belief in another life and in a resurrection appears
afresh in later literature, beginning with the age of dis-

[a] Job xvi. 18.

[1] 2 Sam. xxi. 17; cf. 1 Kings xi. 36, and the ' coal ' in 2 Sam. xiv. 7.

[2] To scatter or burn the bones of the dead was shocking (Jer. viii. 1 f.,
Amos ii. 1); and if the dead could be recognized (1 Sam. xxviii. 12, Isa.
xiv. 16), those who were maimed in their life-time would remain maimed
(Matt. xviii. 8 f.).

[3] Exod. xxiv. 11. In the Garden of Eden the ' tree of life ' (Gen. ii.
9, iii. 22; cf. Rev. ii. 7, xxii. 2) conferred immortality; it was perhaps
believed that had it not been for the disobedience of Adam (he is called
' the son of God ' in Luke iii. 38), man would have been immortal.
Even the ' fallen angels ' had once been divine (Gen. vi. 1-4). So, in
the N.T., through Adam all die, but through Christ all shall be made
alive (1 Cor. xv. 22; cf. Rom. v. 12-21).

integration round about the exilic period. From the vivid
description of the resurrection of Israel in Ezekiel's vision
(ch. xxxvii) and the obscure destiny of the Suffering
Servant in that remarkable chapter, Isa. liii, we pass to the
explicit statement of a bodily resurrection in late apocalypses
(Isa. xxvi. 19, Dan. xii. 2; cf. also 2 Macc. vii, xiv. 46).
Beliefs naturally varied, as they do everywhere and always.
While one Psalmist expresses pessimistic doubt (Ps. lxxxviii.
10 ff.), a beautiful passage in Ps. lxxiii. 23–25 breathes the
purest faith.[1] And while, on the one hand, the death and
revival of vegetation were a convincing proof that man's
death is not his extinction (cf. 1 Cor. xv. 36 ff., John xii.
24), on the other, Job (xiv. 7 ff.) sees more hope for the
stump of a tree than for the man who has been cut down.
Ecclesiastes is sceptical, but *Wisdom* (iii. 1 f.) asserts that
the souls of the righteous are in God's hands, they only
seem to have died; we may compare the lot of those
who have Yahweh the God of Jacob for their help in
Ps. cxlvi. 3–5. The two sects of the Sadducees and
Pharisees were hotly divided, the former contending that
there is neither resurrection nor angel nor spirit (Acts xxiii.
8 f.). If in John xvii. 3 to ' know ' God and Jesus Christ is
eternal life, this is no intellectual knowledge or Gnosticism—
which was always repudiated—but was to be seen in good
works.[2] The ' pure in heart ' shall see God (Matt. v. 8; cf.
1 John ii. 3, Heb. xii. 14); their citizenship is in heaven
(cf. Phil. iii. 20 f.); and life after death, or rather the
quality and value of that life, depended, not upon the belief
in itself, but upon its place in men's whole body of thought
and conduct.

The belief in a life after death has always had strange
fluctuations, and it is only gradually that we approach the—
to us—more familiar idea of a place of happiness above and
of misery and torment below. There are two main stages,
the later apparently dating from the period of *Jeremiah*,

---

[1] ' And yet I am continually with thee, thou hast taken hold of my
right hand. According to thy purpose thou wilt lead me, and after-
ward receive me with glory. Whom have I (to care for) in heaven?
and possessing thee I have pleasure in nothing upon earth.' (Cheyne's
translation.)
[2] Jer. xxii. 16.

Ezekiel and the *Second Isaiah*, the last of whom proclaims anew the reality, majesty and omnipotence of Yahweh and his renewed bond with Israel. The earlier—as apart from the persisting belief in an underground Sheol—is bound up with ideas more popular, and liable to be associated with cults which the reforming minds condemned. If, as seems probable, the great reformers of Israel were responsible for destroying earlier beliefs in existence after death, they succeeded in clearing the way for the growth of new ideas; and the earlier solidarity of Yahweh, his land and the Israelite, whether alive or dead, was replaced by the new solidarity of the 'Israel of God' (Gal. vi. 16) and the members of the Body of Christ.

Ancient psychology was hardly more inconsistent than that of to-day. Life and death were thought of (*a*) from the human side, more physiologically or biologically, or (*b*) more morally or spiritually; and it is not always easy in each case to decide which is intended. The sick who recover are, literally, said to 'live' (2 Kings viii. 9; cf. Joshua v. 8, 'be whole'); but when Ephraim sinned he 'died' (Hos. xiii. 1), for one can be 'dead' through one's sins (cf. Eph. ii. 1–10, 1 Tim. v. 6). 'Life', then, is life worth having, through obedience to Yahweh;[a] it is life in the Kingdom of God, even though one be (physically) maimed;[b] it is the passage from death into life.[c] Man is 'spirit' and 'flesh', and both come directly or ultimately from God, who is the Creator and Source of all flesh;[d] his care is for animals, birds and flowers.[1] He fashions men in the womb, forms them as clay, and therefore knows their frailty.[e] At death the flesh becomes dust, and the spirit returns to God until He sends it forth again.[f] In what form the dead were supposed to exist, seeing that embalming as in Egypt was not and could not be practised in Palestine, can hardly be conjectured; but that the spirit or soul could

[a] Lev. xviii. 5, Ezek. xx. 11. [b] Mark ix. 43 ff.
[c] John iii. 4. [d] Num. xvi. 22.
[e] Ps. ciii. 14, cxxxix. 15 f., Job x. 8–11.
[f] Ps. civ. 29 f., Eccles. iii. 20, xii. 7.
[1] Jonah iv. 11, Luke xii. 6 f., 22–28; cf. Ps. cxlvii. 9, Job xxxviii–xl. Similarly the Egyptian god Aton in Ikhnaton's reform is an All-Creator (see *The Cambridge Ancient History*, II, 117 ff.); cf. p. 28.

have a spiritual body is set forth by Paul in 1 Cor. xv. 42–44.[1]

Spirit is identified with breath, and in ancient Palestine one spoke of the life-giving breath of the divine Pharaoh. By spirit is meant an active and effective power; but the use of the term varies. ' Spirit ' is the source of any special quality, character or activity, *e.g.*, the strength-giving spirit of Yahweh which moved Samson (Judges xiii. 25, xiv. 6). It is the source of wisdom [a] or it is the inclination or will in contrast to the weak flesh.[b] It can be symbolically transmitted;[c] and in the story of Eldad and Medad the point is that Yahweh's spirit came upon them although they were not in the sacred tent (Num. xi. 17, 25 f., 29). More characteristically, Yahweh's spirit distinguishes Israel from other peoples: Israelites are spirit and not mere flesh (Isa. xxxi. 3, 2 Chron. xxxii. 8). His spirit does not merely give life—biologically; it regenerates (Ezek. xxxvi. 27; cf. Isa. xxxii. 15) and the outpouring of his spirit is life-giving, creative and inspiring.[2]

Flesh, then, is more than body. It is man's ordinary constitution. But the terms flesh and spirit overlap; for while both can be psychic, the former can include the physical, mental and emotional activities, and the latter can be on the highest plane, denoting rather the will, character and body of principles actuating men at their highest. Hence there can be a threefold division, as in 1 Thess. v. 23, into body, soul (the normal psychic aspect) and spirit (the definitely Christian principle). In this case soul and spirit are not synonymous, and the soul is psycho-physical and not the permanent principle surviving death. On the whole, the emphasis lies on the relationship with

---

[a] Isa. i. 2.   But note Hos. iv. 12.   [b] Matt. xxvi. 41.

[c] 2 Kings ii. 9, 15.

[1] Cf. Phil. iii. 21.   In 1 Cor. xv. 4–8 Paul mentions in one breath the appearances of Jesus after his death to the twelve disciples and many others and his own vision on the road to Damascus, and of the latter there are three accounts (Acts ix. 3 ff., 17, xxii. 7–11, 14, xxvi. 13 ff.; cf. xviii. 9, xxiii. 11, Gal. i. 15 f.).

[2] Joel ii. 28, see Acts ii. 16 ff.   The question of ' false ' prophets and of distinguishing between true and false claims to be inspired is too complicated to be dealt with here; see *e.g.*, Deut. xiii. 1–5, xviii. 20–22, Jer. xiv. 14 ff., xxiii. 30, xxviii. 9, xxix. 8 f., Mark xiii. 22, 1 John iv. 1.

God, and not upon speculations as to the nature of existence after death, though these are not wanting. Christ came in the likeness of flesh,[a] and flesh lives—at its highest—only because Christ lives in his followers.[b] Sin alienates man from God; therefore—Paul enjoins—dying and rising again with Christ ' present yourselves unto God as alive from the dead ' (Rom. vi. 1–14).

Both body and spirit (or soul) come from God, and the Divine Spirit itself impels men unto Him.[c] Some are ' called ' from the womb : Israel,[d] the Servant of Yahweh,[e] Jeremiah[f] and Paul;[g] and Christians are preordained in Christ.[h] ' Wisdom ' (see p. 68), like Christ, pre-existed the world, and—again like him—it is the source of man's immortality and fellowship with God.[i] The ' body ' is frail and corruptible;[j] hence one should ' sow ', not unto the flesh but unto the Spirit;[k] and be begotten again of incorruptible seed and be sinless.[1] Further, there are different sorts of bodies corresponding to each ' seed ',[l] and in the *Testaments of the Twelve Patriarchs* it is said that God makes the body after the likeness of the spirit and implants it according to the capacity of the spirit.[2] The ' soul ' can be weighed down by its corruptible body;[m] and in a difficult passage Paul longs for an eternal habitation in place of this earthly bodily frame of ours, for as long as we are at home in the body we are absent from God.[3]

On the question of life and death, then, the Bible does not speak with one voice; and it is to the influence of Greek thought that the increased speculation is due. On the one

---

[a] Rom. viii. 3 ff.   [b] Rom. viii, Gal. ii. 20.
[c] Rom. viii. 11; cf. James iv. 5.   [d] Isa. xliv. 2.
[e] Isa. xlix. 5.   [f] i. 5.   [g] Gal. i. 15.   [h] Ephes. i. 4 f.
[i] Wisdom vii. 27, viii. 17.   [j] Rom. viii. 21 ff.
[k] Gal. vi. 8; cf. 1 Cor. xv. 42 ff.
[l] 1 Cor. xv. 38–41.   [m] Wisdom ix. 15.
[1] 1 Pet. i. 23, 1 John iii. 9, v. 1, 18. Isaac is born after the spirit (Gal. iv. 23, 29; cf. Gen. xxi. 1 f.).
[2] Test. of Naphtali, ii. 2. Wisdom viii. 19 f., though evidently important, is excessively obscure. ' On this famous passage almost volumes have been written ' (A. T. S. Goodrick).
[3] 2 Cor. v. 1–8; cf. Rom. vii. 24, viii. 23. In Josephus, *War*, VII. viii. 6, § 343 f., the idea that death liberates the soul and permits it to depart to its own pure abode is even said to be an ancestral belief. Actually, it echoes the Greek sōma-sēma catchword, ' the body (is) a tomb '.

hand, between God and man there is here and now a real, or at least a potential fellowship; but, on the other, this seems to be impaired so long as one lives the bodily life. Paul felt the dilemma: was he to live on for the sake of his mission, or was he to depart and be with Christ, which is ' very far better ' (Phil. i. 22 f.)?   The same dilemma was felt in another form in Buddhism: was the goal Nirvana, release, or the Bodhisattva who is to save men?   The O.T. takes us to a people who lived an active practical life in a world which was Yahweh's world; whereas in the N.T. we are at a period when an entirely new order was anticipated —the Kingdom of Heaven and the Body of Christ, and all that these meant for the living and the dead.   Behind lies the fundamental problem of the celestial and terrestrial realms—are there two worlds or realms, or only one?   But the Kingdom of Heaven and the Body of Christ are scarcely identical conceptions, the former predominates in the Gospels and the latter—and also the Church—in the rest of the N.T.   They are, when taken separately, respectively monarchical and social, and both grow out of the O.T. and non-canonical writings.

V. *Sin and Suffering*

Misfortune, suffering and disaster had their cause, if only it could be ascertained—*e.g.*, the defeat at Jericho (Josh. vii), the fall of the tower of Siloam (Luke xiii. 4) and the man born blind (John ix. 2).   There were evil spirits and demons; and the more powerful a god, the more natural was it that he should be the direct or indirect cause of all things.   Yahweh was the cause of both good and misfortune or evil;[a] and even nature-gods of sun and rain could be destructive as well as beneficent.   Yahweh could send an evil angel or spirit;[b] he could stir up Saul against David.[c] But although he moves David to do wrong, it is the Satan, a celestial messenger (Job i. f.), who, according to the later account, is responsible (2 Sam. xxiv. 1; 1 Chron. xxi. 1).

Sin disturbs the relations between Yahweh and Israel. Sin is rebellion, it is ' missing the mark ' (the verb is thus

[a] Amos iii. 6, Isa. xlv. 7, Job ii. 10, Lam. iii. 38.
[b] Judges ix. 23, 1 Sam. xvi. 14 f.   [c] 1 Sam. xxvi. 19.

used in Judges xx. 16; cf. Prov. xix. 2 mg.), it is ' turning aside from the way ',[a] being in the ' wrong ' as opposed to being ' righteous ' or ' in the right '; it is doing what simply is ' not done ' in Israel.[b] Sin, in fact, is a very general term. It is not necessarily ethical; though in Egypt and Accad offences include lying, saying ' yes ' for ' no ' and ' no ' for ' yes ', and setting members of a family one against the other (p. 23). While there were various well-understood offences—ritual and ethical—sin was felt to alienate man, and a profound feeling and fear of alienation —the absence of a harmonious relationship with God— pervade the Bible.

Sins are against Yahweh, see especially the words of Joseph and David;[1] and when against another Israelite, as in the Book of the Covenant (Exod. xxi–xxiii), it is Yahweh's laws men break. Only in the later Wisdom Literature do we meet with specifically ethical, humanist and even conventional injunctions (p. 66), though they are to be found much earlier outside the Bible.

The presence of Yahweh's holy ark among the Philistines brought them plagues (1 Sam. v. 6–12); men of Beth-Shemesh who looked into it were destroyed (vi. 19), and when Uzzah carefully steadied it to save it from falling, he was promptly slain by Yahweh (2 Sam. vi. 6 f.). Any offence against the ' holiness ' of Yahweh was punished automatically, so to speak.[c] Offences might be ritually, ethically or even aesthetically obnoxious; they include contact with a corpse, women in child-birth, animals that were ' unclean ' and therefore not to be eaten, leprosy, and mould on garments or the walls of houses, eating with non-Israelites, taking part in their ceremonies, or swearing by the names of their gods.[2] But the ' Law of Holiness ' (p. 62) excellently shows that ethical ideas were not neg-lected (cf. also Ps. xv); and it goes without saying that ethical demands and ideas of the nature of God's demands upon man were naturally capable of undergoing change and

[a] Judges ii. 17.   [b] 2 Sam. xiii. 12.   [c] Cf. Lev. x. 1 ff.
[1] Gen. xxxix. 9, 2 Sam. xii. 13; cf. Exod. xx. 16, Ps. li. 4, Luke xv. 18.
[2] Cf. 1 Cor. viii. There was a firm belief in the reality of heathen deities and spirits; cf. 1 Cor. x. 20 f., xii. 2, etc.

development—thus the ethics of the N.T. represent a great advance in the realization both of man's frailties and short-comings and of ideals of a better and fuller life in company with his fellows.

To ensure the smooth working of society there were also lots and ordeals for the purpose of fixing guilt and responsibility. These were determined by Yahweh, and the offender was expected to confess, and so justify the divine decision.[a] There were numerous rites and ceremonies, whether for the general welfare (good crops, success in war), or for more individual occasions, such as making and paying vows.[b] Sacrificial offerings must be made to Yahweh—and not to the *baals* (Hos. ii)—for he is the giver of all good things.[c] There were family and household ceremonies,[d] and laymen could act as priests, though this is deprecated.[1] David's sons were priests (2 Sam. viii. 18); the A.V. is shocked at the idea and renders 'chief rulers'. But kings held a very prominent place in the old religion, though this too was repudiated later.[e]

The increasing prominence of the priesthood and the supremacy of Jerusalem and the Aaronites are the most noteworthy facts in O.T. history; and the attempt to trace the actual development constitutes one of the most intricate problems of O.T. criticism. The High-Priest, clad in royal diadem and purple, took over the glory and prestige of the pre-exilic monarchy. His death, like that of the kings before him, marked an epoch;[f] and the enthusiastic description of the High-Priest Simon in BS l. 1–24 illustrates the respect and veneration for one who was the founder of the Hasmonaean priestly and royal dynasty (*c.* 142 B.C.).

The sacrificial system, particularly at Jerusalem, was elaborate, if not extravagant; and to the present day in the East the shedding of blood is necessary on all important

[a] Prov. xvi. 33, Num. v. 18, Joshua vii. 19 f.
[b] Gen. xxviii. 20 ff., 1 Sam. i. 22 ff., 2 Sam. xv. 7 f.
[c] 1 Chron. xxix. 14 ff.; cf. Exod. xiii. 12 f., Ezek. xx. 31, 1 Cor. iv. 7.
[d] 1 Sam. xx. 6.
[e] Cf. 2 Chron. xxvi. 18 ff., Neh. vi. 10 f., Num. xvi. 40.
[f] Num. xxxv. 28, Joshua xx. 6.
[1] Judges xvii. 5 f., 13; cf. 1 Kings xiii. 33. Especially noteworthy is the Passover, which remains a home festival in spite of Deut. xvi. 1–8.

ceremonial and inaugural occasions. Blood ' makes atonement (*i.e.*, at-one-ment) by reason of the " soul " that is in
it ' (Lev. xvii. 11):[a] this is the only explanation that was
offered. Blood must not be eaten,[b] spilled on the ground, or
left unburied. The sacrifice itself was not so much a gift,
as a means of ensuring or securing the desired relationship
between man and the unseen powers, and a gift was only one
among other means. The psychological effect of the blood-
shedding and accompanying ceremonies was to produce
feelings of strength, peace, unity and forgiveness: on the
more ' spiritual ' level, true repentance and a man's attitude
to Yahweh take the first place. The individual through the
ceremony and/or through his psychical state felt that he
came into relation with the Holy God; and oneness with
Christ is the keynote, especially of Paul's writings. The
occasion gave a man, as it were, a fresh start-off; and this
feeling of newness, of a new beginning, is in line with what is
met with in other religions.[1] Quite apart from the fixed
ceremonial occasions when men had a feeling of guilt, there
was also the fear lest they might sin unwittingly, and to
meet this there were sacrifices.[2]

The old sacrificial system of Israel raises intricate questions
of its variations and developments; and it must suffice to
refer to the two great supreme occasions in biblical history.
The second is that of the sacrificial interpretation of the
death of Christ, and that consciousness of a newness of life,
a rebirth,[c] and a new creation through Christ, which
distinguishes the earliest Christians.[3] The earlier turns
upon the enigmatic Servant of the Lord, who died as a
guilt- or trespass-offering, an atoning sacrifice, and who
brought about a sense of forgiveness which makes all the
difference between the desperate state of Israel which is
presupposed in the first part of the *Second Isaiah* and the

---

[a] Cf. Matt. xxvi. 28, Eph. i. 7, Heb. ix. 22.
[b] Lev. iii. 17, Ezek. xxxiii. 25.   [c] Cf. John iii. 5.
[1] There, too, the interconnexion of mental and physical health is
often found; cf. also the illuminating examples in Mark ii. 1–12 and
John v. 14.
[2] See Num. xv. 22–31, Lev. iv. f.; cf. Job i. 5.
[3] 2 Cor. v. 17, Gal. vi. 15, Rom. vi. 4. Resurrection to a new life
and salvation are associated; cf. 1 Cor. xv. 17.

far more settled conditions in the later chapters (see p. 57).
Upon questions of the identification of the Servant, however,
scholars are not agreed.

The value attached to *animal* sacrifice in the O.T. is to be
noted; but inferior victims must not be used.[a] In the
history of religion human sacrifice has in general come to be
replaced by that of animals; but human sacrifice, especially
that of the firstborn, had by no means been unknown in
Israel, whence the vehement protest in Mic. vi. 7.[1] Abraham
was prepared to sacrifice Isaac, but was stopped in time:
the story in Gen. xxii justifies the use of the animal instead
of the human victim.   But the death of the Servant 'for
the transgression of my people' (Isa. liii. 8), and that of
Christ, the Lamb (as often in *Revelation*), mark the beginning
of new eras in religion.   The blood of Christ, the human
victim, was more efficacious than that of animals (Heb. ix.
11–14).

Such were the ideas of solidarity that, just as an
Abraham or a David could be a benefit and a blessing to
others, so the guilt of one falls upon the whole community,
e.g., David's offence,[b] Achan and the army of Israel,[c] the
region wherein a dead man is found,[d] an evil king,[e] Cain's
murder of Abel[f] and the Fall of Adam.[g]   But there are
protests against this: the sin of the evil-doer should fall
upon him alone.[2]   On the other hand, the righteousness of
the righteous saves him alone, and it is not possible for the
few who are righteous to save the many who are wicked
(as in Gen. xviii. 23 ff.).   The protests are of great interest,
in that they represent the effort to solve the perennial
problem of the relation between the individual and his
environment, and his responsibility for good and evil.
Indeed, the evil-doer who becomes righteous is thereupon
delivered (cf. the penitent criminal, Luke xxiii. 42 f.), and the
righteous who becomes an evil-doer suffers forthwith

[a] Mal. i. 7 f.   [b] 2 Sam. xxiv. 13 ff.   [c] Joshua vii.
[d] Deut. xxi. 1–9.   [e] Jer. xv. 4.   [f] Wisdom x. 3 f.
[g] Rom. v. 12–15, 1 Cor. xv. 21 f.
[1] See p. 112; cf. Judges xi. 31, 34 ff., Jer. vii. 31, Ezek. xvi. 20 f.,
xxiii. 37, and the redemption-price in Num. xviii. 15 f.
[2] Num. xvi. 22, Deut. xxiv. 16, 2 Sam. xxiv. 17, Jer. xxxi. 29 f.,
Ezek. iii. 16–21, xiv. 14, 18, 20, xviii, xxxiii. 1–20.

(Ezek. xviii). The problem is that of the effects of a man's course of life upon his destiny; it seems to have arisen during the social and political disintegration in the exilic age, when religion became a personal matter apart from locality and social surroundings. The individual's conscience is involved, not that of the social group; he is not less but more responsible to himself, for all men are Yahweh's (Ezek. xviii. 4). The increasing emphasis laid upon the value in the eyes of God of every individual, and not merely of men of outstanding merit or authority, distinguishes the great turning-points in biblical religion.

Although sacrificial ideas are prominent in the Bible again there are some noteworthy protests. ' To obey is better than sacrifice and to hearken than the fat of rams ' (1 Sam. xv. 22); mercy, justice and the true knowledge of Yahweh are better than burnt offerings.[1] As for sacrifices—not all the animals of the earth would really suffice for the God of the Universe; [a] as for fasts—fast from wrong-doing; [b] as for Sabbath-keeping—do not walk in your own ways.[c] You rely on Yahweh's Temple, and think that therefore he is with you—but seek good and not evil, and then he shall be with you, as you say.[d] You think your ritual unites you with Yahweh—but the Holy One dwells with the contrite and humble.[e] The most outstanding of all passages is Mic. vi. 8: 'He hath shewed thee, O man, what is good; and what doth Yahweh require of thee, but to do justly, and to love mercy, and to walk humbly with thy God?' (cf. Deut. x. 12).

That the great reformers were uncompromisingly opposed to the sacrificial system is often disputed, in spite of some striking utterances (Amos v. 25, Jer. vii. 21 f.). Undoubtedly, they laid more weight upon moral and spiritual character than upon rites and ceremonies. The true relationship with the God of Righteousness was ensured by righteous conduct; and although the great figures are sometimes regarded as primarily social reformers, it was a theistic

[a] Isa. xl. 16, Ps. l. 8–13.   [b] Isa. lviii. 3 ff.   [c] Ver. 13 f.
[d] Amos v. 14, Mic. iii. 11, Jer. vii. 4 ff.
[e] Isa. lvii. 15, lxvi. 2, Ps. li. 17, cxxxviii. 6.
[1] Hos. vi. 6; cf. Matt. ix. 13, Amos v. 21 f., Isa. i. 11 ff., Jer. vi. 20, Prov. xxi. 3.

social order founded upon the covenant-relation between Yahweh and Israel that they demanded; it was more than the attractive humanism that characterises the Wisdom Literature. While the line of thought of the ' priestly ' parts of the O.T. is ritualist and supernaturalist—there is a gulf between God and man; that of Deuteronomy and the prophets is ethical—God's Law is near at hand and attainable,[a] and did not involve priestly mediation. On the one hand, the sacrificial system becomes exceptionally prominent in the post-exilic Temple, though it had certainly been purged (p. 140); while, on the other hand, along the ' prophetic ' line of thought is developed the conception of the Kingdom of Heaven, although not only are sacrificial ideas focussed upon the death of Christ, but the influence of the Temple system upon Christian thought pervades *Hebrews* and *Revelation* (pp. 76, 151).

Reflection upon sin and suffering raised what seemed to be unanswerable questions. Can man be sinless and escape retribution? Are all suffering and calamity merited? Was the end of the righteous always peace? Was trust in God always justified? That the righteous and the wicked receive their appropriate recompense on earth was the orthodox conviction.[1] But the prosperity of the wicked is not always short-lived; and if they prosper, why should I cleanse myself (Ps. lxxiii. 13)? How can a pure and holy God tolerate evil (Hab. i. 13)? He is patient and long-suffering;[b] but when one is beset by foes the cry goes up: How long?[c] Suffering may be disciplinary,[2] even Paul's ' thorn in the flesh ' led him to experience God's power and grace (2 Cor. xii. 7–10). But in the long run Yahweh will avenge his people.[d] One may hope for a long life (cf. Prov. iii. 2, 16); but Ecclesiastes and Job see no justice in this world,[e] though Job appeals from the God who has caused

---

[a] Deut. xxx. 11–14; cf. Jer. xxxi. 33 f.; Matt. xi. 29 f.
[b] Exod. xxxiv. 6, Jer. xv. 15; cf. Gal. v. 22.
[c] Ps. lxxiv. 10, xciv. 3.
[d] Isa. lxiii. 4, BS xxxv. 18 f.; cf. Luke xviii. 7, Rev. vi. 10.
[e] Eccles. ii. 14, vii. 15; viii. 10, ix. 2, Job xxi. 7 ff.
[1] Cf. Ps. xxxvii. 25, 37 ff., Prov. xi. 31 (with the turn given to it in 1 Pet. iv. 18), xxiii. 18, BS ii. 10, 1 Macc. ii. 61, Col. iii. 25 (cf. Eph. vi. 8).
[2] Ps. xxxiv. 19 ff., BS ii. 1–6, 2 Macc. vi. 12–16; cf. vii. 18, 33, 37 f., 1 Cor. x. 13, Jas. i. 2 f., 1 Pet. i. 6 f., Heb. xii. 7 ff.

him to suffer to the God in whom he has faith (see p. 67). And of the two, the former is the intelligent sceptic and the latter a man truly overwhelmed by pain and disaster.

Not only does Yahweh appear to let men sin and suffer, but he even tempts (tests) them, lays stumbling-blocks before them,[a] 'hardens' their hearts,[b] causes them to be deceived,[c] and gives them laws which are subsequently denounced.[d] Israel is obstinately dull of understanding,[e] she is intractable clay.[1] Yet Yahweh has no pleasure in men's sins,[f] and men must repent;[g] the choice lies before men—a blessing or a curse.[h] Yahweh may propose to destroy a sinful people, but if it turns from evil he will build it up; and if the people whom he proposes to build up does evil he will destroy it.[i]

The writers are struggling with the ever-perplexing problem of the cause of wrong-doing and suffering in themselves or in others. There is not the convenient dualism of the religion of Zoroaster (p. 19); but because Yahweh is supreme in nature and man, all things must in the last resort be traced back to him, the creator of all. What we call 'good' and 'evil' had, primarily at least, no necessarily or exclusively ethical meaning. It is essentially the nature of Yahweh's world which exercises men's minds; and God must justify Himself.[j] Psychologically speaking, what we call sin or wrong-doing is actually self-destructive; false ideas, aims and ideals, false gods (*i.e.*, false conceptions of God)—all must bear their natural fruits. Continuance in what is contrary to the good, the true and the beautiful must have its inevitable psychological effects upon man's character, else there could be no conviction that right must prevail. *Quem Deus vult perdere prius dementat*: and it is the tragedy of individual and national life that men can become the victims of their character and tradition.

[a] Jer. vi. 21, Ezek. iii. 20.   [b] Exod. x. 1, Isa. lxiii. 17, Ps. lxxxi. 12.
[c] 1 Kings xxii. 21 ff., Ezek. xiv. 9.
[d] Ezek. xx. 25 (contrast Jer. vii. 31), Matt. xix. 8, Mark x. 5.
[e] Isa. i. 3, vi. 9 f.   [f] Ezek. xviii. 23, 32.
[g] 2 Pet. iii. 9; cf. Jonah iii. 8–10.   [h] Deut. xxx. 15–19.
[i] Jer. xviii. 7 ff., xxxi. 28, xlv. 4.   [j] Gen. xviii. 25, Job ix f.
[1] For the simile of the potter and clay, see Isa. xxix. 16, xlv. 9–12, lxiv. 8, Jer. xviii. 1–6 and 7–10, Wisdom xv. 7, BS xxxiii. 13, Rom. ix. 20 ff.

Prophets, ' shepherds ' and ' watchmen ' are held responsible for their people.[a]   Moses,[b] Samuel,[c] and Nehemiah [d] identify themselves with their people or appeal on their behalf.   One can bear the ' iniquity ' of another, *i.e.*, his penalty;[e] and this is symbolically performed by the priest-prophet Ezekiel (iv. 4).   Finally, the High-priest on the great Day of Atonement made expiation for Israel (Lev. xvi); it was an annual purgation, testifying to the deep-felt need for preserving the relationship between Israel and Yahweh.   The ceremony passed over into Judaism; but *Hebrews* sets forth the superiority of the priesthood of Christ by the one and only offering of Himself on behalf of men (p. 76).

Suffering is not only a mark of Yahweh's displeasure or a discipline, it is also redemptive.   This is the highest idea in the O.T.   It comes to the front in Isa. liii, and associates the Suffering Servant of Yahweh with Jesus of Nazareth. That Israel was to be a light to the Gentiles,[f] a covenant people,[g] a blessing to other nations [h] turning many to righteousness,[i] was an intelligible idea.   But although the idea of suffering for others is found later, in the books of Maccabees,[j] that of bearing guilt for others (Isa. liii. 8) was not one that Israel could accept.   Yet, the unique relation between Israel and Yahweh meant, as Amos had warned her, that she would be the more severely tried.   ' Unto every one that hath shall be given ' (Matt. xiii. 12), but ' to whomsoever much is given of him shall much be required, and to whom they commit much of him will they ask the more ' (Matt. xxv. 29, Luke xii. 48).   That high office brings with it misunderstanding, pain and suffering was the truth that the Christian Messiah had to incarnate.

In the Bible we see men grappling with the hard facts of individual and national history.   To them God is either the direct or the ultimate cause of all that happens, and the belief that He cared for his world shines out as a clear light in all the darkness of suffering and wrong.   The Creator

[a] Isa. lvi. 10, Ezek. iii. 17 ff., xxxiii. 1–9, xxxiv, Zech. x. 3.
[b] Exod. xxxii. 32.   [c] 1 Sam. xii. 23.   [d] i. 6.
[e] 1 Sam. xxv. 24, 2 Sam. xiv. 9.   [f] Isa. xlix. 6.   [g] xlii. 6.
[h] Gen. xii. 2, Gal. iii. 14.   [i] Dan. xii. 3; cf. Isa. liii. 11.
[j] 2 Macc. vii. 37 f.; cf. 4 Macc. vi. 27–30.

had created the earth to be inhabited.*a* He knows men's frailties, and will not contend for ever.[1] A remarkably fine passage in Wisdom xi. 21–26 breathes the conviction that God must love his creatures: ' thou sparest all things because they are thine, O Sovereign Lord, thou lover of men's lives '. Later, to a Jewish writer plunged in grief at the destruction of the Holy City and the desolation of Israel, whose deeds had surely not been worse than Babylon's (2 Esdras iii. 31), comes the assurance that he could not love that people better than He that made them (v. 33, cf. viii. 47). And an almost contemporary Christian, at an age when the crucifixion of Christ might seem to be the death-blow to all hopes of a new Messianic age, sees in this voluntary sacrifice the manifestation of God's love for the world (John iii. 16).

VI. *The Messiah and the New Age*

Israel always cherished the hope of a bright and glorious future for herself. There might be grave internal wrongs, evils of which she was guilty and which called for punishment, or there might be disastrous attacks, persecution and oppression by her foes. But, in the long run, Yahweh would intervene and introduce a happier age. The hope takes a variety of forms. Yahweh had never left himself without his witnesses, though Elijah (1 Kings xix. 14) and Jeremiah felt their loneliness and defeat (Jer. xv. 10–21, xx. 7–18). Or a ' remnant ' would be preserved—so characteristically Isaiah.*b* Yahweh would return to an Israel that sought him,*c* the offerings of a purged people he would accept.*d* The ' Day of Yahweh ' would surely come, but whereas Israel was wont to expect a triumphant vindication, she was warned that Yahweh would appear as an upholder of righteousness. The day of victory was not necessarily the victory of Israel, but of righteousness, and a judgment not

---

a Isa. xlv. 18; cf. Ps. cxv. 16, Wisdom i. 13 f.
b *E.g.*, Isa. iv. 3, vii. 3 mg., x. 20 ff.
c Hos. iii. 5, v. 15.
d Mal. iii. 3 f.
[1] Isa. lvii. 16, Ps. lxxviii. 39, ciii. 9. The meaning of Gen. vi. 3 is quite obscure.

upon Israel's foes, but upon herself.[1]   The ' Day of Yahweh '
is an old conception to which Amos is the first of the extant
prophets to give an ethical and universal meaning; it
belongs to that larger body of ideas which unite the O.T.
and the N.T., and of which the ideal king, the Messiah, and
the ideal kingdom or realm, made the deepest impression
upon subsequent thought.

The outstanding idea is that Yahweh is sole king of
Israel, supreme over all nations and their gods.[a]   He intervenes in history, either directly or through his emissaries,
or his representatives on earth, or indeed through other
nations.   Now, Israel's forerunners had recognised the
divinity of the Pharaoh of Egypt, himself a subordinate to
the great national god.   Nor is evidence wanting that in
Israel also the king or his office could be regarded as divine.
He was anointed, his person was sacred.[b]   Neither he nor
Yahweh might be reviled;[c] and at Jerusalem David sat
upon the throne of Yahweh.[2]   Yahweh was behind the
election to kingship;[d] and the head of the kingdom might
be called not king, but ' prince ' or ' chief ', so especially in
Ezekiel, where the ruler holds a subordinate position (chh.
xl ff.).   He provides the materials for the sacrifices
(Ezek. xlv. 17, 22–25), but must not approach the inner
shrine (xliv. 3, xlvi. 2, 8, 10–12).   There were, in fact,
varying ideas as to the king's place in the religion, depending
largely upon the recognition of Yahweh as sole king, or upon
the power of the priesthood.   The longing for an ideal king,
the ' shepherd ' of his people, now apparently asleep,[e] had
appeared many centuries earlier in Egypt; but there was
not that persistence and development of idea that characterize the Bible.   The Israelite expectation is that of a
king who is spoken of in human, or even in almost divine

[a] Jer. x. 7, xlvi. 18, Ps. xcv. 3.
[b] 1 Sam. xxiv. 6, xxvi. 11.
[c] Exod. xxii. 28, 1 Kings xxi. 10.
[d] Cf. Hos. viii. 4, 1 Sam. ix. 15 ff., xvi. 1 ff.
[e] Cf. Ps. xliv. 23.
[1] See Amos v. 18, Isa. ii. 12, 17, Zeph. i. 7–12, Obad. 15 f., Joel i.
15, ii. 1 ff.
[2] 1 Chr. xxix. 23, 2 Chr. ix. 8.   The earlier source calls it the throne
of Israel (1 Kings x. 9).   In 1 Chron. xxviii. 5 it is the throne of Yahweh's kingdom.

terms.[1] David, the founder of the lengthy Judaean dynasty, is the prototype (see esp. 2 Sam. vii. 12 ff.); and Zerubbabel is a conspicuous example of Messianic ideas at the time when the Second Temple was being built (Hag. ii, Zech. iv).

Indications of rivalry between the kingship and the priesthood are, however, to be seen, the high-priest having the greater authority (Zech. iii. 7 f., vi. 12 ff.); and the royal priest of the old-time order of Melchizedek in Ps. cx belongs more naturally, not to the days of the actual monarchy, but much later. Note the inauguration of a princely priest in the person of Simon in 1 Macc. xiv. 4–15, 41 (cf. BS l. 1–21). Later still, outside the canonical books, expectation varies between a Levitical or priestly and a Davidic Messiah; but the latter, because of the tradition of David and the utterances of the prophets, was naturally the more popular.

Neither the Davidic nor the Messianic idea appears everywhere in the O.T., and certain passages demand special attention. The first are the ' Servant ' sections in the *Second Isaiah*, wherein Yahweh's Servant is entrusted with a mission, but is despised and rejected.[2] The references point to (*a*) Israel as the Servant, (*b*) an inner ideal or spiritual Israel who must win over the body of the whole people, and (*c*) an individual. But there is conflict of opinion among scholars as to the best interpretation, Isa. liii being particularly difficult. Now, just as Israel and Jacob are names of ancestral individuals and also of the whole people,[a] and just as ' Son of Man ' is a title given to an individual, viz. Ezekiel (*e.g.*, ii. 1), to the ideal Israel in the vision of Daniel (vii. 13 f., 27), and to Israel or to an individual in Ps. lxxx. 17, so it is possible that the conception of the Servant could be equally fluid. That the Servant— above all in Isa. liii—cannot be dissociated from Jesus of Nazareth is undeniable; but opinions differ as to whether we have here only the most remarkable anticipation in the

[a] Cf. Deut. xxxiii. 10.

[1] The chief Messianic passages are Isa. ix. 6 f., xi. 1–10, Jer. xxiii. 5, xxxiii. 15, Ezek. xxxvii. 24; cf. Isa. iv. 2, xvi. 5, xxxii. 1 ff., lv. 3 f., Mic. v. 2, also Ps. ii. 6–11.

[2] Isa. xlii. 1–4, xlix. 1–6, l. 4–9, lii. 13–liii. 12.

O.T. of the sufferings of Jesus and the glory that should follow, or an actual prophecy fulfilled in Him alone. But since the prophets always had in view the conditions of their own age, the former is the more probable; and it would seem that—in some passages, at least—an actual individual is intended, one whose function it was to achieve for his age what in a higher degree was achieved by Jesus a few centuries later at another great period of upheaval.

Accordingly, there is a striking parallelism between (a) Jesus Christ and the conception of the Body of Christ and the special nucleus of apostles and the Church, and (b) this unknown individual, Israel, and the inner or spiritual Israel. The ' Servant ' passages come between a period of distress and disaster and one where a reorganized Israel has fallen away from the lofty idealism of the *Second Isaiah.* Nowhere else in the O.T. has the spiritual imagination risen to so lofty a height; and, whatever view be taken of the ' Servant ', we can ignore neither the brilliancy of the conception nor its influence upon early Christian thought and onwards.[1]

Another unresolved problem is presented in Zech. xii. 1–xiii. 6 by the words ' they shall look unto him whom they have pierced' (xii. 10 mg., cited in John xix. 37). The historical background is wholly obscure. A great wrong had been committed upon an individual or, it may be, upon a body of righteous men; but repentance would be the prelude to better conditions, and Jerusalem would be delivered. Again, while in Plato's *Republic* ii. 362 (400–350 B.C.) the just man is tortured and crucified, but remains steadfast, in Ps. xxii the individual (or the faithful community), afflicted and deserted (verse 1 is cited in Mark xv. 34), ends on a joyous note, and looks for the recognition of Yahweh's kingship among the living and the dead. Moreover, Wisdom ii. 10–20 describes at length the denunciation and persecution of the righteous by the unrighteous. The ' righteous man ' professes to have knowledge of God, and calls himself the Lord's child (or servant); he boasts that God is his father,

---

[1] See Acts viii. 26 ff. The Suffering Servant was interpreted as a Messianic figure by the older Jewish Targum or paraphrastic translation into Aramaic.

and is condemned to a shameful death. But though the righteous die despised, he is reckoned among the sons of God, and his portion is among the saints (iv. 7 ff., v. 1–5). Here, Enoch seems to have been in the writer's mind (iv. 10, cf. Gen. v. 24); but Christian interpolation (or influence) or only a striking coincidence has been varyingly suggested. At all events, we have illustrations of the way in which different minds were concerned with undeserved suffering.

In general, the Messianic and other ideas of the future cannot be classed under one heading. They are influenced by actual internal or external conditions, so, *e.g.*, in the time of Zerubbabel, and no doubt also during the Maccabaean age to which *Daniel* is ascribed. But they take a wider sweep; they look into the future, and are universal and cosmic, replacing old mythological ideas of creation and of cosmic contests by ' eschatological ' notions of an approaching end. They are of the most varied description. There are both moderate and immoderate ideas of what the new order will bring: peace and plenty, and long life, but also extravagant fancies of the good fortune of Israel and the evil fate of sinners and foes. There are natural expectations of the reassembling of exiles or of scattered tribes.[a] Israel's foes will be subjugated or, indeed, they may be converted to Yahweh,[b] for Yahweh is to be found in Israel alone.[1] One striking passage even foreshadows a religious alliance of Israel, Egypt and Assyria (Isa. xix. 19–25); but some of the old versions and the Jewish paraphrase (the Targum) intentionally or otherwise miss the point here. Throughout, Jerusalem and Zion are usually pre-eminent, and this is to be borne in mind when one turns from the O.T. and the apocalypses to the N.T.

Two writings first call for special mention. In the so-called *Psalms of Solomon* (ch. xvii f.), of about fifty years before the birth of Jesus, there is hope of a king, the son of David, raised up by the Lord who Himself is King. He is the ' anointed of the Lord ', or the ' anointed one ', the Lord (cf. Luke ii. 11); he will be a victorious ruler over a

[a] Amos ix. 14 f., Hos. xi. 11, Mic. ii. 12, iv. 6 f.
[b] Zeph. iii. 9 f., Jer. xii. 14 ff., xvi. 19, Ps. xxii. 27 ff.
[1] Isa. xlv. 14, Zech. viii. 22.

holy people, ' all sons of their God '.   ' Blessed are they
that shall be in those days.'   More striking are the passages
in the *Book of Enoch* which undoubtedly influenced Christian thought; it is referred to in *Jude* (see p. 77).   Here we
meet with one who is called ' the anointed one ', the
' righteous ' (cf. Acts iii. 14), the ' elect ' (cf. Luke ix. 35), the
' Son of Man '; he is with the ' head of Days whose hair
was white like wool ' (cf. Dan. vii. 9), and is seated on the
throne of his glory as Judge (cf. Matt. xix. 28).

In Palestine, besides these and other expectations of
Israel's recovery, kindled by the biblical and apocalyptical
literature, there were serious revolts (cf. Acts v. 36 f., xxi.
38); and these disturbances, which Josephus so vividly
depicts, combine to form the background to the rise of that
Jewish sect which became Christianity.   In the N.T., as in
the earlier writings already referred to, we have beliefs of
diverse periods and presenting different points of view.
Jesus came and was crucified; a new age was expected, and
we see something of the hopes in the poems in Luke i. 46–55,
67–79, ii. 29–32, and also of the subsequent disappointment
(xxiv. 21).   The restoration of Israel would be in God's
good time.[1]   The Messiah had come, but Israel was not
yet restored—compare the similar sentiment in Jer. viii. 20.
Jesus had been rejected and crucified; but his spirit lived on
among his followers.   This was not the end; there would
be a Second Coming, a judgment, a final consummation of
past hopes.   The increasingly grave disasters (Jerusalem
fell in 70 A.D.), the persecution of the Christians, and the
difficulty of reconciling the threatening daily situation with
the unshaken confidence inspired by Jesus—these lie behind
the growth of the writings of the N.T.   There would be
false prophets and false Christs.[a]   An evil age is passing
away, an age under ' the god of this world ';[b] and Christians
are contending, not against men, but against powers of
wickedness,[c] for the idols are real demons.[d]   There would
be a last fight of good against evil, until Christ had

[a] Matt. xxiv. 5, 24.   [b] 1 Cor. ii. 6, 2 Cor. iv. 4.
[c] Eph. vi. 12.   [d] 1 Cor. x. 20, xii. 2.
[1] Acts i. 6 f., where the ' Western text ' reads: ' no one can know '
(cf. Mark xiii. 32, Matt. xxiv. 36).

abolished death;[a] and, apparently harking back to Israel's battles at Megiddo,[b] the greatest of the apocalyptists sees the overthrow of the Antichrist Nero at Armageddon (Rev. xvi. 16, xix. 19 ff.).   See further, p. 142.

Actual history and symbolism are blended, and thought passes to and fro between the events of the day and the destiny of Israel, of the New Israel, of mankind and the world.   But in the O.T. the convulsions of nature,[c] even the belief in a new heaven and earth, are not to be taken too literally and unimaginatively; the world remains, but it is one transformed, transfigured, with a happier Jerusalem and a joyful and everlasting Israel.[1]   Nicodemus could not understand how a man must be born again to enter the Kingdom of God;[d] and the parables of Jesus could perplex men of his time as well as of to-day who confuse the letter with the spirit: why must he speak in parables?[e]   The conviction that the Second Coming was imminent might lead Paul to warn men to avoid the distractions of life (1 Cor. vii. 29 ff.), and the expectation of imminent disasters calls forth a similar warning from a rather later writer in 2 Esdras xvi. 40 ff.; but there is no reason to suppose that the ethical injunctions of Jesus were only temporary, and were not meant to be lasting.

VII. *The Kingdom of Heaven*

The long-expected Messiah came;[f] the Kingdom of Heaven—God's sovereignty—was at hand.   The promises of the past had been fulfilled,[g] and Jesus was the cornerstone which the builders of the New Age—and they were many—rejected.[h]   He came to ' save ' men,[i] as was indicated by his name, which is the Greek form of the O.T. Joshua and Jeshua.   He sought out the lost ' sheep ';[j] and, as the Good Shepherd,[k] he gave a deeper meaning to a very old

[a] Cf. 1 Cor. xv. 24 ff.   [b] Judges v. 19, 2 Kings xxiii. 29.
[c] *E.g.*, Isa. xiii. 9 f.   [d] John iii. 3 ff.
[e] Matt. xiii. 10 ff., 34, Mark iv. 10 ff., Luke xii. 41.
[f] Luke i. 17, 32, 43, ii. 11, 25 f., 38.   [g] Gal. iv. 4, Heb. i. 1 ff.
[h] Mark xii. 10.   [i] Matt. i. 21, Acts v. 31, 1 Tim. i. 15.
[j] Matt. xv. 24; cf. Luke xix. 10.   [k] John x. 14.
[1] Cf. Isa. li. 6, lxv. 17 ff., lxvi. 22.   Note the language used even of past or present events in Amos vii. 4, Ps. xviii. 7 ff.

and pre-Israelite idea.[a]   He laid down his life as a ' ransom '
(Mark. x. 45)—a recipient of payment is not implied (cf.
Jer. xv. 21, Job'v. 20, vi. 23); and through his sacrificial
death men were freed from sin and no longer alienated from
God who had reconciled them to Himself through Christ.[b]
Distinctive of the Gospel teaching is the search for the
wandering and perishing; but God's pity and forgiveness
are a gift,[c] an act of grace, and do not justify continuance
in sin,[d] man's fight against his lower nature has not ceased.[e]

Jesus is addressed as Rabbi (Mark ix. 5, and especially in
John). He spoke with a compelling authority—with the
frequent ' verily, I say unto you ', or ' but I say '[f]—and not
as the professional Scribes relying upon past tradition.[g]
The past is dead; one could not weave the new into the old,
or (in the words of Jeremiah) ' heal the hurt lightly '.[h]   The
Law had served its purpose;[i] there is now the ' law of
Christ ',[j] and men should walk after his Spirit and in his
righteousness.[1]   He came not to destroy, but to fulfil;[k] and,
as in the history of religious and other thought (*e.g.*, physics),
the new stage does not annihilate the past, but develops it and
creates a new background.   The line is drawn between John
the Baptist and himself;[l] men must be reborn and be as
children,[m] setting forth upon their new life.   Noble ethical
sentiments and injunctions are to be found in the O.T., the
apocalyptical writings, in Rabbinical Judaism, as also in
other religions; but it is his utter and consistent integrity
that—from the purely humanist point of view—distinguishes
Jesus and sets him apart from all other teachers of ethics
and social compassion and brotherliness.   In the Sermon
on the Mount, in the Parables, and in his whole life he

[a] Cf. Jer. xxxi. 10, Zech. xi. 16, Ps. xxiii. 1.
[b] 2 Cor. v. 18 f., Eph. ii. 11 ff.   [c] Eph. ii. 8 ff.
[d] Rom. vi. 1 f.; cf. John v. 14, viii. 11.
[e] Rom. vii. 19.   [f] Matt. v. 22, 32, 39, etc.
[g] Mark i. 22, Matt. vii. 29; cf. Amos vii. 14.
[h] Mark ii. 21 f., Jer. vi. 14.
[i] Rom. x. 4, Gal. iii. 24; cf. Matt. xi. 13.   [j] Gal. vi. 2.
[k] Matt. v. 17.   [l] Luke vii. 28; cf. xvi. 16.
[m] John iii. 3, 5, Matt. xix. 14.
[1] Rom. viii. 1–11, iii. 21 f.   The Law and the Prophets hang on two
commandments—love of God and love of one's neighbour (Matt.
xxii. 40); cf. ' the Golden Rule ' (Luke vi. 31).

manifests the fact that the highest and truest Self is greater than the daily Self, that it is folly to lay up treasures on earth, or attempt to serve two masters.[a] His sayings, even when paradoxical, are searching; and the ' hypocrisy ' he condemned was an externality and superficiality, condemned by the prophets before him,[b] for the consciousness of the intimate personal relation between God and man is characteristic of Israel's writers.[c] He called for life on the highest plane and for unbounded faith in a Heavenly Father who knows men's needs.[d] There was a yoke,[e] and though the gate was narrow,[f] it opened out the way to the fullest life.

The Kingdom of God was at hand, and the first call to a changed life came from John the Baptist. He was evidently of greater importance than even the N.T. passages and references indicate, but his figure has been subordinated, especially in the Fourth Gospel, to that of Jesus. The record in *Luke* and *Acts* (p. 72) aims at presenting a continuous story from the announcement of the births of John and Jesus to the mission of Paul among the Gentiles— that is, from the somewhat distinctively Jewish character of the Baptist to the struggle between Jewish Christianity and the more universalistic teaching of Paul.[1] The *Benedictus* regards John as the prophet of the Most High, the precursor of the Davidic Saviour, and the preacher of salvation to the Jews in the remission of their sins.[g] John's function—that of preparing the way for the Messiah—is connected with the prelude to Yahweh's coming intervention on behalf of his distressed people in Is. xl. 3 ff. (Mark i. 1 ff., Luke iii. 3); and as the Elijah foreshadowed in Mal. iv. 5 f., he is the precursor of the terrible Day of Yahweh and is to turn old and young to repentance.[h] Recognized by the people as a prophet,[i] and actually receiving more attention in the *Antiquities* of Josephus than does Jesus (see p. 165), he was the expected Elijah (Matt. xi. 14; cf. xvii. 10–13). With the exhortation to Israel in Mal. iv. 4 to remember the law of Moses agrees the association of Moses, Elijah and Jesus at

[a] Matt. vi. 19 f., 24 ff., xix. 29.   [b] Mark vii. 6 ff.
[c] Cf. Ps. cxxxix.   [d] Matt. vi. 26 ff., Luke xii. 22 ff.
[e] Matt. xi. 28 ff.   [f] Matt. vii. 14.   [g] Luke i. 68–79.
[h] Cf. BS xlviii. 10, Luke i. 17.   [i] Mark xi. 32.
[1] Cf. Mark i. 1–4, Acts i. 22, x. 37, xiii. 24.

the Transfiguration (Mark ix. 2–8); and Moses and Elijah are probably the 'two witnesses' in Rev. xi. 3. Jesus himself was taken by some to be Elijah, or Jeremiah, or John the Baptist risen from the dead (Matt. xvi. 14, Mark vi. 14–16); but the incident demonstrates his uniqueness and that essential gulf between him and 'all the prophets and the law', a gulf which John may be said to bridge.[a]

John the Baptist came as an ascetic,[b] preaching the near approach of the Kingdom. His teaching is immediately practical—no extortion by the tax-collectors, no violence by soldiers, contentment with one's wages, and a voluntary sharing of food and clothing (Luke iii. 11–14; cf. Acts ii. 44 f., iv. 32). The Israelite reliance upon their ancestor Abraham—*i.e.*, upon Yahweh's promises to their fathers (p. 89)—was futile;[c] the true sons of Abraham do his works.[d] The Kingdom was indeed rightfully Israel's;[e] but she rejected it in the form in which it came. The political Messianic element is wanting in the poems relating to John's birth,[f] and Jesus did not identify himself with the current political movements, though the people sought to make him their king.[g]

But the Kingdom of God was not of this world.[h] It is near at hand, it will come suddenly,[i] though Jesus did not know the hour (Mark xiii. 32). One must be watchful and patient,[j] for God is not 'slack'.[k] Jesus would come again in the glory of his Father with the angels, and would judge the world.[l] On the other hand, the present generation would see it;[m] nay, it had come,[n] it is among, or rather within, men.[o] In the Fourth Gospel the spiritual *event* is superseded by present spiritual *experience*, and the followers of Christ already enjoy fellowship with Him.[p] By their

---

[a] Matt. xi. 12 f., Luke xvi. 16.   [b] Luke vii. 33 f.
[c] Luke iii. 8.   [d] Cf. John viii. 39; cf. Gal. iii. 7, 9, 14.
[e] Matt. xxi. 43; cf. vii. 12.   [f] Luke i.
[g] John vi. 15; cf. xii. 13, Mark xi. 10, and Matt. v. 35.
[h] John xviii. 36; cf. Luke iv. 6, Matt. iv. 8.
[i] Mark xiii. 36, Matt. xxv. 13.   [j] Cf. Heb. x. 36.
[k] 2 Pet. iii. 9 f.
[l] Mark viii. 38, Matt. xiii. 49.
[m] Mark ix. 1, xiii. 30; cf. 1 Thess. iv. 13–17.
[n] Matt. xii. 28.   [o] Luke xvii. 21.
[p] Cf. 1 Cor. i. 9, 1 John i. 3.

attitude to Christ men are already pronouncing judgment upon themselves.[a]

This unity and fellowship with God through Christ[b] constitutes the ' Body of Christ ', the New Israel, the Israel of God.   It is, as it were, a spiritual organism, a ' Church '.[1] Following along the lines of contemporary Jewish active proselytism (Matt. xxiii. 15) membership was open to all [c]— but conditionally; and the difference between the Jewish and the Christian conditions was vital, the necessity of circumcision for Gentile Christians being a burning question. Christian circumcision was spiritual and Christians claim to be the true circumcision.[2]   Jewish, too, in itself is the idea of the ' pre-existence ' of Christ, for what is holy is felt psychologically to have a non-human and pre-human origin—like the Jewish Torah and the Koran in Islām. Christ, like Yahweh, is First and Last, Alpha and Omega.[d] He is eternal, and Christians are pre-chosen in Him through God's eternal purpose.   They are called to glory, their citizenship is in heaven,[e] and their kingdom has been prepared for them from the foundation of the world.[f]

These passages are not all of the same tenor.   We are dealing with a Great Hope—one already now actualized or shortly to be actualized.   Men were struggling with new pregnant experiences and with the expectations and doubts that arose as the years passed.   When a new stage in life and thought is felt to be at hand, can it ever be determined at what point it has dawned or has come into the full light of day? A Gospel that was universal in its scope had not—and has not—reached its goal.   ' Thy Kingdom come ' is still the hope in the Prayer of Prayers.[g]   There were already the ' first-fruits ', an ' earnest ' or pledge of what was to come;[h]

---

[a] John iii. 19 f., ix. 39.   [b] John xvii. 21–23.   [c] Cf. John i. 12.
[d] Isa. xliv. 6, Rev. i. 8.   [e] Eph. i. 4 f., 11, iii. 11, Phil. iii. 20, 1 Pet. i. 10.
[f] Matt. xxv. 34; cf. xx. 23, Heb. xi. 16.
[g] Cf. 1 Cor. xvi. 22 mg, Rev. xxii. 20.
[h] 2 Cor. i. 22, Eph. i. 14, Rom. viii. 23.
[1] The term (lit. ' the Lord's ') has its O.T. root in the ' congregation ', the national body of Israel, and the more restricted ' assembly ' of the people in their religious capacity: a distinction is drawn in Lev. iv. 13 f., though not consistently elsewhere.   Ideally, Israel was a nation of priests (Exod. xix. 6, Isa. lxi. 6; cf. 1 Pet. ii. 9, Rev. i. 6).
[2] Cf. Phil. iii. 2 ff., Eph. ii. 11 ff., Col. ii. 10 ff., and see p. 87.

and the Kingdom of God was like a grain of seed or like leaven.[a] Though Jesus had been crucified, the Paraclete or Advocate, the Spirit of Truth, was with men (John xiv. 16 mg.); and at Pentecost the outpouring of the Spirit in Jerusalem was the sign that God was in their midst, inaugurating the Christian Mission (Acts ii. 14 ff.; citing Joel ii. 27 ff.). The N.T. in common with the vicissitudes of the Early Church clearly shows how readily difficulties and divisions could arise, for the Gospel *of* Jesus and the Gospel *about* Jesus were not one and the same. There were ' schools ' of thought which ' divided ' Christ.[b] There were 'Antichrists ', teachers of false doctrine,[c] men who came in Christ's name [d] and claimed to be his.[e] None the less, the primary test is not doctrinal, but ethical (cf. Mark iii. 33–35, Matt. xxv. 41–46, John xv. 14).

Jesus Christ gathered up into one all that had gone before; all was ' summed up ' in him (Eph. i. 10, the same Greek verb as in Rom. xiii. 9). He is the ' Amen ';[1] He is the climax of the O.T. functions of prophet and priest, the Second Adam superseding the old era which began with the First Adam.[2] The King of Kings,[3] he is the King that comes in the name of the Lord.[f] He is ' Son of David ';[g] but he is far more than the type of Messiah that was awaited.[h] With the ' Suffering Servant ' of Isa. liii, Jesus is clearly identified in Acts viii. 26 ff.; and echoes of that chapter recur in 1 Pet. ii. 22–25 (cf. Rom. iv. 25). The relationship between Jesus and the enigmatic figure in the *Second Isaiah* has been noticed above; there are in fact impressive points of contact between the *Second Isaiah* and the thought at the rise of Christianity: the general conditions behind each were not wholly dissimilar. Jesus is ' Son of Man '—the designation He uses of Himself—and

---

[a] Luke xiii. 18–21.   [b] 1 Cor. i. 12 ff.; cf. 2 Cor. xi. 4.
[c] 1 John ii. 18, 22, iv. 1, 2 John 7 f.
[d] John v. 43; cf. Matt. xxiv. 4 f.
[e] Cf. Matt. vii. 15 ff.
[f] Matt. xxi. 5, Mark xi. 9 f., Luke xix. 38 ff., John xii. 12 ff.; cf. Ps. cxviii. 26.
[g] Matt. i. 1, Luke. ii. 4, Rom. i. 3.   [h] Cf. Mark xii. 35–37.
[1] 2 Cor. i. 20; cf. Rev. iii. 14.
[2] 1 Cor. xv. 22, 45, 47.   [3] 1 Tim. vi. 15.

He is ' Son of God '.[a]   Like Israel herself, He is the Son
(p. 89). And in Him men see God the Father.[b]   He is
not God the Father, for ultimately He will hand over all
things to God.[c]   There is a spiritual unity of God, Christ
and the Christian ' body ', the Body of Christ;[d] and through
faith Christians may become partakers of a divine nature,[e]
begotten again.[f]   See further, p. 44 f.

VIII. *Conclusion*

The ' Kingdom of God ' implies a supreme head; the
' Body of Christ ' implies an organic whole, animated with
his Spirit, a diversity within unity, the parts unified by and
contributing to the whole (Rom. xii. 4–8, 1 Cor. xii. 4–31,
Eph. iv. 11 ff.).   The earlier solidarity of Yahweh and Israel
(p. 88 f.) has taken a new form; and in the N.T. there is a
fresh synthesis of (*a*) Yahweh, the God of Israel, and (*b*)
Yahweh, the creator and ruler of the world.   The uniquely
intimate relationship between Yahweh and Israel, his
spouse and offspring, and the supremacy of Yahweh over
man and the world were already to a certain extent syn-
thesized by the belief in angels and other intermediaries
(p. 97 f.).   But this belief tended to give them too great an
importance and to separate men from their God.   And
against such a separation there is constant protest, especially
in the *Psalms* (cf. Paul in Rom. viii. 38 f.).   Yet Yahweh in
his intimate dealings with the nation and men of Israel and
Yahweh as the supreme God of the world could not be
precisely the same at the same time.   Yahweh, like the
potter with his clay (p. 114 n.), had a purpose which overruled
the vicissitudes of history; though even when he seemed
indifferent or hostile to Israel, there was faith in the righteousness of one who ' would be what he would be ' (p. 87 n.), as
in the impressive confidence expressed in Dan. iii. 17 f. (cf.
Hab. iii. 17 ff.).   Accordingly we meet with a striking
paradox when Job is confident that God who is now tor-
menting him will vindicate him against Himself.   There is

---

[a] Luke xxii. 67–70, Matt. xiv. 33.   [b] John xiv. 9.
[c] 1 Cor. xv. 24; cf. xi. 3, Phil. ii. 11, Acts vii. 56.
[d] John xiv. 20 f., xvii. 16 ff.
[e] Gal. iii. 26, 2 Pet. i. 4, 1 John iii. 2.   [f] 1 Pet. i. 23.

no ' daysman ' between them—let God act as one: ' the defendant implores the plaintiff to be his judge '; ' one God holds him guilty, another knows his innocence ', and he appeals to the one against the other.[1]   Here is, of course, no Trinitarian doctrine, though the belief in the angel of Yahweh and intermediary angels was already preparing the ground for one.   We have ideas which (*a*) in more mythological form lie behind the old Oriental conceptions of father-and-son gods and their respective functions, and which (*b*) in the N.T. issue into the doctrine of God in Christ reconciling the world unto Himself.[a]

There is another line of thought.   Yahweh is the God of an ordered universe; to him all things owe their existence and specific functions.[2]   He has only to say to the sea: ' Thus far shalt thou come and no farther '; for his Word is effective and by it all things consist.[3]   His ' Wisdom ' is manifested in his actions,[b] and later writings treat it as an agency, a personification, if not an agent.[4]   In the Alexandrian Philo, a devout Jew who had assimilated some Greek philosophy, we meet with the *logos* ('reason, rationality').   It is intermediary between God and man, an interceding power, sometimes independent and sometimes an aspect of God's activity.   It takes the place of the angels, Word and Wisdom of the O.T.   It combines God's creative work and man's understanding, but God is an abstract being distinct from the world and men.   To the same region of ideas belong the Prologue to the Fourth Gospel and *Hebrews*, and there are many points of contact.   But there is this vital difference, that in Christ, who is the Power and Wisdom of God,[c] being tempted and suffering like ourselves,[d] the Logos has become flesh, and has ' tabernacled ' among men, *i.e.*, made man its tabernacle or temple.[5]   In Christ the theophanies of the O.T. culminate—the angel of Yahweh,[e] or of his presence,[f]

[a] Rom. v. 10 f., 2 Cor. v. 18; cf. Col. i. 20.
[b] Jer. x. 12; cf. Luke xi. 49.   [c] 1 Cor. i. 24, 30.
[d] Heb. ii. 17 f., iv. 15.   [e] Exod. iii. 2.   [f] Isa. lxiii. 9.
[1] Job xvi. 18–21, xvii. 3. The quotations are respectively from Peake's Commentary, p. 169 f., and A. B. Davidson, *Theology of the O.T.*, p. 288, cf. p. 284.
[2] Job xxviii. 26, xxxvii. ff., Ps. civ, cxlviii. 6, Jer. xxxi. 35 f.
[3] Ps. xxxiii. 6, 9, cvii. 20, cxlvii. 15, Isa. lv. 11.
[4] See p. 68.   [5] John i. 14; cf. p. 151.

or of the Covenant;[a] and as Yahweh is God of the world of nature and men, so Christ combines all functions. Through Christ God made the world, all things consist in Him; and the earlier realistic conviction of Yahweh's presence is superseded, at this later and more developed stage of thought, by the conviction that Christ is the basis of existence.[1] Stated in modern terms, Christ is ' the continuous immanent principle of order in the Universe '; ' the principle of cohesion in the Universe, He impresses upon creation that unity and solidarity which makes it a cosmos instead of a chaos '; ' the Christian Logos is a cosmic principle, the agent in creation, the life of the world, the sustainer in being of all created things.' [2] The sympathy between man and nature, amounting in primitive religions to a virtual relationship, is familiar in the O.T., and appears in later Messianic passages which look for increased fertility of nature; and Paul goes further when he envisages a new universal harmony throughout the ' whole creation ' now groaning and in travail.[b]

Is this ' philosophy '? At least it represents convictions in the light of which the mythologies and philosophies of the day were judged. The Christians were confronted by strange intellectual constructions.[c] There arose curious forms of Gnosticism; these were not necessarily non-Christian, but they were efforts to synthesize Christianity and the best— one might almost say the ' scientific '—knowledge of the day. They represent intellectual and exclusive types of thought; for, outside orthodox or normative Judaism, were men like Josephus (whose ' philosophy ' is of no little interest), Philo, Jews in the Greek cities of the Decapolis, not to mention other curious blends of Oriental and Hellenistic culture. The world of their day was one of contending powers, astral cults, cosmic beings and angels and other tutelary beings.[3] To the popular and widespread belief in spirits, demons and what not, corresponds the

[a] Mal. iii. 1.   [b] Rom. viii. 19–23.   [c] Col. ii. 8, 1 Tim. vi. 20.
[1] Heb. i. 1–4, Col. i. 13–19.
[2] See respectively Gore, *Reconstruction of Belief* (1926), p. 378 f., on the ' activities of the Son of God in nature '; J. B. Lightfoot (1876), on Col. i. 18, and Inge, *God and the Astronomers* (1933), p. 267.
[3] Cf. Rev. vii. 1, xiv. 17 f., xvi. 5, xix. 17.

more detailed analysis of the functions and activities of man and nature. Such were ' the beggarly elements ' to which men were in bondage (Gal. iv. 9). But just as Yahweh in the O.T. is exalted over and supersedes local baals and the various functional and regional gods, so in the N.T. God in Christ is above and supersedes the diverse influences, patrons and agencies which seemed to influence everyday life and answer the demands of the intellect. The vagaries of polytheism, the wealth of demonology and angelology, and the barren wastes of Gnostic speculation may seem to us to be utterly foolish; but they have a very real value, in that they represent efforts, intuitive, or deliberate, or markedly intellectual, to answer questions and to solve problems that are still with us.[1]

The biblical response to these questions is an uncompromisingly monotheistic one: there are not many gods and spirits, but a One and Only God. It is a monotheism that is emotional, practical and subjective (see p. 151, n. 5), before ever it becomes, as it is to-day, also a philosophical issue. In both O.T. and N.T. God is a ' jealous ' God, who will not tolerate the worship of other gods.[a] What this connoted runs through the history of religion in and behind the Bible: God's character and attributes; how men were to reverence and love Him and carry out his will—and what this will was; how they were to think of God's place in the Universe of man and nature. To-day we should call it the problem of positive knowledge, science and religion.

The God of the Bible is also one of wrath; and those of to-day who speak of the ' angry Jehovah ' of the O.T. overlook the stern side of Jesus and the uncompromising discipline of the N.T.: Divine Love and Divine Righteousness are inseparable. Now this ' wrath ' bespeaks men's hatred, contempt, and even their fanatical abhorrence of all that offended their convictions of God; and the background of the N.T.—as the works of Josephus amply testify—represents a time of passion and heat, with fierce, though contradictory and conflicting, ideals and convictions. There was a zeal—in both the O.T. and the N.T.—which led men

[a] Deut. xxxii. 21, 1 Cor. x. 22.
[1] See *Rebirth of Christianity*, p. 69 f.

to fury against their enemies, or which, when thwarted, plunged them in despair; and just as there were extremes of intellectual perversity and perverted mentality when, as Jeremiah could say, ' the false pen of the scribes wrought falsely ' (Jer. viii. 8), so there were the extremes of emotion and passion when their God was at stake. It was zeal for her God that kept Israel alive in her desperation; but it was zeal—and an unwise one—that led to her undoing (Rom. x. 2).

> ' The " Messianic " hope of Israel ', says a recent writer, ' was both her glory and her ruin. In its various forms it inspired some of the great prophetic and apocalyptic utterances and repeatedly brought consolation to Israel in its darkest days. On the other hand, the very revival of such hopes in the first Christian century, to which the N.T. witnesses, led eventually to the catastrophe of A.D. 70 and the destruction of such political existence as remained to Israel.' [1]

In reaching the heart of the Bible we cannot fail to recognize that in it we have the greatest drama of past religious history. But the story of the Election and Rejection of a Chosen People, as we read it in the Bible to-day, is one never to be read in a spirit of self-satisfaction and self-glorying, least of all in an age of trial and testing when one epoch of world-history is passing over into another (see p. 204).

This chapter has been mainly concerned with certain aspects of the continuity between the O.T. and N.T., in particular with the two leading conceptions: the Kingship of God (the Kingdom of Heaven) and the Solidarity of Israel and Yahweh (the Body of Christ). Though not wholly disparate these tend to express, respectively, the Transcendence of God and his Immanence. There is a profoundly real development in the Bible : two great sweeping events lie in and behind it—namely, the exilic period and the rise of Christianity, a third and earlier one has yet to be noticed (p. 135). Moreover, what we call ' spiritual ' ideas were expressed in concrete and realistic act or word (p. 183). But as religion becomes more spiritual

[1] H. Wheeler Robinson in Manson's *Companion to the Bible* (1939), p. 310 f. Cf. V. M. Scramuzza on the policy of the early Roman emperors towards Judaism, in *The Beginnings of Christianity*, by F. Jackson and Lake (1933), v. 277 ff.

the emphasis lies not so much upon the *body*—ritual, conduct, tradition—as upon the *character* of men and the source of their deeds and words; and the ' spirit ' of the religion takes on a fresh ' form ' or ' body '.   Finally, ideas of ' sin ' which are so prominent in the Bible have their root in feelings or experiences of alienation, frustration and haunting uncertainty; and consequently the ' covenant ' idea, the bond between God, man and the world is of all the biblical ideas the most vital.

In this chapter one extremely important subject has not received the attention that it requires, namely Jerusalem and Mount Zion.   What has now to be said partly supplements the preceding pages and partly opens out new lines of thought.

CHAPTER VII

JERUSALEM AND MOUNT ZION

I. *Early History*

How largely have Jerusalem and its holy Mount Zion entered into the religious idealism of Christian lands, and yet how little we think of the development which has given them the value they have for us! They may be said to give a unity to the whole Bible; and, certainly, an enquiry into them will be found to bring into the foreground some remarkable vicissitudes in their history and, as we shall subsequently see, to force upon our attention some of the fundamental problems that confront biblical students (Chap. VIII. § i).

Jerusalem, the sacred city of the three great monotheisms Judaism, Christianity and Islam, ranks among the most ancient of sites. It was known to Egypt of about 2000 B.C. as an important city, and appears a few centuries later, about 1400 B.C., in the full light of history, when, among the cuneiform tablets discovered at Tell el-Amarna in upper Egypt, were numerous letters from the kings and chiefs of Palestine, Syria and neighbouring lands. It was an influential city, and among those threatened by the widespread revolts and invasions with which these tablets are mostly concerned was Abdi-khiba, the king of Jerusalem.

He recognizes, as do other kings, the suzerainty of the Pharaoh; he is his loyal ' servant ', and wholeheartedly he admits the divine nature of his lord whose ' shepherd ' he is. He addresses the Pharaoh as his ' sun-god '; others call him also their Addu (Hadad). The Pharaoh's breath is life-giving, men cannot live without it (cf. the king in Lam. iv. 20), and they long to see his ' face ' or presence (cf. Ps. xxvii. 8). Abdi-khiba himself declares that the Pharaoh has set his name upon the city for ever, therefore it cannot be neglected (cf. 1 Kings xiv. 21 ; Isa. lxiii. 19). He has set his name ' at the rising of the sun and the setting of the sun '— it is one of many phrases which find a parallel in the O.T.

134

(see Isa. xlv. 6, Mal. i. 11). The king owes his position to the human representative, or incarnation, of the supreme god of Egypt. ' Neither my father nor my mother set me in this place,' he says, ' the mighty arm of the king has caused me to enter into the house of my father '. Another king writes: ' Tunip thy city weeps and its tears run down (cf. Lam. i. 2), and there is no one taking hold of our hand ' (cf. Isa. xlii. 6). A third asserts that his eyes are upon him, ' if we go up into heaven (or the sky) or if we descend into the earth, yet is our head in thy hands ' (cf. Ps. cxxxix. 7 f.). Between Ps. civ and the hymns of the famous reforming and monotheïzing Pharaoh Ikhnaton (Amenhotep IV) there is a resemblance which cannot be accidental; and in general there are many striking points of contact between the ideas and phraseology of Egypt, Palestine and Syria of this age and even the later parts of the O.T.

In this 'Amarna Age ', as we may call it, we have a very definite starting-point for tracing and understanding the growth of biblical religion. From the way in which the petty kings of Palestine address the divine Pharaoh we can see how they could address their own native gods; indeed, among the Psalms are passages which could well have been used in the worship of Palestinian deities other than Israel's Yahweh. There is also the same lyricism, the same unrestrained if not extravagant language in the Amarna tablets that we meet with in the O.T.

Of the many deities recognized in Palestine and Syria in and about the Amarna Age, the most prominent were Shamash, the Sun-god, Hadad (also called Baal), the Storm and War-god, and a goddess like the later Ashtoreth or Astarte (the Accadian Ishtar) and the Queen of Heaven.[1] But there were tendencies to recognize a supreme god or king of gods, even as a great monarch would be supreme over lesser rulers; and Ikhnaton's famous though unsuccessful effort to make his god Aton supreme, when viewed along with other evidence,[2] points to impressive political and

---

[1] The name Hadoram in 1 Chron. xviii. 10 is probably a compound of Addu (= Hadad), for which 2 Sam. viii. 10 (see mg.) has Joram. The names mean ' Hadad or Yo (*i.e.*, Yahweh) is high '.

[2] See ' *Truth* ' *of the Bible*, Index, under 'Amarna Age '.

religious activity roughly contemporary with the age of Moses, the Mosaic age, and before Israel's national history opens. The Amarna Age was an international one, Palestine was practically an Egyptian protectorate; and since Jerusalem was always in close contact with Egypt, we may safely say that archaeology and the monuments allow us to assume that the religious history of Jerusalem began before 1400 B.C.

Jerusalem lay off the main trade-routes. The scene from the Mount of Olives (on its east) ranged over the sacred city and Judah, the desolate region running down to the Dead Sea, and the rich growth of the Jordan Valley.[1] The area was one of striking contrasts, and the dependence of the people of Palestine upon the gifts of nature made their religion and their Messianic hopes realistic and practical. Nature-cults prevailed, and nature-gods—sun and rain—were both indispensable for their beneficence, and terrible for their destructive powers. They were more universal in their sway than local clan or tribal gods, and were both propitiated and feared. Such deities were no mere nature-powers—e.g., Ikhnaton's god Aton, the visible sun-disc, was creator and sustainer of all life, the god ' satisfied with truth whose abomination is lying ', and the Pharaoh was the ' beloved son ' of his god: ' there is none other that knoweth thee save thy son Ikhnaton'. Israel's Yahweh, too, has many nature-attributes (p. 93); but the history of the steps from the Amarna Age to the establishment of Yahweh is a fundamental problem of the O.T.

Ancient thought could speak of the invisible deities in highly anthropic terms, and this anthropism is sometimes extremely crude. But the deities could also be deemed accessible and near at hand; and ideas swung between placing them in the sky or close at hand on earth. They could be approached at their temples or shrines—the ' high places ' which the prophets condemned (p. 95 f.); or they were embodied in or represented by specific individuals

---

[1] From the Mount of Olives ' the scene is an appalling picture of the terrible forces which wrought it ', enough to breed ' an austere and fanatic temper '. See respectively Breasted, *The Dawn of Conscience* (1934), p. 416 f., and Sir George Adam Smith, *The Historical Geography of the Holy Land*, pp. 314 ff.

(like Ikhnaton), by idols or images, or by other sacred objects. Religion was realistic, concrete, and often seemingly materialistic. The deities were distant, but under proper conditions approachable. If the latter, they were ' natural ' beings, here and now, though none the less ' sacred '; if the former, men sought for them or for others more in touch with their needs. Hence (1) early thought could conceive of a heaven or sky abode for the supernatural beings; and upon them mythology ran riot (cf. p. 93). But (2) earthly things corresponded to those above, and there could be, as it were, a heaven upon earth in so far as these beings had their abode on earth among men. Such cosmic myths and ideas, as in Egypt and Accad, have left their traces in the Bible, where they are focussed upon Yahweh; and all the evidence goes to indicate that the Temple at Jerusalem, like some others, was itself of cosmic significance. It was built after a divinely-given pattern;[a] and Yahweh was there.[b] What was once realistically conceived survived in more symbolical form even in the time of Josephus (*War*, V. v. 4 f., §§ 214 ff.); and rather earlier it could be said that the High-Priest wore a cosmic robe symbolizing the world.[c]

II. *The O.T. Period*

Josephus admits that the original founder of the temple was a Canaanite (*War*, VI. x. 1, § 438); and long before him Ezekiel had spoken of the tainted origin of Jerusalem—half Amorite (or Canaanite), half Hittite (Ezek. xvi. 3): we recall the Hittite Uriah, the husband of Bathsheba (2 Sam. xi. 3). . Tradition identified Jerusalem with the Salem where Melchizedek was king and priest of God Most High, and the founder of a priestly order.[d] With it was also identified Mount Moriah (? Amorite), the scene of Abraham's sacrifice of Isaac.[1] But the more ' canonical ' tradition ran that Jerusalem, once in non-Israelite hands, had been seized by David; and from his time onward ' the stronghold of

[a] Exod. xxv. 9, 40, xxvi. 30.   [b] Ezek. xxxv. 10, xlviii. 35.
[c] Wisdom xviii. 24.
[d] Gen. xiv. 18, Ps. cx. 4, lxxvi. 2, Heb. vii. 1–3.
[1] 2 Chr. iii. 1, Gen. xxii. 2.   Among other sacred mountains were Horeb (' the mount of God ', Exod. iii. 1), Sinai, Carmel, Tabor and Hermon.

Zion ' (on the southern part of the Eastern Hill), or ' the city of David ', stands at the head of the history of Jerusalem.[a] 2 Sam. xxiv. is ' the charter for the sacrificial service'; David, visited at the threshing-floor of Araunah by an angel of Yahweh about to destroy Jerusalem, buys the site and sets up an altar; and the Temple is erected there by his son Solomon after a divine pattern.[b] The original bare rock still survives in the *sakhra* in the Dome of the Rock (the Haram esh-Sherif): whether it was actually the Holy of Holies, the ' hinder part ' of the Temple,[c] is disputed. David and the preparations and Solomon and the actual building of the Temple thus inaugurate Israelite worship.[1]

The whole region had sacred associations. Hard by was the village of Anathoth, named after Anath, a famous goddess associated with Yahu (Yahweh) even in the fifth century B.C. by a Jewish colony at Elephantine in Upper Egypt, and related to the inveterate Queen of Heaven of Jeremiah's day.[d] Beth-Shemesh and the more distant Timnath-Heres testify to the sun-cult, which was also associated with the Temple. With its ' horses of the sun ' (2 Kings xxiii. 11; cf. xi. 16) compare Yahweh's chariots (Hab. iii. 8, Ps. lxviii. 17). At Jerusalem the valley of Rephaim (the ' shades ' of the dead?), the valley of Hinnom (= ' sleeping ' [?], the later Ge-henna), and the infamous Topheth[e] speak for themselves. Carite and other foreign guards served in the Temple till the time of Ezekiel,[f] who also was the first to sever the Temple from the Palace and the burial-place of the kings (p. 101). Deities of other peoples had an honourable place from the time of Solomon,[g] and Ahaz did not hesitate to erect an altar after a Syrian pattern.[h] Even the decoration and furniture of the Temple point to ideas which we do not naturally associate with Israelite

[a] 2 Sam. v. 7.
[b] 1 Chron. xxviii. 11 f., 19, Wisdom ix. 8.
[c] 1 Kings vi. 16, Ps. xxviii. 2 mg.
[d] vii. 18, xliv. 17 ff.
[e] 2 Kings xxiii. 10, Jer. vii. 31.
[f] xliv. 6 ff.
[g] 2 Kings xxiii. 13.
[h] 2 Kings xvi. 10 f.; cf. 2 Chron. xxviii. 23.
[1] See 2 Sam. vii (1 Chron. xvii), 1 Kings v, 1 Chron. xxii and xxiii ff.

religion.[1]   The account of Josiah's reforms [2] throws a most vivid light upon what had hitherto prevailed; but that they had little or no lasting effect appears from the repeated condemnation by Jeremiah (*e.g.*, xxxii. 28 ff.) and Ezekiel (*e.g.*, ch. xxiii); cf. also Lam. iv. 6, 13.   The history of the Monarchies in 1 and 2 *Kings* vehemently condemns the calf-cult and other idolatrous practices of the northern kingdom (2 Kings xvii), and upholds the single and central sanctuary of Jerusalem; but the centralizing of religion and the character of that religion are two very different matters. See pp. 95, 98, 162.

Jerusalem, with its magnificent and wealthy Temple, acquired a reputation for rebellion and sedition.[a]   The small kingdoms of Palestine and Syria were hot-beds of intrigue, and we hear of one occasion when the Temple treasures were sent to Damascus to bribe its king to break his treaty with Israel.[b]   An outstanding event was the deliverance of the city from the Assyrian Sennacherib in the reign of Hezekiah;[c] it encouraged the belief in its inviolability by reason of Yahweh's presence.[d]   But a century later Jeremiah condemns blind confidence in the Temple, as though it were a fetish; and calls for decent humanity and a purer religion (vii. 4 ff.).   Yet Jerusalem was the City of the Great King;[e] in Zion he dwelt,[f] from Zion he roars,[g] and upon his holy hill sat the Davidic king.[h] Yahweh was *there*, and more spiritual minds taught that he who ' filled earth and heaven ' had placed his Name there, and men could effectively resort to his altar.[i]   The conviction persisted that all that Yahweh could do and all that he could be for his people depended upon the existence of his Temple.

The fall of Jerusalem, the destruction of the Temple (in 586 B.C.) and the Exile did not destroy Israel's faith in

---

[a] Ezra iv. 15, 19.   [b] 1 Kings xv. 18 f.   [c] 2 Kings xviii f.
[d] Isa. xiv. 32, xxviii. 16, xxxvii. 22 ff; cf. Lam. iv. 12.
[e] Ps. xlviii. 21, Matt. v. 35.   [f] Ps. ix. 11, lxxiv. 2.
[g] Amos i. 2.   [h] Ps. ii. 6.   [i] 1 Kings viii. 27 ff., Ps. xliii. 4.
[1] *E.g.*, the ' brazen sea ', the pillars Jachin and Boaz, the cherubim, the brazen serpent (2 Kings xviii. 4).
[2] But Jeremiah (xxii. 15 f.) only praises the king's just and righteous rule.

Yahweh, even as the catastrophic end of the Jewish state several centuries later (in A.D. 70) failed to quench the spirit of Judaism (see p. 150). Men found within themselves the source of religion, even though, as is the wont of men, visible, external and institutional media are needed to give an embodiment to their faith. Although Yahweh had left his Temple at the fall of Jerusalem, he returned again,[a] and in the reorganization of life and religion in the post-exilic age the Temple-service was more elaborate, though, to be sure, Yahwism had evidently been purged of its worst features. Jerusalem was again, what it had once been, ' the city of righteousness ',[b] and the habitation of Wisdom or the Law.[c]

This conception of righteousness, or right-ness, is an old one; it is not confined to Israel, though it is especially connected with Jerusalem. It recurs in the names of the priest-king Melchizedek[d] and of the king Adoni-zedek,[e] both non-Israelites, in Zadok, who represents Jerusalem rather than does Abiathar (1 Kings ii. 35), the head of the later Zadokite priests, and in Jehozadak the high-priest (Hag. i. 1). The general meaning of the word is that of the harmony or conformity of a thing to its nature: it is ' what is right ' and as it should be (p. 84). Its ethical or other value depended upon current standards or ideals. Yahweh would be what he would be (p. 87 n. 1); but he was ' right-(eous) ' in all his deeds, and he expected ' rightness ' from his people. The prophets elevated the ideals of social, national and religious rightness, and Jesus demanded a higher standard than that of his day,[f] when it had been narrowed down more specifically to almsgiving. ' Right-ness ' was the ideal, and it had its corresponding ' right ' effects. But earlier, with the greater emphasis upon all that was for the material welfare of land and people, the ethical and spiritual aspects were less prominent. Ancient myth and ritual were more particularly concerned with the func-tions of authoritative individual priests, chiefs or kings, who, through their intimate relations with supernatural powers,

---

[a] Ezek. xi. 23, xliii. 2, Zech. i. 16, viii. 3.
[b] Isa. i. 26; cf. Isa. xxxiii. 5, Jer. xxxi. 23, Ps. cxviii. 19.
[c] BS xxiv. 8.   [d] Ps. cx. 1, 4.   [e] Josh. x. 1.   [f] Matt. v. 20.

were responsible for land and people in a way and to an extent that our modern thought can with difficulty understand.

The prophets insist that it is Yahweh and not the *baals* who supply Israel's needs,[a] that it is he and not the soothsayers or objects of cult who sends rain.[b] Rainfall depends even upon keeping the Feast of Tabernacles.[c] Impure ritual and an illegitimate priesthood were fatal,[d] inferior sacrifices were condemned,[e] and the failure to rebuild the Temple had disastrous practical effects.[1] Beliefs in the efficacy of sacrificial rites are familiar in other ancient religions (*e.g.*, Brahmanism, p. 16), and were evidently once prominent in the old religion of Israel. The daily offerings on behalf of the people and the extravagance of the sacrificial system as a whole indicate that what Jerusalem, the ' city of righteousness ', once meant was more in harmony with early types of belief. Yahweh was god of nature as well as of Israel (p. 95), and Israel was to be a blessing to the world. The more spiritually minded of the prophets, indeed, held that Jerusalem and Mount Zion would be the source and centre of true religion, the just arbiter in international disputes;[f] but we should not forget how Jerusalem and its wonderful Temple must have stood for all that satisfies men's deepest and most urgent practical needs.[g]

Jerusalem, with its Temple, the centre of Judaism, aroused the enthusiasm of Israel and sustained her hopes. It was the joy of the whole earth,[h] elevated above all else,[i] the centre of the universe[j]—it is an idea found elsewhere— and the mother of nations.[k] Such a holy city was one never

---

[a] Hos. ii; cf. 1 Kings xvii. 1, xviii.
[b] Jer. v. 24, xiv. 22, Zech. x. 1.
[c] Zech. xiv. 17–19; contrast Matt. v. 45, Acts xiv. 17.
[d] Ezek. xliii. 27, xliv. 12; cf. Lev. x. 1 ff., 1 Kings xiii. 33 f.
[e] Mal. i. 7 f., iii. 7–11; see also Judith xi. 12 f.
[f] Isa. ii. 2 ff., Mic. iv. 1 ff.; cf. Ps. xlvi. 9.
[g] Cf. Luke xii. 30 f.   [h] Ps. xlviii. 2, Lam. ii. 15.
[i] Isa. ii. 2, Ps. lxxviii. 69.
[j] Ezek. xxxviii. 12, Jubilees viii. 19.   [k] Ps. lxxxvii. 5.
[1] Hag. i. 9–11. Human sacrifice is condemned (Hos. vi. 9, Jer. vii. 31, xix. 5, Ezek. xvi. 20 f., xxii. 3 f.); and although in Deut. xxiii. 18 the harlot's hire might not be brought into Yahweh's house, Isa. xxiii. 17 f., does not hesitate to use the practice figuratively of the profit that Tyre would bring to Jerusalem (cf. the figure in Rev. xviii. 3).

to be forgotten.[a] But Israel knew of the ruin of her city, the desecration of the Temple, and the Exile in 586 B.C. In fact the historical disaster, calling forth the lyrical *Lamentations* (p. 64), became the type for subsequent occasions, notably in the two apocryphal and apocalyptical writings ascribed to Jeremiah's secretary Baruch and in 2 *Esdras*, all three being just before or after the final catastrophe of A.D. 70.

The passages now to be referred to are of different dates and represent diverse historical situations or eschatological anticipations. One day the disunited people would be united and the scattered tribes would reassemble.[b] No more would strangers and traders enter the city;[c] least of all would they desecrate the Holy of Holies, as did Pompey the Great in 63 B.C. (referred to in *Psalms of Solomon*, ii. 26 ff.). But nations would serve Israel,[d] and bring their gifts and tribute.[e] Yahweh is the mighty king, reigning in Mount Zion;[f] the nations would be converted[g] and one day he would be acknowledged as God. He is one and his Name one.[h] There will be an era of peace, when Yahweh shall be supreme judge.[i] Above all, the *Second Isaiah* stands out for its flights of impassioned utterance, consolation and rebuke, the glory of Jerusalem, and the final grim description of the loathsome doom of Yahweh's enemies in the valley of Hinnom, the later Gehenna (lxvi. 24).

But Jerusalem will first be attacked and looted,[j] and Gog the prince of Magog with all his host warring against Israel will be overwhelmed.[k] Ezekiel's lurid picture of Yahweh's majesty as he manifests his ' holiness ' (xxxviii. 16, 23) and glory (xxxix. 13) is not inaptly followed by a vision of the new Israel, the Temple, and the resettlement of the tribes. Yahweh takes up his stand on the Mount of Olives confronting the nations fighting against and occupying Jeru-

[a] Ps. cxxxvii.
[b] Isa. xi. 12, xxvii. 13, Jer. iii. 17 f., xxxi. 6, Ezek. xxxvii. 21 f.
[c] Ezek. xliv. 9, Isa. lii. 1, Joel iii. 17, Zech. xiv. 21; cf. Acts xxi. 28, Rev. xxi. 27.
[d] Isa. xiv. 2.
[e] Isa. lx. 5–7, lxi. 6, Ps. lxxii. 10, Zeph. iii. 10.
[f] Mic. iv. 7, Ps. xlviii. 2. [g] Jer. xvi. 19.
[h] Isa. xi. 10, xlv. 6, 14, Zeph. iii. 9, Zech. viii. 20 ff., xiv. 9, Ps. xxii. 27.
[i] Isa. ii. 2–4. [j] Zech. xii. ff. [k] Ezek. xxxviii; cf. Rev. xx. 8.

salem,[a] or he contends against the nations, the Phoenicians and Philistines are especially mentioned (Joel iii). There are wild pictures of Yahweh's terrible sword.[b] On Mount Zion there is a coronation feast by Yahweh of Hosts, now universal sovereign.[c] He prepares the sacrifice for Israel's enemies;[d] at his table there is a sacrificial feast of the slain.[e] The wine cup of his fury is to be drunk by all the nations.[f] In a variety of forms in the O.T. and apocalyptical writings what is said of Jerusalem, the coming Messiah and Yahweh's manifestation of his plans and actions indicate the range of ideas that were familiar to the Jews at the rise of Christianity.

III. *The N.T. Period*

Christianity arose in an age of Roman overrule, profound unrest, divided parties and the keenest anticipations. It was natural, therefore, that the writings to which reference has been made should play a conspicuous part in the rise of the new religion. The Temple, Jerusalem, and Judah are prominent in the accounts of the births of both John the Baptist and Jesus.[g] When only twelve years old, Jesus is found discussing with the Rabbis in the Temple.[1] Jerusalem was ' the City of the Great King ',[h] and Jesus was hailed as the King.[i] The visit of Jesus at Passover time— often one of excitement and disturbance—which the Synoptists place at the close of his career—marks in the Fourth Gospel its opening (Mark xi. 15 ff., John ii. 13 ff.). The cleansing of the Temple on that occasion links up with the protest of Jeremiah (vii. 11) and the prophets' detestation of the presence of strangers or traders (p. 142 ; cf.

---

[a] Zech. xiv. 4.
[b] Deut. xxxii. 41 f., Isa. xxxiv. 5 f., Jer. xii. 12, xliv. 6.
[c] Isa. xxiv. 23, xxv. 6 ff.; cf. 1 Chron. xxix. 21 f.
[d] Zeph. i. 7 f.   [e] Ezek. xxxix. 17–20; cf. Jer. xlvi. 10.
[f] Jer. xxv. 15 ff.   [g] Luke i. 9 ff., ii. 22, 27 ff., 37 f.
[h] Matt. v. 34 f.   [i] Luke xix. 38; cf. Mark xi. 10.
[1] Luke ii. 41 ff. To this precocity two parallels can be cited. Josephus relates that at the age of fourteen he was consulted by priests and leading men (*Life*, § 9), and in our own day the Indian philosopher, S. Dasgupta, avers that at the age of five to eight years he was consulted on matters of Indian religion and philosophy. See Radhakrishnan and Muirhead, *Contemporary Indian Philosophy* (1936), pp. 175 ff.

Zech. xiv. 21 mg.). His deep grief at the refusal of his
people to recognise him,^a again associates him with Jeremiah, and his warning of coming doom and of the fate of
city and Temple ^b would inflame popular and religious
sentiment, even as the fear that he would lead a revolt
against the Romans would alienate the Jewish authorities
who were for mediation and compromise. ' Jerusalem,
which killeth the prophets ' ^c—how inevitable it was that
the Prophet who came from Galilee of all places (Matt. xxi.
11) should meet his end in that proud and ancient city, so
rich in tradition and prophecy! His final visit to Jerusalem
was made with deliberation and with fore-knowledge of his
sufferings.^d The request of the two sons of Zebedee that
they might sit on his right hand and left hand in his Kingdom and his reply are highly significant in this context
(Mark x. 35–45; Matt. xx. 20–28); and with it should be
noticed the dispute among the disciples (Luke xxii. 24–30)
where, however, their destiny, to be judges of the tribes of
Israel, has a markedly Jewish tone,¹ like the reference to
eating in the Kingdom (Luke xiv. 15; cf. xiii. 29).

The Jews were the natural ' sons of the Kingdom '; they
had the prior claim.^e But those who were ' bidden ' to the
marriage-festival of the king's son and held back should not
partake in it; even those guests who were not rightly attired
should be cast out.² The Jews had not made use of their
gifts: note the Parable of the Pounds (Luke xix. 11 ff., Matt.
xxv. 14 ff.). They were the ' vineyard ' (cf. Isa. v. 1–7); but
they slew even the master's heir, and it was given to others

---

^a Luke xiii. 34 f., xix. 41 ff.   ^b Luke xxi. 20 ff.
^c Cf. Luke xi. 49–51, xiii. 34, Acts vii. 52.
^d Luke ix. 51, xiii. 22, xvii. 11, xviii. 31 ff.
^e Matt. viii. 11 f.; cf. Rom. i. 16, ii. 9 f., iii. 1 ff., ix. 5.
¹ Luke xxii. 30; cf. Matt. xix. 28. But see 1 Cor. vi. 2, ' the saints
shall judge the world ' (cf. Dan. vii. 22, 27, Wisdom iii. 8, 2 Tim. ii. 12,
Rev. ii. 26).
² Luke xiv. 15–24, Matt. xxii. 1–14; cf. the ritual preparation in
Exod. xix. 10, 1 Sam. xvi. 5 and Zeph. i. 7 (the guests are ' sanctified ').
For the marriage-festival, cf. the marriage of the Lamb in Rev. xix. 7,
and the ' foolish virgins ' who were not ready for the bridegroom's
feast (Matt. xxv. 1–13; cf. Luke xii. 36). The disciples of John fast,
but not those of Jesus, for the Bridegroom is with them; the old order
has passed away and, as the parable continues, new garments and new
wine-skins are needed (Luke v. 33 ff.).

(Mark xii. 1 ff.).   They were the barren fig tree, which is cursed, or—strikingly enough—given another chance.[1] They were men who could not read the signs of the times.[a] The seed is sown, but not everyone receives it or can make it fruitful;[b] their house is not built upon a rock.[c]   The good and the bad fish drawn up by the net are at once separated;[d] or the goats are to be separated from the sheep at the final judgment.[e]   Similarly the tares will be separated from the good wheat:[f] we may compare Gamaliel's advice to those who sought to kill the apostles: time would show whether their work was of men or of God.[2]   Jesus had come to help the sick and needy and, by consorting with the detested tax-collectors and outcasts, was offering them a share in his Kingdom.[g]   But he condemns those who trusted in their own righteousness.[h]   Jealous of their own ancestral privileges, the Jews are told that men shall flock from all quarters and sit with Abraham, Isaac and Jacob in the Kingdom of Heaven and they themselves shall be cast out.[i]

One may fittingly close this cento of passages with a reference to two Parables.   The Jews had toiled diligently in the vineyard and had borne the heat of the day, but were to receive the same privileges as the most recent labourers; was that fair (Matt. xx. 1–16)?   The extravagant younger son had left his father's house, but returns a repentant prodigal; and, to the disgust of the elder son, who had served his father faithfully, is received with open arms; was that fair (Luke xv. 11–32)?   But God was not unjust; He has complete freedom of action with those who are his own (cf. Rom. ix. 14 ff.).   Jesus came to call sinners to repent-

---

[a] Matt. xvi. 3.   [b] Matt. xiii. 19 ff.
[c] Matt. vii. 24 ff.   [d] Matt. xiii. 47 ff.
[e] Matt. xxv. 31 ff.   [f] Matt. xiii. 24–30, 36–43.
[g] Mark ii. 15 ff., Matt. ix. 11 f., xxi. 31 f.
[h] Luke xvi. 14 f., xviii. 9–14.
[i] Matt. viii. 11 f.; cf. Luke xiii. 28 ff.

[1] Luke xiii. 6–9.   In Matt. xxi. 18 ff., Mark xi. 12–14, 20 ff., it is cursed and dies, a case of disappointed expectation (cf. Isa. v. 2, 4); on the other hand, it was not the season of figs (Mark xi. 13).   The incident is a difficult one to interpret.   Cf. the comparison of Israel with figs in Jer. xxiv.

[2] Acts v. 38 f.: the Western text has a fuller rendering.   Even men who cast out devils in the name of Jesus would not necessarily be received by him (Mark ix. 38–40, Matt. vii. 22 f.).

ance (Mark ii. 17), and God could say to the Jew, ' Son, thou art ever with me, and all that is mine is thine ' (Luke xv. 31).[1] The Jew might ask, What advantage had Israel, the first-born of Yahweh, over the Gentiles? ' Much in every way ', Paul replied (Rom. iii. 1 ff.); and with Paul's treatment in Rom. ix–xi of the question that tormented many a Jew we can read a Jewish point of view in 2 *Esdras*.

The passages referred to in the preceding paragraph and earlier do not strike the same note; and for the question whether they are all from the mouth of Jesus, or whether they also reflect diverse standpoints in the troublous events in Palestine and Jerusalem at the rise of Christianity, the Commentaries must be consulted. Anti-Jewish feeling cannot be ignored, least of all in Matt. xxvii. 24 f., which whitewashes the Roman Procurator Pilate and harshly intensifies the guilt of the Jews. Matt. xxvii. 25 has been truly said, by a well-known Liberal Jew, to be ' a terrible verse; a horrible invention '.[2]

This condemnation of the Jews is carried on in *Acts*, which culminates in Paul's speech at Rome: the Jews had rejected Jesus, God's salvation is now sent unto the Gentiles, it is they who will hear.[a] This is the motive of the book. The ministry of Jesus had been ' beginning from Galilee ';[b] his gospel was now to be preached ' beginning from Jerusalem '.[3] The book tells of the forty days after his Resurrection when Jesus was ' speaking of the things concerning the Kingdom of God ' (i. 3 ff.), the inaugural outpouring of the Spirit at Pentecost a few days after his Ascension (ch. ii), and the increasing importance of Jerusalem as the cradle of Christianity under James the brother of Jesus (xii. 17, xv. 4, 13, xxi. 18). The conversion of Saul (Paul) introduces a new stage. His subsequent visits to Jerusalem to ' get to know ' (or ' enquire of ') Peter, and fourteen years later to discuss doctrinal questions (Gal. i. 17–19, ii. 1–10), his trial at Jerusalem amid scenes of uproar (Acts xxi. 17 ff.), and

[a] Acts ii. 23, iii. 14 f., v. 28, vii. 52 f., xiii. 46, xxviii. 23 f.
[b] Acts x. 37.
[1] Jesus came to save Israel: salvation was from the Jews (Matt. xv. 24, John iv. 22; cf. Acts xiii. 23).
[2] C. G. Montefiore, *The Synoptic Gospels* (1927), ii. 346.
[3] Luke xxiv. 47; cf. Matt. x. 5 f., xv. 24, Acts iii. 26 ' unto you first '.

finally his removal to Rome to appeal to Caesar, gradually take us away from the centre of Judaism to the Christian mission among the Gentiles.

The Gospel had been spreading beyond Jerusalem (Samaria, Acts viii), Peter had taken the step of converting and receiving Gentiles (ch. xi), and the question of determining the conditions of membership became acute. The Council of Jerusalem (ch. xv), in spite of the difficulty of interpreting the details in the light of Paul's own words (Gal. ii), is the official recognition that Jewish and Gentile Christianity could not be identical. Jews were hopelessly divided among themselves; there were Jewish Christians, Gentile Christians and hostile Gentiles—amid these conflicting factors the Christian Church gradually established itself as an independent entity distinct from Judaism and other religions, though the steps in this growth cannot be at all clearly traced. Even as regards its Founder, one cannot but echo the words of a well-known authority: ' It is idle to attempt to write anything like a biography of Jesus from our Gospel sources; the materials for it do not exist.' [1]

IV. *The End of the Temple*

Jesus came at an age of political, social and religious crises, and through him there was the greatest change the world has ever seen. He came ' to cast fire upon the earth ', and the domestic divisions which he envisaged (Matt. x. 34 ff.) separated, as with a winnowing fan (cf. Matt. iii. 11 f.), those who were for from those who were against Him— there was no other alternative (Matt. xii. 30; cf. Mark. ix. 40). Jerusalem was doomed; and Josephus gives a horrible picture of the last scenes.[2] She had hoped to produce a world-ruler; false prophets had said God would help, but the Jews did not deserve it; they had inflicted too many wrongs on their own countrymen. God had blinded their eyes because of their transgressions, and had gone over to their enemies. Jerusalem had given birth to a generation which caused her overthrow; and in a silent prayer to God

[1] C. H. Dodd in Manson's *Companion to the Bible*, p. 369.
[2] *War*, III. viii. 3, § 354, V. viii. 2, § 343, ix. 4, § 412, VI. v. 4, § 312, VII. v. 5, §§ 148 ff., 7, §§ 161 f., viii. 7, § 376.

he begins with the words, ' Since it pleases Thee who didst create the Jewish nation to break Thy work '. For three years Jerusalem held out; but she was no longer inviolable. The city that was believed to have God for her Founder perished. Vespasian was proclaimed emperor on Jewish soil, and the Romans set up their standards in the court of the ruined Temple. In Rome there was a great triumphal procession in honour of Vespasian and Titus, parading some of the spoils of the Temple, its golden vessels being ultimately laid up in the Temple of Peace which Vespasian founded (75 A.D.).

The Temple was burnt by the Romans, and there were terrible massacres. But revolts continued. Finally, in A.D. 132, Hadrian, aiming at divinity at Rome and Athens, founded the new city of Aelia Capitolina on the ancient site, and set up a temple on the ruins of the sanctuary to Juppiter Capitolinus. It was the last blasphemy. With the short-lived and luckless Messianic revolt of Bar Kochba (A.D. 135), which led to more widespread destruction, our story of the sacred and mysterious city comes to an end.

The God of the Jews was a ' jealous ' God (p. 87), and aught that threatened his supremacy would move them to fury. At an age when Jerusalem was being dangerously influenced by the widespread Hellenism, or Greek culture, Antiochus Epiphanes, the ' god manifest ', who was devoted to the cult of Zeus (Juppiter), killed the high-priest, the ' anointed one ', and ravaged the city. In 169 B.C. this blasphemer of the ' God of gods ' set up in the Temple an image of Zeus which, as on his coins, may have portrayed his own features. This is the ' abomination that causes appal-ment ',[1] which is mentioned in the so-called ' Little Apoca-lypse ' as the height of sacrilege (Mark xiii. 14, Matt. xxiv. 15). Here the reference is presumably to the insistent attempt of Caius Caligula, about 40 A.D., to erect in the Temple a colossal statue of himself as Zeus. The Jews, who were willing to sacrifice daily to the Roman Emperor, were prepared to die rather than tolerate this; but fortunately

---

[1] Dan. xi. 31, 36; cf. 1 Macc. i. 54, 59, 2 Macc. vi. 2. The term a derisive alteration of the ' Baal of Heaven '. The cult of the youthful Dionysus (Bacchus) was also enforced.

Caligula opportunely died. More obscure is the ' man of lawlessness ' who will sit in God's sanctuary, setting himself up as God, though now held in check; his fate is to be slain by the Lord Jesus (2 Thess. ii. 1–12). Next Nero, a fierce persecutor of Christians—he numbered some among his household (Phil. iv. 22)—claimed to be the world's saviour and was regarded as a veritable Antichrist; he is referred to in Rev. xiii. 3, xvii. 11, and is the beast whose number is 666 (Rev. xiii. 18). Domitian in turn claimed deification; but his death put a stop to what his persecution of the Christians might have led to. Finally, Hadrian is represented on the coins of Aelia Capitolina, where what is presumably his bust is held in the hand of the city-goddess, the Tyche or Fortune of Jerusalem. Such city-goddesses were familiar,[1] and coins of Vespasian and Titus had already depicted Judaea captured or conquered as a mourning woman—a last illustration of the Virgin Daughter of Zion of long-past days.[a]

In these conflicts the ancient myths of cosmic struggles between good and evil take their latest and most vivid form.[b] The ideal of the universal reign of Yahweh involved his identification with other great deities; in the Greek age it was Zeus, earlier it could be gods of Accad or Egypt. Similarly with Christ. It would not have been difficult, as comparative religion and archaeological material have shown, to identify Him with, or at least to find parallels with Him in, Marduk, or Osiris, or Apollo. But this would have meant to obscure, indeed to destroy, the most characteristic features of Yahweh and of Christ; and while Israel and the Jews fought to preserve the uniqueness of their Yahweh, it was the aim of the Christians, as their Church grew up, to secure the uniqueness of Christ.

We have only to look outside the confines of Judaism and Christianity to perceive the impressive difference between the development of religion in the Bible and the persistence, outside, of inveterate forms and types of cult. Here, round about the first century A.D., we should find Hadad and Baal, and Astarte, or the Queen of Heaven, in new shapes.

[a] Isa. xxxvii. 12, xlvii. 1.   [b] John xii. 31, Eph. vi. 12, Rev. xii.
[1] Cf. the Queen of Heaven in Jer. xliv. 15 ff.

Mithras, known already in the Amarna Age, is soon to be the great rival of Christ. Human sacrifice long persisted in Carthage; and in Baalbek religious prostitution was put down by Constantine the Great (A.D. 306–337)—to the furious indignation of the populace. Portable shrines or arks were drawn by oxen;[a] and other archaic usages persisted. Old myths of Phoenicia survived, though in Greek form (p. 46); the combination of a senior and of a junior god recurs,[1] and a solar monotheism aimed at unifying religion.[2]

Jerusalem had suffered two terrible catastrophes, in A.D. 70 and A.D. 135. But they did not destroy the faith of the Jews. After the former, Johanan ben Zacchai established a new centre at Jamnia, and a new era in Judaism was inaugurated. The citadel of sacrificial religion had been destroyed, but in a famous utterance he cried: ' We have still an atonement which is worth that of the sacrifices: the practice of charity, for it is written " I desire mercy and not sacrifice " ' (Hos. vi. 6; cf. Matt. ix. 13). And in the Apocalypse of Baruch (lxxxv. 3) a contemporary writer can say, ' Zion has been taken from us and we have nothing now save the Mighty One and his Law '. For the Christians the Kingdom of God remained the ideal and the hope. Already Paul had spoken, not of the Jerusalem on earth, but of the symbolical one in heaven, as ' our mother ' (Gal. iv. 26). In *Hebrews,* too, there is the belief in a symbolical Mount Zion (xii. 22); and Christ is the High-priest of a greater and more perfect tabernacle, the Mediator of a New Covenant, one whose single sacrifice cleanses men and makes at-one-ment between them and God (ix. 11 ff.). In this epistle the earthly sanctuary is but the shadow of the true heavenly reality.

Three noteworthy lines of thought may be mentioned: (1) Instead of a complete renovation of the earthly city and temple, there is a temple in heaven, or rather, heaven is a

[a] Cf. 1 Sam. vi. 7 ff.

[1] Even Hadrian, besides his self-deification, deified his dead youthful favourite Antinous as the giver of fertility, the symbol of youth, and the mediator between heaven and earth (*Camb. Anc. Hist.,* xi. 321).

[2] See the writer's *Religion of Ancient Palestine in the Light of Archaeology* (1930), ch. iii, esp. pp. 216 ff.

temple, with ark, altar, etc.   So in *Revelation* (*e.g.*, i. 12, iv. 6, viii. 3, xi. 19), where the earthly city is a veritable Sodom and Egypt.[1]   (2) There is a new heaven and earth; and the new Jerusalem descends as a bride from heaven (Rev. iii. 12, xxi. 9 f.); but there is no temple, for God and the Lamb are the temple (xxi. 22–xxii. 5).   And (3) God fills the whole Universe (Isa. lxvi. 1), the world and man are the temple, God's house is without bounds (Bar. iii. 24f.); neither in Jerusalem nor at the sacred-mountain of the Samaritans shall men worship God, but in spirit and truth, for God is Spirit.[2]   So, men, united in Christ, informed by the spirit of God, are to grow into a spiritual house (1 Pet. ii. 5, Heb. iii. 6; cf. Num. xii. 7), a holy temple (Eph. ii. 21 f.); not God's temple among men, but men as his temple.[3]   We have travelled away from the old notion that the temple and other earthly things are the counterpart of the heavenly— that the earth is a symbol of heaven (p. 137); and instead of the transference of the earthly temple to heaven, we have the hope of a Kingdom of God on earth.[4]

Here we leave our account of some of the contents of the Bible.   We have been dealing with the literature of an oriental people which has made our western world.   If we have not refrained from referring to the less pleasing sides of that people, let it be said (with a renowned scholar of a past generation) that the very tone of mind which makes the heathenism of the old Oriental world the most hideous of worships enabled Israel to grasp with unparalleled tenacity and force the spiritual idea of Yahweh.   And another more recently has observed that the Arab feels no incongruity in bringing God into his weaknesses and appetites.   Allah rules his eating, his fighting and his lusting, and is his commonest thought and companion.[5]   The very intensity of Israel's *psyche* is seen in her fanaticism and in her faith,

[1] xi. 8; cf. Isa. i. 10, Ezek. xxiii. 8, Wisdom xix. 14 f., also Rev. iii. 9, John viii. 44.
[2] John iv. 21–24.   Shortly before the destruction of the Temple some Jews had said that the world was a better temple for God than that one (Josephus, *War*, V. xi. 2, § 458).
[3] Cf. 1 Cor. iii. 16 f., vi. 19, 2 Cor. vi. 16.
[4] See further G. B. Gray, *Sacrifice in the O.T.* (1925), ch. 10 f., and the commentaries on *Revelation*.
[5] W. Robertson Smith and T. E. Lawrence respectively.

reminding us that the distinction between an unethical and an ethical spirituality, mysticism or religion is more important than that between religion and all that lies outside it.   See p. 198.

Moreover, in the O.T. we are moving at a relatively early stage of thought; and it is the spiritualizing and ethicizing of mythological and crude anthropic types of belief that are particularly impressive.   The Bible reflects its age and its environment: the desert and relatively advanced forms of civilization, the simple tribal life and the stress and strain of the city, the family, clan or tribal organization and the monarchy.   The kingship of Yahweh and the more closely knit structure and organic body as seen in the conviction of the real solidarity of Israel and Yahweh are two conceptions which, if pressed, are irreconcilable: but the ideal was to combine them, to preserve at once Yahweh's supremacy or transcendence and his immediacy and directness or immanence.   These two leading ideas appear to be those which most closely unite the two Testaments, and illustrate both the true continuity between them and the development. That these raise many problems of greater or lesser complexity will have been noticed, and to some of them the next chapter will be devoted.

CHAPTER VIII

SOME FUNDAMENTAL PROBLEMS OF THE BIBLE

I. *Introductory*

THE preceding chapters have brought us to some fundamental problems of the Bible upon which a few words are
necessary. We have found varieties of belief and of development, and evidence that books have been compiled and
revised. The more deeply we study the Bible in the light of
modern knowledge, and in particular of our knowledge of
the lands of the Bible, the more unavoidable are the questions of criticism, most of which scarcely occur to the
ordinary reader. While the so-called ' lower criticism ' is
concerned with the preliminary task of getting back to the
writings as composed by the original authors, the ' higher '
criticism deals with questions arising out of their contents:
their trustworthiness, the relation between them and other
similar but conflicting material, and so forth.

Today it is generally agreed among scholars that there are
four main sources in the Pentateuch—viz., J and E, the
Yahwist and Elohist, named after their respective preference
for the divine names Yahweh (Jehovah) and Elohim (God,
lit. ' gods '), D (Deuteronomy, and ' Deuteronomic '
passages, p. 48 f.) and P, the post-exilic priestly narratives
and laws. The ' Deuteronomic ' hand can be readily traced
throughout *Joshua–Kings*; but P has given the whole
(*Genesis–Kings*) its present form, so that it is now a post-
exilic series, though of course much of the contents is
earlier. Also the dates of the rest of the O.T. have been
broadly fixed, though throughout opinions differ, often
widely, when it comes to more precise questions of authorship, compilation and exact date.

As regards the N.T., it is generally agreed that Mark's
Gospel is the earliest of the Synoptic Gospels, and that the
Pauline Epistles are of the first importance for understanding

primitive Christianity. There is no doubt that the rise and earliest stages of the Christian Church, so far as they can be ascertained, have influenced the actual form in which all the four Gospels, with their record of the Founder, now survive.

Modern knowledge has altered our perspective of the Bible. It is not easy, at first, to realize that the great prophets in their earliest form precede and illuminate the historical or narrative books as they lie before us; or that of the two accounts of Creation in Gen. i. 1–ii. 4 a and ii. 4 b–25, the latter is the earlier. Moreover, in spite of the importance of the endeavour to trace the rise and growth of Israel from the Exodus out of Egypt to the Invasion and Settlement in Palestine, and thence to the monarchy (and divided monarchies), it is precisely archaeology and the monuments, as well as the thread of history, starting with the pre-Mosaic Abraham, which allow, or rather force, the student to concentrate upon Palestine, its pre-Israelite culture, its place in the history and civilization of the Middle East, and, ultimately, to consider the actual political and cultural conditions amid which the Jewish sect that became Christianity sprang up.

It must be emphasised that it is not so much questions of historical fact—the credibility of statements—as the character of the broad religious development that is of prime value. Indeed, it is the essential difference between the spirit of the great prophets and that of the priestly writings that lies at the basis of the convenient formula 'the Prophets precede the Law'. It is the difference between the general spirit of the religion of Israel and that of neighbouring lands, and again between Christianity and the trend of later Israelite and Jewish thought, that proves to be the chief outstanding fact in biblical study. It is the nature of the underlying continuity that now runs through the Bible, and our conception—or theory, if you like—of the nature of the development or evolution and the profound questions that are thereby raised that make the Bible, not only a Book of unique religious value, but a unique source for our knowledge of the growth of ideas on the relations between God, man and the universe. To this we shall turn later. Meanwhile, we may state that the fundamental problems turn on

(a) Israel and the land of Palestine, or Canaan; (b) the rivalries between the two kingdoms of Judah and Israel, and also between the Jews and the Samaritans; (c) the exilic period; (d) the popular narratives (J and E), and—in the N.T.—(e) the rival claims of Jerusalem and Galilee. The problem of the development of the priesthood is too intricate to be handled in our space.

II. *Israel and Canaan*

The keynote of the O.T. is the distinctiveness of Israel, and her superiority over other peoples, of Judah over her (North) Israelite or Samaritan kinsfolk, of the Aaronite priests over the rest, and, when we come to the N.T., the superiority of the New Israel over the Old. Now, Israel traced her national history back to the Exodus from Egypt. On her settlement among the Canaanites in Palestine there was much intermarriage, which even later writers vehemently condemn.[a] Palestine was a land of ancient culture, and obviously had its own traditions, customs and beliefs. It is commonly agreed that not all the tribes of Israel had been in Egypt; and there are conflicting traditions of the length of Israel's sojourn there.[1] Moreover, not only was it the natural result of the intermarriages that Israelites learnt much of native Palestinian or Canaanite lore and custom, but there are traditions of the patriarchs which imply an actual settlement once and for all in pre-Mosaic times and have no place for an Exodus.[2] Hence there are two quite independent views of the ancestry of Israel.

From what is known of the 'Amarna Age' (p. 135), and from inspection of the O.T. itself, it is clear that much that we call ' Israelite ' was of native origin and not due to the invading tribes from Egypt or the desert. The old cults of the Sun-god (Shamash) and the Storm- and War-god (Hadad) did not disappear at a stroke. Very late forms

---

[a] Judges iii. 6, Ps. cvi. 35 ff., Ezra ix. 12 f.

[1] The chronological scheme allows 400 or 430 years (Gen. xv. 13, Exod. xii. 41), or half that period (LXX in Exod.); but Joseph actually lives to see the children of his grandson Machir who subsequently entered Palestine (Gen. l. 23, Num. xxxii. 40).

[2] For this very important fact see Skinner's commentary on *Genesis*, pp. xxiii n., 418, 422, 450, 507, 512.

survive into the Christian era of myths, of which the O.T. preserves only the merest echoes, *e.g.*, the ' fallen angels ' (Gen. vi. 1–4), the Mount of Assembly (Isa. xiv. 13), a myth of Paradise other than that in Gen. ii. ff. (Ezek. xxviii. 1–19), and various creation and dragon myths.[1] They are associated with the worship of Yahweh, and it is possible in some cases to see how cruder or polytheistic elements have been omitted or re-shaped. In fact, a careful comparison of the O.T. with the life and thought of the surrounding lands, and in particular with the myths and poems discovered at Ras Shamra, relates the religion of Yahweh to the surrounding religions as closely as Christianity is related to the Judaism of its day. There are essential points of contact in spite of essential differences, but opinions differ as to the precise extent of each.

In the O.T. narrative the story of Joseph (originally of independent origin) links together the patriarchal narratives and an early settlement once and for all with the descent of the ' sons ' of Israel into Egypt and the subsequent exodus of the Israelite ' tribes '. According to the present thread of the narrative, the name Yahweh is now revealed (Exod. iii, vi. 3). It supersedes the earlier El-Shaddai (a name probably meaning ' God-mountain ' or ' mountain-God '), which is associated with Edom, the mountain region from which Yahweh was believed to come.[a] But according to quite another view, the worship of Yahweh dated back to Enosh, the grandson of Adam (Gen. iv. 26): both names mean ' man '. Thus, behind the ' canonical ' tradition are other traditions, and one can scarcely conjecture how they ran.[2]

III. *Judah versus Israel and the Samaritans*

The blessings of Jacob (or Israel) and of Moses (Gen. xlix, Deut. xxxiii) indicate the fortunes of the twelve sons or tribes of Israel.[3] During the time of the divided mon-

---

[a] Deut. xxxiii. 2, Hab. iii. 3.

[1] Ps. lxxiv. 12 ff., lxxxix. 10, Isa. li. 9 f., Job xxvi. 12.

[2] Note also Joshua's farewell speech (Josh. xxiv, especially ver. 14 f.), which refers back to the days of Terah the father of Abraham.

[3] There are two accounts of the origin of the name Israel (Gen. xxxii. 28, xxxv. 10).

archies, however, Judah and Israel are rivals,[1] whereas prior to them and after this period the term Israel includes Judah and the other tribes. There is some ambiguity in the use of the term, especially after the downfall of (North) Israel, which, however, is sometimes called Ephraim or Joseph (*e.g.*, Ps. lxxviii. 67, lxxx. 1). This rivalry becomes fiercer when Judah, claiming to be the true Israel, confronts the mixed Samaritans who are named after the important city of Samaria.[a] The narratives as a whole betray a bias against Judah's northern neighbours; and its first king, Saul of Benjamin, is rejected by Yahweh almost as soon as he has been anointed.[b] Indeed, although he was chosen by Yahweh to deliver Israel from the Philistines (1 Sam. ix. f.), according to another and later account the institution of the monarchy was an affront to Yahweh, who himself was their king (cf. viii. 7, x. 19, xii. 12). We hear little of the Israelite point of view; yet Saul was a great king, devoted to Yahweh (1 Sam. xiv. 35, his first altar), opposed to witchcraft (xxviii. 39), holding sway even over Judah (xv, xxvii. 10–12), and famous for his victories (1 Sam. xiv. 47 ff., 2 Sam. i. 17–27). But the ' canonical ' history concentrates upon David; it is he who finally defeats the Philistines and captures Jerusalem (2 Sam. v. 6–9), although, according to another tradition, it had been seized by the Ephraimite (or North Israelite) Joshua (Josh. x). Again, one cannot conjecture how the latter and now suppressed tradition would have run.

Similarly, the history in *Kings* has little to say in favour of Israel; though here and there are exceptions, *e.g.*, the Elijah and Elisha stories, the rise of Jehu (2 Kings x), and Yahweh's compassion (2 Kings xiii. 4, xiv. 25–27). But the northern kingdom was at times very powerful, even more so than Judah; the writings of Amos and Hosea testify to the worship of Yahweh, however imperfect it might have been; Hosea (himself of the North) is proof of a lofty spirit, and the E portions of the Pentateuch (which probably are northern), also are in several respects less primitive than J

---

[a] 1 Kings xvi. 24.   [b] 1 Sam. xiii. 13 f.; cf. xv. 11.
[1] According to 2 Sam. xix. 43 (when corrected by the LXX) Israel claims to be firstborn rather than Judah.

(which is probably Judaean). Some of the Psalms, too, appear to have the same home. The cities of Abel and Dan in the North were renowned for their good old Israelite character (2 Sam. xx. 18, LXX), and, of the northern sanctuaries, Shiloh and Shechem were especially famous. Indeed, it has been conjectured that the central sanctuary which *Deuteronony* demands was a northern one (Shechem itself), and that the insistence upon Jerusalem as the one supreme sanctuary represents a later stage in the growth of the biblical tradition.[1] At all events, in due course the Samaritans accepted the Pentateuch, and were virtually a sect of the Jews.

With the collapse of the northern kingdom the Judaean history of Israel comes to an end; Judah is the heir of the true Israel, and renounces her northern neighbour. Compare the treatment in *Chronicles* (p. 49 f.). The predominant tradition is that the Ten Tribes were carried off into exile [a] and their place taken by foreign colonists settled there by Assyria.[b] This fateful event and the future assembling of the twelve tribes have become one of the major curiosities of speculation. But when we consider the boundaries of the northern tribes [c] no land is absolutely denuded. Ezekiel regards the north (Samaria) with more sympathy than he has for Judah; Anna was of the northern tribe of Asher;[d] the woman of Samaria [e] can speak of ' our father Jacob '; and Josephus tells us that the relation between Judaeans and the Samaritans was sometimes admitted, sometimes repudiated.[f] There is no reason to suppose that the worship of Yahweh had come to an end in the north;[2] rather do the political and religious differences and the proud position of Jerusalem and Zion account for the age-long rivalry. So also the rivalry between the ' brothers '

[a] 2 Kings xvii. 6, 23; cf. Tob. i. 2.   [b] 2 Kings xvii. 24 ff., Ezra iv. 9 f.
[c] Josh. xvi. ff.   [d] Luke ii. 36.
[e] John iv. 12.   [f] *Ant.* IX. xiv. 3, § 290 f.
[1] There is also reason to believe that Joshua's covenant-ceremony at Shechem in ch: xxiv, which has been supplemented by his final oration in ch. xxiii, represents a tradition older than the now ' canonical ' account of the Law-giving at Sinai-Horeb.
[2] Jer. xli. 5, Zech. vii. 2, 2 Chron. xv. 9, xxx. 11, 18. See Gaster, *The Samaritans* (1925), p. 11 f., and Adam Welch, *Post-exilic Judaism* (1935), ch. ii.

Esau or Edom and Jacob or Israel becomes ' canonical ' in spite of their close intimacy and periodical occasions of friendship; and Edom in post-biblical times was a symbolical name for Rome. Moreover, the despised ' uncircumcised ' Philistines are ' canonically ' repudiated; although there could be alliance or close contact [1]; and in the days of Sennacherib's attack upon Jerusalem (701 B.C.) the boundaries shifted and the relations between Judaeans and Philistines tended to vary.

IV. *The Exilic Period*

At the fall of Jerusalem and the destruction of the Temple in 586 B.C., Judah suffered some devastation; the leading classes were carried off into exile, and northern Israel after the fall of Samaria, now nearly 140 years previously, had had time to establish settled conditions. We read of the return of exiles in the first year of Cyrus; [a] but the rebuilding of the temple was not successfully undertaken until the second year of the reign of Darius and was finished in his sixth year, *i.e.*, 516 B.C.[b] The contemporary prophets Haggai and Zechariah do not presuppose any earlier important return of exiles, but proclaim that Yahweh has now taken pity upon his people; he has returned to Jerusalem, and his ' house ' shall now be built.[c] But Zerubbabel, the Messianic figure whom they proclaim, was not destined for success; there is a gap in the history, and not until the return and activity of Ezra and Nehemiah was there any real reorganization. The work of the layman Nehemiah should, for a variety of reasons, be placed before that of Ezra: the visits of the former to Jerusalem to which he refers [d] must apparently be dated at 444 and 432 B.C., and that of Ezra (as scholars now tend to urge) as late as 398-7. Accordingly we have very little history of Jerusalem between 586 and 444 and later—an immense gap!—and it is only then that successful efforts seem to have been made to

---

[a] Ezra i. 1.   [b] vi. 15.
[c] Hag. i. 2–4, Zech. i. 12–17, ii. 4, 7 ff.
[d] Neh. xiii. 6.
[1] See Gen. xxvi, Zeph. i. 9 (cf. 1 Sam. v. 5), 2 Kings i. 2, Isa. ii. 6, Neh. xiii. 23 f.

draw a rigid line between the Judaeans and the Samaritans who had hitherto continued to take a real interest in Jerusalem and its temple.[a]

Contemporary papyri from a colony in Elephantine in Upper Egypt testify to a temple of Yahweh (under the name Yahu); the Jews, persecuted by Egyptians, appealed to Jerusalem (but received no answer) and to Samaria. It had a strange syncretistic cult. It evidently did not recognize Jerusalem as the sole and central sanctuary of Yahweh, and Yahu is associated with two consorts.[1] Yet many of the names borne by these Jews have a familiar stamp, *e.g.*, Azariah, Isaiah, Micah, Nathan and Zephaniah.

Accordingly, the ' Chronicler's ' history (*Chronicles–Ezra–Nehemiah*), when it tells of the fall of Jerusalem, the Exile, and the return ' everyone unto his own city ' (Ezra ii. 1), aims at establishing a perfect continuity between the pre-exilic and post-exilic Jerusalem. It ignores the native population even as, in the account of the earlier history, the sons of Jacob–Israel go down into Egypt and return as tribes,[b] and a prior settlement is ignored. On the events that lay behind the *Second Isaiah* and the ' Servant of Yahweh ' the history is silent. See pp. 118 f., 163.

The exilic period, now under consideration, was one of sweeping changes in and outside Palestine, and it is not so much in the biblical narratives as in the prophets that we find an interest in a wider world. The wars of Medes and Persians in the far north, Scythians pouring south towards Egypt, the decline and fall of Egypt, Assyria and Babylonia— these combine to make the rise of the Persian empire under Cyrus a decisive break in the long record of these lands. Nearer home, among the tribes to the east and south of Palestine, were considerable movements which affected Palestine itself.[2] Desert influences, never wholly lacking in Judah and Israel, were now stronger; their effect upon the thought and phraseology of the people, never extinguished,

---

[a] Ezra iv. 2 f., Neh. ii. 20.
[b] Gen. xlvi, Exod. vi.
[1] Both Abraham and Jacob had two wives; cf. also Ezek. xxiii (*e.g.*, ver. 4 f.).
[2] See Jer. xlix. 1, Ezek. xxxv, xxxvi. 2, 5.

was now more weighty.[1] As is only to be expected, social and political conditions were more unsettled and primitive; and while there had been changes in Samaria after 720 B.C., the population in Judah itself contained more ' desert ' elements than before, and the tribe was largely of semi-Edomite blood (1 Chron. ii, iv). The Samaritans might be regarded as foreigners by the Judaeans; but the latter were not the same ' Israelites ' as previously.

There were impressive reforms in Jerusalem, the ' high-places ' had been cleansed of their worst features; and if in the north men once had to learn how to worship Yahweh (2 Kings xvii. 26, 28), in the south the new social and religious changes must have made it necessary to give the people guidance and instruction; compare the account of the measures ascribed to Jehoshaphat by the late writer in 2 Chron. xix. 4–11.[2] If so, a later parallel can be found in the *Testaments of the Twelve Patriarchs*, which contains much ethical teaching, apparently for the Jewish converts of the new ' Israelite ' kingdom (towards 100 B.C.); the book may be said to be one of ' instruction in Jewish morality as well as in Jewish patriotism and the Jewish law '.[3]

V. *The Popular Narratives*

The O.T. narratives are didactic. *Deuteronomy* essentially appeals to the people and their responsibility (p. 48); but in its present form and in writings of its spirit it is Jerusalem that is of central importance (p. 95). The O.T. narratives as a whole explain the supremacy of Jerusalem, the presence of the ark, the superiority of the Zadokite priests of Jerusalem over other priests, and of the Aaronites over all. They represent an Israel which fell apart after the reigns of David and Solomon once and for all, though there were times of the closest interrelations when Judah was even subordinate to (North) Israel (cf. 1 Kings xxii. 4, 2 Kings

---

[1] Cf. the tent-living ascetic Rechabites and their part in the rise of Jehu (Jer. xxxv, 2 Kings x. 15–23), and the Kenites (Judges i. 16, 1 Sam. xv. 6) who, with the families of ' scribes ' (1 Chron. ii. 55), may be suspected of having had a hand in the prominence given to South Palestinian tradition in our narratives.

[2] The lofty and impassioned chapters of the Second Isaiah (xl–lv) also read like the inauguration of a new religious impulse.

[3] F. C. Burkitt, *Jewish and Christian Apocalypses* (1914), p. 36.

iii. 7). In the exilic period the north probably had the upper hand and might have planned a new All-Israel; and in the time of Zerubbabel there were probably hopes of restoring the Davidic dynasty along with the new or Second Temple. But the priesthood gains the upper hand, and some centuries later there is even a priestly kingship (p. 118).

The narratives tell how Yahweh had chosen, guided and protected Israel; but we really do not know how the religion of Yahweh supplanted the conditions in the Amarna Age (p. 134 ff.). The popular narratives treat the local sanctuaries favourably in contrast to the prophets who denounce them and their cults (p. 95 f.). It is therefore possible, not that the prophets grossly exaggerated the conditions, but that these narratives arose after they had been purged. Certainly Jerusalem comes in for the most severe condemnation by the prophets; and while this ancient city is scarcely mentioned in these narratives, the story in Judges xix (ver. 12) regards it as non-Israelite—though it had been captured by Joshua!—and the patriarchs Abraham and Jacob pass by it without mention.[1] The seat of the dynasty and Yahweh's great Temple are not of surpassing interest for the simple culture of the people; it was enough to explain how both were inaugurated. Like other great cities (*e.g.*, Damascus, Tyre and Sidon), its general culture severed it from the masses; and it was the latter, who ' dwelt among their own people ' (2 Kings iv. 13), that the didactic history and the popular narratives have in view.

In fact, in the light of archaeology and criticism we have to conclude that the picture given in the O.T. as it stands affords a very inadequate account of the actual development. The Amarna and Ras Shamra tablets, the allusions in the prophetical writings, and those, much later, in the apocalyptical books, represent types of thought other than the popular narratives which instruct and discipline their readers, and by their simple charm have always been a delight to the western world.[2]

[1] Note Gen. xii. 6–9, xxxv. 6, 19, 21. The only references are to Mount Moriah and Salem (p. 137).

[2] Among the Jews, too, such stories as those of Cain and Abel, Isaac, Joseph and Phinehas were at an early date related to children; so 4 Macc. xviii (about 50 B.C.–A.D. 50).

Accordingly, just as when we go behind the Hebrew *text* of the O.T.—the Massoretic Text—we find evidence for considerable variation (p. 42), so, when we examine the ' canonical ' *history* there are many signs that we now have only the last stages in a complex growth. It is as difficult to recover the earlier stages as it is to determine when the consciousness of national unity and destiny became firm enough to give rise to the ' canonical ' thread of history and influence subsequent writers. The ' prophetic ' spirit now pervades it. The far-reaching vision of the prophets made Israel conscious of her place in God's world, and the people read their history through the glasses which her seers made for them. Scholars differ seriously in their treatment of the fundamental problems of the O.T.; and whereas there is a natural desire to substantiate the traditional view of it as far as possible, there are not wanting those—of whom the present writer is one—who find themselves forced by archaeology and/or criticism to bring down even the earlier writings to a lower date than is the view of ' orthodox ' criticism. For any return to pre-critical, compromising, conservative, or traditional positions there is no justification.[1]

The exilic period with its drastic internal and external vicissitudes forms a clear landmark; and in the *Second Isaiah* there is a remarkable spiritual freshness and force, notably in the Suffering Servant. There is the feeling that a corner has been turned, and that Israel is entering upon a new stage in her career. But as time passed, Israel was no longer aware of her indebtedness to the great reforming prophets; the history that must lie behind the *Second Isaiah* was entirely unknown. Centuries passed, and Jesus of Nazareth, the prophet, appeared; there was a new prophetic impulse. It aroused, as usual, bitter opposition among the custodians of the old tradition. Jesus was crucified, but he was not dead; he had given birth to a new

---

[1] Do the intermarriages with the natives as denounced by Ezra (ch. ix) date from the invasion and settlement? Was the destruction of Shiloh, named by Jeremiah as a warning to Jerusalem (vii. 12–15, xxvi. 6), that of about the time of Samuel, when it disappears from the story? Judges xviii. 30 f. implies that it was contemporary with the captivity of the land (cf. Ps. lxxviii. 60 ff.).

Israel animated by his spirit, and what might have been yet another stage in Jewish religion became the foundation of Christianity.

VI. *Jerusalem and Galilee*

The scope of this book does not permit us to discuss the many problems which the N.T. raises. Like the O.T., it has changing social and political backgrounds. It represents the rise and first steps in the growth of a new religion out of its parent, a transition recalling in many respects that of Israel in the age of the *Second Isaiah*. More than Judaism it reflects the influence of Hellenism, of Greek thought and the LXX (p. 38); but throughout there is the undercurrent of the O.T. and of Jewish experience and tradition. Besides the Jews, who were hotly divided among themselves, there were Jewish Christians, Gentile Christians and Gentiles; and these four main groups and their controversies have left their mark on the growth of the N.T., and notably on the treatment of the work and teaching of Jesus. That there was an actual historical figure, the Founder of Christianity, no intelligent individual can doubt; but as regards his life and utterances there is considerable variation of opinion, owing to the variation in the N.T. itself. In our oldest sources Jesus is already divine. We cannot get behind them; and we are left, therefore, with such questions as—to mention only three—his belief in an imminent advent of the kingdom of God or in its actual presence (p. 125), his teaching with regard to signs,[1] and the details of the Last Supper.[2] A fourth question, the early rise of the Church, will be briefly outlined later on.

The evidence from non-biblical sources is extremely slight.[3] Josephus, who wrote his *War of the Jews* about

---

[1] Thus, he warns against signs (Mark xiii. 22; cf. 1 Cor. i. 22, Rev. xiii. 13 f., 2 Thess. ii. 9–11 and, in the O.T., Deut. xiii. 1 ff.). He repudiates cosmic signs in Mark viii. 11, Luke xi. 16; cf. the account of the Temptation in Matt. iv. 1 ff. Men who did not believe in him would not be persuaded even though one rose from the dead (Luke xvi. 31); but he foresaw his own death and resurrection (Matt. xii. 38 ff., Luke xi. 29 ff.).

[2] Mark xiv. 22–25, Matt. xxvi. 26–29, Luke xxii. 16–20, 1 Cor. xi. 23–25; but see also John vi. 41 ff.

[3] See *The Cambridge Ancient History*, vol. xi. 253 ff.

A.D. 75–79 and his *Antiquities* about 93–4, is unfortunately ambiguous and perplexing. He knows of John the Baptist, and something of his teaching, but not as a forerunner of Jesus. He knows that Herod Antipas slew him, but as a possible influential rebel. He knows that Herod divorced the daughter of Aretas and married the ambitious Herodias, thereby arousing ill-feeling. He does not know of John's rebuke, but states that some of the Jews believed that Herod's defeat by the incensed Aretas was a divine punishment for John's death.[1] He reports that ' James, the brother of Jesus, who was called Christ ', was accused before the Sanhedrin by the High-priest of breaking the Law and was stoned to death, to the distress of some of the Jews, even those who were uneasy at the breach of the law.[2] To ' Jesus (the) Christ ' he denotes a brief paragraph which precedes a full account of ' another sad calamity '.[3] He refers to his wonderful works, his conversion of many Jews and Gentiles, his crucifixion and resurrection as foretold by the prophets, and the fact that the Christians are not extinct in his day.[4] Considering the date at which Josephus wrote, one is inclined to suspect that he knew more than he wished to say about the Christians, who had long been ' upsetting the world ' (Acts xvii. 6, cf. xxvi. 26).[5]

Jesus had been rejected and crucified by the Jews and had risen again : this is the keynote of the N.T. But it was the question of the circumcision of converts and of intercourse

---

[1] *Ant.* XVIII. v. 2, §§ 116 ff., Mark vi. 14–29.

[2] *Ant.* XX. ix. 1, § 200. He does not mention the earlier death of James, the brother of John, at the hands of Herod Agrippa I (Acts xii. 1 f.); and his account of the king's politics and end and that in Acts xii. 20 ff., are independent of each other.

[3] The authenticity of the paragraph has been questioned, and the one that precedes may be referred to in the other ' calamity '.

[4] *Ant.* XVIII. iii. 3. The additions to Josephus in the Slavonic version are of mixed value. See Creed, *Harvard Theological Review*, XXV (1932), pp. 277 ff.; J. W. Jack, *The Historic Christ* (1933). Josephus does not mention Christians among the sects described in *War* II, viii, *Ant.* xviii. 1. It may be added that, like Paul, he was shipwrecked on his way to Puteoli (*Life*, iv, § 16), and that at the fall of Jerusalem he succeeded in liberating three of his friends who had been crucified—two died in spite of medical attention, the third survived (*Life*, lxxv, § 421).

[5] Josephus lived at Rome for some twenty or more years after the Fall of Jerusalem in A.D. 70.

with them that soon sharpened the difference between Judaism and Christianity. Not only did Jews demand the circumcision of their converts, they would even require that aliens settled among them should submit to it. Josephus asserts, however, that to this latter requirement he was averse.[1] During the disastrous famine in the time of the Roman Emperor Claudius, to which there are several references in the N.T.,[2] an interesting incident occurred at the conversion to Judaism of Helena, a generous benefactress, and her son Izates. The circumcision of the latter was demanded; but one Jew held that Izates could worship God though uncircumcised, such worship being superior to circumcision. The incident, which Josephus narrates at length (*Ant.* XX. ii), appears to be contemporary both with Acts xi. f. (that is, with Paul's visit to Jerusalem) and—so it can be argued—with the important Council at which the circumcision of Gentile Christians was the issue (ch. xv). The coincidence would be noteworthy, though it must be admitted that the chronology of Paul and his epistles, especially Gal. ii (with its important allusions), is full of difficulties.

The foregoing has led us to the question of the prominent part taken by Jerusalem in the rise of the Church. Jesus had travelled round, healing, and teaching the Kingdom of God. Moreover He had sent out his disciples on their mission: the Twelve (Mark vi. 6–13, Matt. ix. 35–xi. 1, Luke ix. 1–6) and the Seventy (Luke x. 1–12, 17–20), and these, too, preached and healed the sick. According to *Matthew*, after his Resurrection he appeared to them in Galilee, giving them authority to baptize, teach and make disciples of all nations; and the Gospel closes with the impressive words, ' Lo, I am with you alway, even unto the end of the world.' [a] But in Acts Jerusalem is the radiating centre,[b] after the day of Pentecost at which many nations were represented,[c] and after the martydom of Stephen.[3]

[a] Matt. xxviii. 16–20.   [b] i. 8; cf. Luke xxiv. 49.   [c] Acts ii. 5 ff.
[1] *Life*, xxiii, § 113, xxxi, § 149.
[2] Acts xxiv. 17, Gal. ii. 10, Rom. xv. 26, 1 Cor. xvi. 1–3, 2 Cor. viii. 1–3.
[3] Acts viii. 1.   Note the healing and deeds of wonder by the apostles (ii. 43, iii. 6, 16, viii. 7, etc.).

Philip goes to Samaria,[a] whither Peter and John come from Jerusalem; Peter visits Caesarea,[b] and Barnabas is sent to Antioch.[c] But at Damascus, where there were many converts to Judaism (as Josephus relates), and also some Christians, the hitherto unknown Ananias can baptize Paul and impart the Holy Spirit.[d] At Puteoli (the modern Pozzuoli), the port for Rome, there was a Jewish colony (Josephus), and Paul was cordially received by ' brethren ' of both towns.[e] A few years earlier (A.D. 49–50), Claudius had expelled Jews from Rome, because ' Chrestus ' had instigated disorders, but whether this not uncommon name refers to a ' Christian ' movement is uncertain. At all events, Aquila and his wife Priscilla, whom Paul met at Corinth, were from Rome, and either already were, or became, trustworthy Christians.[f] But at Ephesus the Christian converts were immature; they had not received the Holy Spirit, but represented the teaching of John the Baptist.[g] There, also, Apollos of Alexandria, though eloquent and fervent in his teaching, knew only the baptism of John, until taken in hand by Aquila and his wife.[h] Now, Alexandria was the port for traffic to the west, to Puteoli and Rome, and it would seem, therefore, that there was a stage in or even before the growth of the Christian Church when John the Baptist, and not Jesus, was notably prominent. The Gospels—and especially *Luke*—testify to John's singular importance, while insisting upon his subordinate position to Jesus (especially the Fourth Gospel); but beyond this we can scarcely go. We know only that Paul refers to different parties among the Corinthians, and regards Apollos of Alexandria as his predecessor in teaching Christianity.[i]

There were stages in the rise of Christianity. As in the O.T., we should expect rivalries and jealousies, as regards not only the necessity of circumcision, but also the gift of

[a] viii. 12 f., 16 f. [b] x. 48, xi. 16 ff.
[c] xi. 19 ff., xiii. 2, 4; cf. xv. 22.
[d] ix. 10 ff.; cf. xxii. 16.
[e] xxviii. 13 ff.   xviii. 2, 1 Cor. xvi. 19.
[g] Acts xix. 1 ff.; cf. i. 5, xi. 16.
[h] xviii. 24 ff.
[i] 1 Cor. i. 10–12, iii. 4–9.

the Holy Spirit.[1]   Just as in the O.T. Jerusalem came to be
of central importance, so too in the N.T. it is no less prominent; and in both the O.T. and the N.T. it is clear that its
claims were not undisputed.   This brings us to the title of
this section: Jerusalem and Galilee.   No good could come
out of Nazareth of Galilee, Nazareth had never produced a
prophet;[a] the Messiah was to come from David's city of
Bethlehem.[b]   Nevertheless, Galilee of the Nations,[c] a semi-
Gentile district, had been promised a great light and future
glory.[2]   The Galilean ministry of Jesus is prominent in the
Synoptic Gospels.   On the other hand, *Luke*, which looks
forward to the redemption of Jerusalem,[d] treats the rejection
of Jesus at Nazareth more harshly than the other Synoptists,[3]
and Jesus after his Resurrection appears to his disciples in
Jerusalem, bidding them wait there until they were clothed
with power from on high.   This and his instruction to
them unite *Luke* and *Acts* (Luke xxiv. 45 ff., Acts i. 2 ff., ii).
But in *Matthew* Jesus, as already mentioned, appears to the
disciples in *Galilee*, as he had said, and then sends them on
their mission (Matt. xxviii. 7, 10, 16).   Moreover, his
promise to go before them into Galilee is wholly obscured
by *Luke*.[4]   *Mark* narrates the promise (xiv. 28, xvi. 7); but
this Gospel ends in the middle of a sentence, and the present
conclusion (xvi. 9–20) is not authentic.[5]   If, as is thought,

[a] John i. 45 f., vii. 41, 52.   [b] Matt. ii. 1–6; cf. Mic. v. 2.
[c] Joshua xii. 23, 1 Macc. v. 15.   [d] ii. 38, cf. ver. 25.
[1] Cf. the story of Eldad and Medad who receive the spirit of Yahweh
though they were not elders of the people (Num. xi. 23 ff.); but by
the evident addition of the words that they were 'of them that were
written' (ver. 26) it is suggested that they were, so to speak, 'on the books'.
Also of the rivalries and compromises between the priests of Jerusalem
and other priests there are a good many indications in the O.T., though
it is not easy to disentangle the references and treat them historically.
[2] Matt. iv. 14–16, see Isa. ix. 1–7.   The obscure verse, Isa. ix. 1,
links together ch. viii (with which it is joined in the Hebrew Bible)
and ix. 2–7, with its Messianic promise for the throne of David (*i.e.*,
Jerusalem).
[3] Luke iv. 28–30; cf. Matt. xiii. 53 ff., Mark vi. 1–6.
[4] Matt. xxvi. 32; see Luke xxiv. 6 and note the wording in Acts
xiii. 31.
[5] It refers to the scepticism of the disciples (cf. Matt. xxviii. 17,
Luke xxiv. 25, 41, John xx. 24 ff.), and is clearly associated with Acts
(see verse 17 f.).   John xxi (an Appendix) records an appearance in
Galilee following that in Jerusalem, and the story of Peter is closely
related to the one in Luke v. 1–11 (Galilee).

Mark was written at Rome, as also was *Luke–Acts*, we can understand both its broken conclusion and the fact that it never enjoyed popularity, as did the longer composition which, ' beginning from Jerusalem ', narrates the spread of the Church—omitting Damascus and Alexandria—and ends with Paul at Rome.[a]

There are two divergent streams of tradition: Galilee and Jerusalem, and their relative value is keenly debated. If the Risen Jesus had been seen in Galilee, one would expect that the Church of the New Israel would have had its centre there, and not in Jerusalem. Even in the O.T. the reformed and purer worship of Yahweh certainly appears to have been (North) Israelite in its origin, though Judah and Jerusalem gave it its setting and lasting significance. And here the problem remains. The City of Righteousness (Isa. i. 26), whose name, like that of her great king Solomon, associates her with peace,[1] gained an imperishable place as the holy city of the three great monotheisms which arose in the East, and the story of her fortunes involves that of the history of religion itself.

Chapters VII and VIII deal with certain phases of the thought of the Bible, the beliefs that prevailed, and the continuity between the O.T. and N.T., one which the non-canonical writings enable us to strengthen. We find, indeed, many examples of divergence of practice and belief; but these are not unexpected when we remember that the Bible relates to the history of a religion extending over many centuries, and that this religion underwent some sweeping developments. The religion of Israel was not that of the Amarna Age; and between the pre-exilic and the post-exilic epochs there were great changes. Finally, between the Old Israel and the New there is fundamental difference.

An outline of some of the difficult problems that arise when we more penetratingly examine the Bible has been given in this chapter. They are familiar to scholars, and agreement of opinion has not yet been reached. They are due to the stages through which the religion of Israel passed;

[a] Acts xxviii. 16 ff.
[1] 1 Chron. xxii. 9, cf. Isa. ii. 4 (contrast Joel iii. 10), lx. 17 f.

but just as religious faith and confidence in the past was able to rise above the stresses and shocks of history, and indeed to be enriched by them, so may it always be. The letter of history and the letter of the Bible may seem to be gravely disturbed by harsh events and by the course of modern life and thought, but they are transcended by the Spirit of History and by the Spirit of the Bible, and that these two are one we have next to recognize.

CHAPTER IX

ON UNDERSTANDING AND TEACHING THE BIBLE

I. *The Approach to the Bible*

FROM what has been said in the foregoing pages it will be evident that we approach the Bible in a way other than that which was usual in past generations. Modern thought is building up a new background to it; we cannot say that it is more difficult or more easy to understand it; the fact is simply that we approach the Bible in a new light. The title of this chapter opens up three lines of thought: (*a*) that of teaching the Bible to the young and adolescent; (*b*) that of ensuring that the teachers understand their task; and (*c*) that of realizing what the Bible has to teach us. The more seriously we take ourselves, the more necessary is it to keep before us these three aspects of the subject. There will always be varieties of temperament, experience and competence among both teachers and taught. The world in which the former now live and in which the latter will one day find themselves is one that ranges from *Green Pastures* and popular biblical romances (*e.g.*, of the life of Moses or David) to the advanced works of Samuel Alexander, A. N. Whitehead, and all whose writings bear directly or indirectly upon Christianity and the Bible. And this world ranges from somewhat narrow and intolerant types of religion to a scepticism and a not always veiled hostility which merits the same adjectives.

It is easy for the teacher to start off with a selection of biblical passages upon the moral and spiritual value of which there would surely be universal agreement. There are, in fact, some admirable syllabuses drawn up for the purpose. But as we proceed we encounter unavoidable questions of the trustworthiness of our biblical passages, the disputed value of the Old Testament, and, in particular, the difference between the more ' conservative ' and the

171

more 'radical' students of the Bible. In addition to this, there is the divergence of opinion when we find that the study of the Bible sooner or later involves questions of religion, science and philosophy. That is to say, the Bible cannot ultimately be severed from the *cultural* problems of the day; and just as it has played a unique part in the growth of the general culture of the West, so its place in the future growth of culture—in the Western world, at least—is a question that cannot be answered by mere appeal to prejudice, emotion or passion. The teacher must help those who are to be helped, and also help them to hold their own with specialists and experts in the relevant fields outside biblical study. This means that the Bible must be studied more comprehensively than is usually the case—a task that is not the concern of the Churches alone. The primary question is, How is the Bible to be taught in the best way? And with it is, of course, the question, How is it *not* to be taught?

Old Testament history once seemed to end with the Fall of Jerusalem in 586 B.C. and the Exile: the immense significance of the post-exilic period is the outstanding discovery of modern research, dating from about 1878. But now we carry the history down to the latest books of the Bible (*Daniel* dates about 166 B.C.), and include the apocryphal and apocalyptic writings as late as the first century A.D. A sound view of the history of Palestine and its neighbours forbids us to sever the Old Testament and the New Testament. Similarly, archaeology unites the pre-Israelite, Israelite, Persian, Greek, Roman and Islamic stages in the vicissitudes of Palestinian civilization. As we peruse the writings of the old Jewish historian Josephus we pass almost insensibly from the Old Testament to the New Testament periods; the interconnexion between the periods as regards the religion has been shown in Chapter VI. For purposes of O.T. study and teaching it would be preferable to make the Exile and the *Second Isaiah* both the climax of one period and the inauguration of the next. And the New Testament, in turn, should be treated as the final stage of the Old Israel and the beginning of the New Israel.

In this way the Bible is seen to enshrine the story of the

election and rejection of a Chosen People and the rise and conditional permanence of its successor. It impresses upon us the vital difference between the regeneration or rebirth of the Old Israel at the exilic age, when Israel seemed to be on the point of extinction, and her inability to meet the new situation when an obscure Jewish sect that scarcely made any impression upon the historians of the day gave birth to Christianity. Old Testament study leads inevitably to the New Testament, the rise of Christianity, and its separation from Judaism; and the New Testament in turn cannot be understood apart from the Old Testament, which alone makes it intelligible. The Bible cannot be rightly understood if we sever it from the history of the lands which contributed to its growth; and in this great history-making age of ours we should take a more dynamic view, and realize that there lies before us the possibility, either of the failure of Christianity to respond to the conditions of our day, or of the inauguration of a new era, a restatement or rebirth of Christianity. History does not repeat itself, but there are from time to time typical turning-points not dissimilar to each other: there is in any event no inevitable progress.

The familiar objections to the Old Testament are superficial and can be more readily met to-day than in the past. We have to do with an ancient virile and passionate people, strong in its loves and in its hates. The Old Testament is to be compared and contrasted, not—as is usual, and to its detriment—with the fresh spiritual idealism of the New Testament and its 'programme'; rather should the vicissitudes of the Old Israel be viewed along with those of Christendom. In both we find much that is contrary to the highest ideals. Both Israel and Christendom bear witness to what they conceive God requires, or indeed what He seems to tolerate. Man evidently has freedom to do evil as well as good; and the Bible brings problems of a lower morality, of true and false leaders, prophets or Messiahs, and of unethical spirituality or religiosity. These problems are not dismissed by refusing to recognize as idealism or religion that which we condemn: even our own may be imperfect relatively to our stage of development. Reject the Old Testament and we reject deeper insight into the sort of problem that is always with us, and not in non-Christian lands alone.

When we pass unfavourable judgment upon the Old Testament we implicitly lay down principles. We may be shocked at the Psalms of Vengeance or at the divine command to destroy the Canaanites (p. 93 n.): we imply that there are limits to the hatred of evil and wrong-doing—though sentimentality and toleration can be carried too far! We may call the Psalms of Vengeance un-Christian; but if we find their spirit in Christendom, it is not merely because of the Old Testament—there are many Old Testament passages that breathe another spirit—but because they correspond to one phase of human nature. If the outspokenness of the erotic and sensual elements in the Old Testament is distasteful, we may be forgetting the character of the life and thought of the Ancient—and Modern—East. Moreover, we may be treating literally what was meant symbolically. There is, in truth, a sexual element in religion and mysticism which is symbolical; but we are led on to recognize that symbolism, metaphor and imagery, however inevitable or invaluable, can, unless safeguarded, direct thought or action along spiritual, moral or intellectual lines that are misleading and unwholesome.

Again, we may condemn the particularism and exclusivism of Israel. But there certainly were times when it preserved her genius; it was the shell that guarded the kernel. Moreover, the feeling of 'election', of being divinely chosen, must involve a particularism such as belongs to every high mission.[1] The attractive note of universalism in the Old Testament in no sense meant that all religions were equal: Israel and Jerusalem were to remain supreme, the heart of the organism, the centre of the religion of Yahweh. Israel was conscious that she stood in a unique relationship to her God; but the warning of Amos (iii. 2) that this entailed a greater responsibility, laid down a principle that applies to every religion that claims superiority over others. It was granted to Israel to play a unique part in human history; individuals and nations have each their unique contribution

[1] H. W. Robinson, *Record and Revelation* (1938), p. 327; H. H. Rowley, *Israel's Mission to the World* (1939), pp. 48–50, 57, 71, 129.

to make to the common welfare: to whom much is given, of him much shall be required, whatever be his endowment—as in the Parable of the Pounds (Matt. xxv. 14–30). The sense of worth and selfhood can lead to selfishness and egotism; but the Christian doctrine of the supreme worth—and inescapable responsibility—of every individual does also mean that the highest realization and expression of Self may be self-sacrifice for others, for the whole of which one is a part.

Yahweh's anger, his vengeance even ' to the third and fourth generation', jars upon us. But this is only one side of his character, *i.e.*, it represents, of course, only one side of Israel's character, whereas the persisting conviction of his love for Israel is the most impressive testimony to her undying faith. To say that ' God is love ' is to attribute to Him no sentimentality or amiability, but an ultimate quality that lies behind whatever divine justice and righteousness must entail for men's wrong-doing. And if it is not merely a theological or intellectual statement on our part, but the result of living religious experience, we clearly have to ask how far it has succeeded in motivating our own life and thought. We should take no superficial view of the chain of cause and effect, or of prelude and sequel; Israel's sturdy and uncompromising monotheism traced all good and evil to God. She had a unifying or integrating view of God's universe; and however imperfect we judge this view to be, we ourselves, owing to the collapse of the world-view we have inherited, have as yet nothing to take its place.

Modern criticism has doubted or rejected various long-accepted beliefs and traditions. But this has been inevitable. The earliest ' criticism ' is found in the prophets of the Old Testament; and in the New Testament it is more sweeping. But criticism now as then can be constructive as well as destructive: its aim is to restate and enhance the value of the Bible as a Sacred Book—that is, its sacramental value. If some modern critics seem at times to be too ' radical ', some ' conservative ' writers with the best intentions hold views which, though meant to substantiate the Bible, are as drastic as those of the most radical appear to be. At the rise of Christianity the Jews no longer knew what their own religion owed to their own ' critics ', the prophets. In a sense they were the victims of their perspective of the past.

The aim of biblical study is to reach a sound and reasoned perspective of the past that shall offer the best prospect in facing the future. But when men see in the past the Logic of History, Fate, or the Hand of God we do well to scrutinize their evidence and their methods, for their views may be as imperfect or misleading as the idol or fetish that is believed to embody all that is sacred for its worshippers. In other words, a world-view, a theory, a doctrine or a ' body ' of thought can be as materialistic as any object we call ' matter ': materialism is not to be found only in ideas based upon matter. In emphasizing the embodiment, the form, or the letter we may lose the ' spirit ' they are meant to express. It is the aim of biblical study to recover the Spirit of the Bible, and to re-embody it in a way that shall re-establish harmony between religious and secular knowledge, between the Bible and the best thought of the day. This is the search after Truth.

What do we mean by ' spirit '? At the outset it is the indivisible, intangible and incalculable power or energy, animating and inspiring life and thought, character and action, and giving meaning and intelligibility. Spirit is recognizable only in its effects; and it is separable only by our mind. It is a neutral term, as also is the ' corporate spirit ', or *esprit de corps*, without which no people, society or closely knit group could endure. The most hide-bound materialist, positivist or rationalist manifests ' spirit ' in the way he makes intelligible to himself the evidence before him. Where religion is concerned, the *spiritus sanctus*, or Holy Spirit, is said to ' open ' the mind (cf. Luke xxiv. 32, 45); one sees, then, in Bunyan's words, ' with the eye of the soul '. The unifying or integrating act of the mind makes the Bible more than a miscellany; and through the Holy Spirit one discerns its permanent religious value.

Our experiences normally start from the physical world, nature, and what is accessible to our senses; it is the ' spirit ' of our activities which guides us, even as our invisible and intangible mental processes, with their concepts, categories, and patterns, shape or direct our lives. The ' spirit ' and the way in which it is manifested are correlative; and when we speak of the Spirit of the Bible we have to ensure that letter and spirit answer to one another. Were it not for the possibility of this divergence we should not all differ as we do, and range between the extremes of a crude literalism or rationalism and an extravagant mysticism or symbolism.

When we speak of the Truth of the Bible, we may mean the Truth it can teach us, or the Truth we expect to gain from it. The two are not necessarily the same, else we should all be of the same opinion. In teaching others, the young especially, it is worth while considering what sort of Truth their young minds expect, as well as what we believe they ought to expect. In the Bible are many 'truths'—true principles, lessons and beliefs. Their value can even be independent of the question of the historical trustworthiness of the passages involved. In the faith of Abraham, the courage of Joshua, the penitence of David, or the courage of the Three Youths—here and elsewhere are truths which we can not only appreciate, but can embody afresh in our own lives and thus endorse. Even the most 'unhistorical' of narratives will prove to have some value, apart from its original intention. Much in 1 and 2 *Chronicles* which cannot be used for our knowledge of the two monarchies illuminates the later period when these books were written. Lists of 'unclean' beasts, genealogical tables, the furniture of the Tabernacle and Temple—these and much else are of value for building up our knowledge of the conditions in Israel when the Bible was taking shape.

The 'antediluvian' stories in Gen. i–xi, whatever anyone may think of their 'historical' value, have many interesting and important features. There were variant traditions of Creation and Paradise; one perspective of the past had no place for the Deluge, and another traced the worship of Yahweh back to Adam's grandson. The chapters contain traditions of the origin of civilization; they illustrate the development of ideas and the variety of literary composition. In a word, they bring questions the answers to which involve the Old Testament as a whole. Admittedly the Bible as a source brings many difficult problems; and all our hand-books, in their desire to simplify the study of the Bible, are obliged to leave out points which one scholar or another will consider vital. Serious students should know the Bible better than the handbooks; as it is, when the young are sent out into the world with a knowledge of one or other of the views which simplify the Bible they are too often unable to evaluate their own knowledge and that of their opponents, or to hold their own in argument or controversy. But all should remember that they are dealing with the convictions and beliefs—and also the prejudices—of the biblical writers. These latter had their aims and purposes; they represent the ' history ' and ' science ' of their day. To suppose that they were stating ' facts ' and nothing more is to destroy the spirit of biblical religion. Past generations would trace the story of man and the universe back to the first chapter of *Genesis*; to-day the Bible, viewed in the light of modern knowledge, is being placed in a vaster framework; it is an immensely impressive one, and therefore one with an enhanced meaning for religion. If we have lost the old Bible-view of the universe, it does not follow that, despite appearances to the contrary, a new one cannot be restated.

The chief stages in the religious development in and behind the Old Testament gave new meanings to earlier written or oral traditions of the past; and Christianity, in its turn, found a new value in the Old Testament. In every case the past is being transformed, and is re-interpreted in accordance with the conditions of the age and its outlook. This is a process which has not necessarily come to an end. The Bible tells of some great turning-points: Abraham (Gen. xii. 1 ff.), Israel (Exod. iii. 7 ff.), the injunction ' Ye shall not do after all the things that we do here this day, every man whatsoever is right in his own eyes ' (Deut. xii. 8, cf. Judges xvii. 6, xxi. 25), Joshua's decision (xxiv. 15), the decisive teaching of Jesus (*e.g., but* I say unto you), Paul's spiritual maturity (1 Cor. xiii. 11), the past which God had hitherto tolerated (Acts xvii. 30, Rom. iii. 25). Every great crisis is a test, a judgment and a sifting; and the most supreme turning-points can be recognized in the Exilic Age and at the rise of Christianity and its final severance from Judaism. That the present age is another crisis is freely and widely recognized.

The efforts to find in the Bible the sort of Truth we desire can sometimes be more well-meaning than justifiable. We are prone to ' rationalize ', to find a meaning in our evidence that shall be intelligible for ourselves. In this way we feel we can understand it, or its origin, or its value for ourselves. Thus it has been suggested that Elijah was fed, not by ravens, but by Arabians (1 Kings xvii. 46): the change in pronunciation of the Hebrew is of the slightest. Or the origin of the story of the miraculous Manna in the Wilderness (Exod. xvi. 14 f.) is found in a snowfall, a novelty to the Israelites from Egypt. Volcanic eruption, it has been thought, accounts for sundry details in the narrative of the Law-giving on Sinai or Horeb (Exod. xix. 16, 18), and for the story of the destruction of Sodom and Gomorrah (Gen. xix. f.). One writer has gone further and has traced the Decalogue back to a curiously marked slab of lava which Moses picked up and deciphered on it the name of Yahweh. That the story of the Deluge may go back to an extensive flood, or to more local inundations traces of which have been found at Accad, need not be doubted. But as a general principle, whenever any narrative which is questioned on reasonable grounds is said to be ' substantially or essentially trustworthy ', or the like, one may fairly consider how much of it may be used if one is teaching young children or older students.

Much is still heard of the bearing of archaeology and the monuments upon the Bible, or more particularly upon the Old Testament. Now, these have confirmed what has never been doubted; they have corrected (*e.g.*, the chronology), they have most helpfully supplemented (*e.g.*, the Assyrian wars); and they have brought much new and important information. But trustworthy details in a passage never substantiate the whole; incredible elements surround historical figures, and much is related of imaginary ones that, taken in and by itself, is perfectly rational and credible. Certain details in the patriarchal narratives in *Genesis* are confirmed by monuments of the pre-Mosaic age to which these refer. But they are not necessarily confined to that age, for even in medieval and modern Palestine travellers have found much that illustrated the Bible.

Hence details of custom and law in *Genesis* that also recur in ancient literature of the pre-Mosaic age do not of themselves prove that the narratives in their present form belong to that early date.

Even more or less contemporary sources are sometimes found to be prejudiced or inaccurate. On the other hand, late sources often preserve ancient details; though we are not impressed when the late Babylonian priest Berosus (280–260 B.C.) reports that ten antediluvian kings of Babylonia reigned for not less than 432,000 years and a cuneiform tablet nearly 2,000 years earlier gives the figure as 456,000. Moreover, writers referring to the past will often observe a certain consistency. The very late Apocalypse of Baruch names no one later than the day of the historical Baruch, Jeremiah's secretary; the equally late Assumption of Moses prefigures the post-Mosaic history of Israel, but mentions no names; and although we can identify details in the ' predictions ' in *Daniel* the writer is careful not to betray himself.[1] The popular narratives avoid the term ' Lord of Hosts ' (see p. 93), not because they date before the first mention of it elsewhere, but because they are didactic and have been ' censored '. As already noticed, there is a closer continuity between the early conditions in Palestine and the prophetical books and later writings than between either of these and the popular narratives.[2]

Traces of a flood have indeed been found in Babylonia; but no one has doubted that there might have been what was supposed to be a world-wide deluge, it is the account as related in *Genesis*—a twofold account by the way—that is regarded as untrustworthy. Again, excavation has shown that the walls of Jericho fell, but the indications point to an earthquake and not to the blowing of trumpets (Josh. vi); and while, on archaeological grounds, the event has been dated in the fourteenth century B.C., the narrative presupposes the use of iron and the Iron Age, which is later. Hence in every case we have to start from our evidence in

---

[1] F. C. Burkitt, *Jewish and Christian Apocalypses* (1914), p. 18 f.
[2] See p. 162 n. 2. The assumption that the Israelites enter a land of long-established culture, but come under its influence only many centuries later, is quite untenable.

its present form.   The use of writing in Palestine was known before the time of Moses: it is not denied that Moses *could* write—the question is whether our Pentateuch goes back to his day.[1] As a matter of fact, the numerous Amarna tablets from Palestine show that Egyptian couriers travelled round, and that they and not the royal correspondents were sometimes the scribes.   In general, external evidence (archaeology and the monuments) has illuminated the background of the Old Testament to a remarkable extent, though not in the way that may still be hoped for.   But the anxiety to find external confirmation at all costs unfortunately tends to direct attention away from all that wherein the permanent value of the Bible lies.   Archaeology is often thought to confirm, and comparative religion and psychology to impair or destroy; but whatever in any way enables us to understand the Bible is to be welcomed. ' When I see evidence for facts,' said Principal Robert Rainy on a notable occasion, ' they are God's facts, and they will only be my help in the end if I can duly make use of them.'[2]   In the wise words of Erasmus (d. 1536), ' By identifying the new learning with heresy, you make orthodoxy synonymous with ignorance.'[3]

Now, rationalizing is in itself a legitimate proceeding: it renders things intelligible to our reason.   Miracles of healing can often have a therapeutic explanation, and the Crossing of the Red Sea might be explained by a strong east wind which caused an unusually low tide.[4]   But the procedure lends itself to abuse; and, as when a difficult or dubious reading is emended, critical tact is necessary.   There are some cases where we do not trouble to go behind our records; but there are others (*e.g.*, the Gospels) where we demand a substratum of fact.   Some of the early Church Fathers treated as allegory what some people still wish to regard as authentic, *e.g.*, the Creation of the world in seven

[1] In Judges viii. 14 RV mg. ' wrote down ' is to be preferred to the EV ' described ', which is based on the Latin version, ' descripsit '.
[2] When the late Sir George Adam Smith was charged with heterodoxy; see the *Life of Rainy* by P. Carnegie Simpson, ii. 269 ff.
[3] The motto on the title-page of *The Modern Churchman*.
[4] Exod. xiv. 21; but verse 22, on the other hand, describes a ' miracle '.

days and the Garden of Eden. We may too readily rationalize, or we may treat as symbol or allegory what was once taken literally;[1] for early peoples will see the miraculous or the supernatural where we do not. There was a strange mystical realism which saw in objects the impression they made upon them or the meaning they had for them, *e.g.*, blood *is* life (p. 83), the Sun-disc *is* the Pharaoh's divine father (p. 136).[2] Between such peoples and ourselves there are differences of mentality or of psychical make-up; and it requires insight and sympathy to understand them. This applies to (1) early and primitive peoples, who in many respects represent stages of growth beyond which our civilization has advanced. It applies also to (2) the young who, as they grow up, may have to unlearn much that they were taught. And in general it applies to (3) the great diversity of temperament and mentality among the grown-ups of to-day. An adequate understanding of the development in and behind the Bible would enable us to grasp the continuity between (*a*) the earlier or more primitive types of thought in the Old Testament, which are akin to those among primitive and ancient peoples generally, and (*b*) the more advanced forms in the New Testament, which link up with the cultural history of Christendom and present conditions of thought. The study of the Bible involves our ideas of both mental and spiritual growth, and of the development or evolution within its pages and throughout history; hence it is of really great importance both for any discussion of theories of evolution and for our attitude to the great variations of life and thought to-day all the world over, in so far as these represent different stages and sorts of development.[3]

We cannot expect to understand minds, whether young or old, that are remote from our own. After all, there are

[1] In his commentary on *Hebrews* (p. xxxi) Moffatt observes that while the author ' often turned the literal into the figurative, his theological interpreters have been as often engaged in turning the figurative expressions of the Epistle into what was literal.'

[2] At our higher stage of development it is not so much visible objects as objects of thought that are for us what they *mean* for us and—as for example in the case of the Bible—we often differ among ourselves.

[3] Evolution and Revelation are not to be severed, see p. 207 n.

obvious limits to our ability to see other people's beliefs in the light in which they themselves see them. Where ancient or primitive peoples are concerned we must often ' leave the dead to bury the dead ': it is more important to attend to our own beliefs. But it is necessary so to teach the young that in the course of their mental growth the stages may be as natural as possible. Now, at early stages of thought there is a sort of mystical realism: the Australian native can see the kangaroo as his brother, Ikhnaton could address the sun as his father. But it is often difficult to draw the line between this realism and conscious symbolism. Note, for example, the ' symbolical ' acts of the prophets (p. 84), the mystical interpretation of Canticles (p. 64 f.), and the sexual imagery of *Ezekiel* (Chh. xvi, xxiii). Moreover, we ask ourselves, did men literally expect a catastrophically transformed universe or one, as we should say, 'spiritually' transformed? How far was language which could be understood literally mainly a way of expressing or evoking underlying ideas?

What to us are ' ideas ' were expressed in concrete material form, *e.g.*, the presence of a god, resurrection and life after death, heaven and hell. Rites of rebirth and visible imitations of the toilet or dress of a god were the forerunners of ideas of spiritual rebirth and of striving after holiness. The former *could* become merely external; the latter *can* be merely verbal, lip-worship (Mark vii. 6). Ancient myths and ritual have been the prelude to theology, and ' redemption, substitution, purification, atoning blood, the garment of righteousness, are all terms which in some sense go back to antique ritual '.[1] Our differentiation between the material and the spiritual, or between the embodiment and the idea or spirit embodied, was not necessarily felt. The ' Body of Christ ' and ' Kingdom of God ' find their earlier forms in the tribe or the region united, maintained and sustained by its god. The gods were not ' outside ' men's world, though that world was conceived differently from our own; and they might be represented by, or incarnate in, special individuals, who, however, were not as such thought

[1] Wm. Robertson Smith, *The Religion of the Semites* (3rd ed., 1927), p. 439, and the present writer's notes, pp. 676 ff.

to be necessarily divine in themselves. A group performing its sacred rites was in a ' holy ' state; and since the god was often believed to be present—as he was in the Temple of Jerusalem (p. 139)—it can be said, to use modern terms, that the heavenly descended to earth for the sanctification of the earthly.[1] There is a sense, then, in which the god is both ' immanent ' in his embodiment, yet is ' holy ' and transcends it.[2]

The essence of religion is found, not only in the Bible, but elsewhere, though in rites and forms of belief often very different from our own. These essentials, as stated in the abstract, do not develop as do their particular forms, embodiments, or expression; and the vicissitudes of the latter are of vital consequence for the peoples concerned. Of Israel it has been well said, ' Behind the people's national life lay the consciousness of redemption as much as it lies behind the life of the Christian ', and ' all the main Christian ideas of atonement and bearing of sin are embraced in the *Second Isaiah* '.[3] Truth must be stated in forms relative to the current conditions of thought—a thing is ' true ' because of its correspondence with our experience and knowledge. But these conditions are not without change; and while the young can be so trained as naturally to accept and assimilate what they are taught, today the penetrating and far-searching enquiries in the various departments of knowledge are changing the background of life and thought. Comparative religion is impressive in its findings. What we call Inspiration and Revelation depend on the receptivity and response of men and of their age. God was in the

[1] Josephus (*Ant.* III. vii. 7, § 181) states that the inmost part of the tabernacle was reserved for God alone, because heaven also is inaccessible to men.

[2] The Lambeth Conference of 1930, p. 75 (on ' The Christian doctrine of God ') observes: ' Spirits are part and parcel of the fundamental unity of the primitive family or tribe. Such a unity is characteristic, and finds ample place for its full expression in the Christian doctrine of God. God Incarnate, the Spirit of God, Salvation and the Sacraments of the Church are fundamental concepts which are readily stated in terms of primitive religion and can be presented as giving a way of life which is a practical thing within that mental outlook '.

[3] A. B. Davidson in Hastings' *Dict. of the Bible*, article ' God ', p. 202; and *O.T. Prophecy*, p. 467.

world before Israel appeared and before Christianity arose; but through the Bible there have grown up conceptions of God, Man and the Universe which have directed the cultural development of the Western World. But whereas the men of old looked for a new and transformed world, it is a new and transformed meaning of it that our age needs. An old world is passing away, a new one is demanded; and if religious conviction and positive knowledge fall apart, both will suffer.

The Bible does not sever God, man and the universe, as we are apt to do. The severance between man and the outside world, or nature, or the world of the sciences is not found in early religion. To the Greeks above all we owe our modern differentiations and, as a consequence, our sciences and humane studies. We can view the world apart from men, biblical criticism and comparative religion apart from religious values, and economics apart from ethics. But it is obvious that, though the actual world has not undergone any significant change since man appeared, it is not what it *meant* for primitive and ancient peoples, or for ourselves when young. The world for us is what we have come to know of it, thanks to our developing consciousness and increase of awareness, our experience of life, and our reflection upon the data provided by our senses. And when we aim at acquiring a *true* knowledge, we judge our data by their coherence with our stock of knowledge, and correct or supplement either as the occasion arises.

Accordingly, the world is effectively for us a ' construct '; and although, as we look back on the past or look around and compare results, the ' constructions ' differ, these differences can be intelligibly explained. The worlds of the primitive, the child, the scientist, the religious and the ' man in the street ' will differ in a way which we can well understand. Hence, when we ask which shall be the best construction, we should not forget these differences, and the fact that men reach a certain stage of maturity before they put the question. The best construction must take into account the mental development in ourselves and throughout the ages. Meanwhile, we are always putting our knowledge to the test; and unless it were tolerably accurate and adequate, our scientific and other enquiries into the nature of the world would continually be hopelessly breaking down.

If the world is our ' construction ' of it, our processes of thought and those in the world outside must be in some way inter-related. When we propose to think about the world, our material consists not only of the visible objects extended in space—stars, the earth, plants, organisms, etc.—but, more especially, our acquired knowledge. The individual is reflecting upon what he is seeing and what he had previously acquired. The ' facts ' with which he is dealing are due to mind; and his interpretation must be tested by independent verification and relevant fresh ' facts '. It is not strange, therefore, that there should be some inter-connection between his mental processes and those in the outside world, for mind (in the widest sense of the word) is reflecting upon what mind had already given him. We are limited, therefore, by our experience and thought; and although we might seem to be moving in a closed circle, the world in which we live does appear to be more or less what we think it is.

There are, to be sure, lunatics, paranoiacs and men of extreme dissociated personality whose ' constructions ' of the world are such that we place them in the classes mentioned. Indeed, we might even conclude that the more a man's world-view diverges from the general trend of accumulated knowledge and experience and of accepted general intellectual and moral principles of life and thought, the more likely is he to depart from the characteristics of *normal* men—does the adjective beg the question?—and not only to suffer himself, but to be more than an annoyance to others. And also from the religious point of view it could with equal right be stated that there are religious principles which cannot be ignored with impunity, and that a world-view which finds no place for them, or even excludes them, is a dangerously mutilated one.

If, then, the world is *effectively* for us what we have come to learn of it, two points may be made. (*a*) From the standpoint of scientific and positive knowledge our world *is* what we think it to be, even though ancient and primitive people did not, and the young of today do not, know this. And (b) from the religious standpoint, the Universe of God and men is not what anyone chooses to think, rather is it what the world's religions are continually endeavouring to formulate. When the religion has been a living one, there has been a coherence between it and the general culture of the age to an extent that emphatically demonstrates the lack of coherence of our day; and because the Bible has played a unique part in shaping the life and thought of the West, the world-view which we gain from it is surely not to be ignored, even though our knowledge of the outside world differs so widely from that of its writers.

A survey of beliefs and customs in the Bible and elsewhere brings to light two fundamental lines of experience and reflection. The one is the widespread belief in gods and spirits, in the supernatural, in a reality outside the visible world, or in an unseen reality with which man is inescapably bound up. The beliefs as a whole are not necessarily ' religious ' in any useful sense of the term; and in the abstract they are logically neutral in that they take so many diverse and contradictory forms. The other is the equally widespread conviction of right, order, law and truth, of conformity to norms and standards, otherwise misfortune, wrong, injustice, and evil would not be recognised as such (pp. 19, 140). But since there are sweeping differences of opinion, this conviction, too, is in itself logically neutral. Accordingly, men are encouraged and stimulated, or they are perplexed and thwarted, as the case may be; and, striving after a certain harmony and intelligibility, they put life to the test and pass judgment upon its vicissitudes.

The history of religion is one of ebb and flow, of decay and revival or rebirth; and since we evaluate a religion on moral or even purely intellectual and ' non-religious ' grounds, the spheres of the ' religious ' and the ' non-religious ' cannot be violently severed. Reason has the last word; and, on the religious plane, even Revelation and Inspiration are reasonable, in that God does reveal Himself and does inspire, and what we call the ' supernatural ' or the ' spiritual ' is a natural part of His Universe. That there can be an even unconscious influence of mystical or religious experience has often been suggested.[1] In fact, Einstein has observed that ' the serious scientific workers are the only profoundly religious people ', and that modern scientific speculations spring from a profound ' religious impulse '. ' Cosmic religiousness is ', he remarks, ' the strongest and noblest mainspring of scientific research ' and he confesses, ' I am a deeply religious man '.[2] Not to multiply quotations, it must suffice to refer to what I have elsewhere called the ' Theory of Religion ' : Religion in general asserts or implies that God and man are in some sort of relationship before ever man recognises a God; religious and mystical experiences intimately unite man, the Universe and the God of the Universe; there is some fundamental and ultimate relationship between the three, however it be implied, manifested or stated.[3]

There are typical deeper experiences which can be classified; they are on a plane of existence of their own. From the intellectual and human side we reach principles of order and right in man and nature; but humanism, secularism or science cannot present a *whole* view of human personality and life. On the other hand, religion will unify and integrate the widest ranges of life—that, at least, is its aim. Starting from the non-religious side, we sooner or later reach the point where religion is involved, and it is very instructive to see how the best humanists, rationalists and scientists will impinge upon or approximate what it has been the function of religion to handle. But they implicate what religion has to explicate, and tend to beg the questions which religion seeks to answer.

Biblical study itself takes us, on the one hand, to a variety of departments of purely critical, rational research, and, on the other hand, to the profoundest and ultimate problems of God, man and the Universe. Hence, the Bible

[1] See The ' Truth ' of the Bible, p. 185 f. Cf. Christopher Dawson, *Enquiries into Religion and Culture* (1933), p. 194; T. Whittaker, *The Liberal State* (1907), p. 180; R. Collingwood, *Philosophical Method* (1933), p. 161.

[2] Biographies by D. Reichenstein (1934), pp. 100, 108, 135 f., and H. G. Garbedian (1939), pp. 314 ff.; cf. J. H. Morrison, *Christian Faith and the Science of To-day* (1936), pp. 97, 214.

[3] See *Rebirth*, Index under ' Religion, theory of '.

and the Christianity based upon it point the way to the completest synthesis conceivable. In the field of biblical study there are problems of the Hebrew and Greek originals, literary composition, historical genuineness, decay and revival, development or evolution. It is found that the several problems cannot indefinitely be handled in isolation; and that there are principles of methodical study in the biblical field that cannot be severed from those in other fields. There comes the time when our own deepest convictions are involved, and critical biblical study is lifted on to another plane. This does not mean that questions of text, compilation, and the rest are treated in a ' religious ' or ' spiritual ' manner; but it does mean that our horizons are widened, we work within a larger, indeed the widest, framework. From one standpoint, the supernatural—or, better, the spiritual—is a ' plus ', an extra, it is something outside and beyond the natural; but from another and higher standpoint it is within the natural and the reality which religion handles is a normal and natural part of God's Universe. That this is not now the prevailing opinion only emphasizes the difference between our day and the periods in the past when religion was more living and real.

A deep consciousness or awareness underlies the profoundest intuitions and convictions; and it is the essential aim of religion to nurture it. In religious experience there are typical feelings of intimate relationship with God and His Universe, but also of the gulf between God and man. He is felt to bound man's life and thought; He pre-exists the limits of our thoughts, and is eternal; and this relationship banishes man's sense of finitude and of his helpless and fleeting existence in an unreal world. Modern science has overwhelmingly demonstrated the almost terrifying littleness of this earth and its inhabitants; but religion incredibly enhances man's status. And even sweeping plans for the social and political betterment of man, though on the secular and humanist plane, will imply an almost boundless limit to man's possibilities—too often ignoring their religious aspect. Religion has its experiences of God's infinite majesty and love; they evoke awe, adoration and humility, though, paradoxically enough, the religious or

related experiences will often give men a conviction of their
own inherent power.

The experience of the gulf between God and man—one
that is bridged by God and not by man—and of man's
falling-away from his best, from what he *knows* he should
be, is in one form or another common in the world's
religions; and it is given a ' historical ' setting in the O.T.
story of the Fall.   Experiences of bliss or of despair, or of
evil (whether by man himself or of which he is the victim)
lie behind the specific beliefs concerning retribution and an
after-life; and they are more fundamental than the precise
forms in which they have taken shape and directed speculation.   There are experiences, sometimes ineffable or too
sacred to discuss, and the individual must needs resort to
analogy, metaphor, image or symbol.   No doubt religious
beliefs and rites can be accepted ' at second-hand ', so to
speak, but the recurrence of the essential elements of
religion, the fact that they are constantly being tested afresh
and restated, and the impressive new stages in the course
of the great historical religions combine to indicate that a
man's religion is in the long run autonomous and is its own
authority.

The fact of the existence of a supreme Power in personal
relationship with man is an immediate religious experience.
But the concept ' God ' is also an invaluable, or rather, an
indispensable one, unifying and integrating one's thoughts.
It answers the demand for an ultimate principle of moral
and ethical worth—God is the supreme Value.   It satisfies
the conviction that there must be a final purpose beyond the
here-and-now.   It provides an absolute cause and ground
of all things, so that there is a Being, not merely less finite
and less imperfect than man, but absolutely perfect,
summing up and justifying the highest ideals and attributes.
The supposition that religion is the result of ' wishful
thinking ' invites a *Tu quoque* to him who seriously and
obstinately upholds it.   The instinct that leads one to
rationalize one's instinctive beliefs is, in itself, neutral;
but the idea of ' God ' is not a mere idea and nothing more.
My belief or conviction that I have a one pound note in my
pocket may be erroneous, and I may be seriously em-

barrassed thereby; but the belief in God can be and constantly is being put to the test. If Israel had not tenaciously held this belief there would have been no Bible! True, the belief in God does not banish our sorrows and tragedies, or solve our problems, or answer all our questions; but we live on another plane, we breathe a purer air, and we meet life—or, rather, are aided to meet it—in a new spirit. And when once this belief becomes a reality, God, and the Bible as the Word of God, are thenceforth the starting-point for convictions as to His nature and attributes.

Some knowledge of the relevant lines of modern study is necessary if one is to understand and teach the Bible; but the Book that has hitherto stood the test of time can be neither understood nor taught in a way that enables one to realize its unique value unless it be approached on the spiritual plane and truly regarded as the Word of God.

CHAPTER X

ON UNDERSTANDING AND TEACHING THE BIBLE

II. *The Word of God*

THE Bible is the basis of Christianity. In it the Christian finds a God who has revealed Himself in history in a personal relationship to men. It is a conviction that has been evoked, sustained and repeatedly confirmed by personal experience. Can it be ' objectively ' justified to-day in the light of modern thought? All the world over are many conceptions of gods or of God; but Christianity is the outcome of a lengthy development in and behind the pages of the Bible and in the history of the Church. This development, when carefully compared with the history of other religions, gives it a more than impressive value. No other religion has been so searching, pregnant and rich in all that concerns man and the world.

Christianity has at times thwarted the free play of the intellect; but attitudes to religion have in their turn at times been misdirected by scientific and other secular research. Christianity has nevertheless profoundly stimulated both intellectual and social activities, even though it might be retorted that it was not precisely Christianity but the general atmosphere of the Christian world to which the credit was often due. Christianity with its doctrine of the Incarnation does not and cannot deny the world; and although an ' other-worldness ', an extreme emphasis upon ' another ' world, has sometimes characterized it, it has no less characteristically aimed at—what might be called— ' making the best of both worlds '. From a purely comparative and objective point of view, therefore, it can be asserted that the influence of Christianity and the Bible has hitherto been immeasurably greater than that of any other religion or sacred writing.

When we say that the Bible is the Word of God we do

not refer to every constituent verse or passage. It is, rather, that we find God in and behind it, even as Christianity is something behind the verbal expression of it in creed, doctrine and dogma. The saintliest individual is not a saint at every moment of his life, but his character and his general mode of life and thought will have entitled him to be so styled. So it is with the Bible: we are impressed by the spirit that prevails in it and dominates it. We cannot say that the Bible is literally inspired in, so to speak, a ready-made or take-or-leave-it way, or that truths otherwise inaccessible or incapable of verification by personal experience or by reason were imparted or dictated. Inspiration quickens and illumines man's insight and his faculties; but, human fallibility being what it is, the Bible is not free from contradictions and errors, and is by no means of equal religious value throughout. The writers were men of their age, and the people were what human beings everywhere are. We recognize their weaknesses and faults, and realize that God can be no ' respecter of persons ' (Acts x. 34). At the same time, we cannot think that His choice is arbitrary. Man's readiness to attend and respond is essential. The potter may find his clay intractable (p. 114 n.), the nation that is chosen and raised up may prove faithless (Jer. xviii. 7 ff.), but ' as many as received Him to them gave He the right to become children of God ' (John i. 12). *He* knocks (Rev. iii. 20), and *we* knock (Luke xi. 9): there is co-operation; and in so far as man is capable He comes into his life. The limit to God's self-giving is the capacity and readiness of man to receive what He has to give; and what we owe to Israel is due to her readiness to accept God's discipline. Israel had no special claim to divine favour; with her as with every individual God's grace is unmerited.

The actual stages in the history of the Bible and of the Church prove that no complete body of truth was given once and for all to the saints, but in divers manners over the centuries. When we take a long and wide survey we find supreme events that were not confined to the relatively few centuries over which the Bible extends. The O.T. is, it is true, regarded as the preparation for the N.T.; but the first steps had already been taken in and around Palestine before the earliest of the writings preserved in the O.T. It is this intrinsic continuity and progressive development of fundamental ideas which is so vital when one is thinking about the future of the Bible and Christianity. Moreover, we cannot draw a rigid line between Christianity and other religions. All peoples are His (Acts xvii. 24 ff.); He has clearly revealed Himself in the world (Rom. i. 18 ff.). The modern comparative study of religions definitely forbids us to narrow our conceptions of God's place in the Universe, but rather calls upon us to ask ourselves what the concept ' God ' should mean for us, provided we use it seriously.

Christianity is indebted primarily to the Bible, but also, and very profoundly, to Greek thought. But today we go back behind both; and since every living religion is inextricably bound up with men's life, we must regard Christianity, not solely as a religion, but as a cultural force. Both religion and science are concerned with man and the world, and we are learning a new approach to both. But learning involves unlearning, and the words of Albert Schweitzer should be pondered over: ' It is because Oriental and Greek conceptions which have had their day are still current among us that we bleed to death over problems which otherwise would have no existence for us '.[1] Naturally, discrimination is necessary.

Now, the biblical view of man regards him as an animated body rather than as a body within which a soul is confined. Hence it was difficult to imagine any existence after death apart from some sort of embodiment. But Yahweh in the O.T. and Christ in the N.T. are the creator and sustainer of both man and the world (p. 130). Man and nature, or the outside world, the world of our sciences, were not rigidly separated by ancient and primitive peoples, and the true interconnection between them should not be obscured today. Two points are to be made: (1) the variety of spiritual gifts in men, and (2) the variety of spirit in nature.

(1) The N.T. recognizes varying ' measures ' of divine grace and diversities of spiritual gifts, dependent upon the variety of members of the Body of Christ with their several

[1] *The Decay and the Restoration of Civilisation*, I (2nd ed., 1932), p. 68.

abilities, endowments and callings.[1] But there are false
ideas of Christ; there are Antichrists, false prophets and
false Messiahs. Both Testaments speak of men who felt
they were inspired, but are condemned as false. And if we
go further afield, we find men who were what we might call
quasi-religious and of a 'demonic' spirituality. God, as
the Psalmist recognized, answers to a man's character
(Ps. xviii. 26). In the O.T. a distinction was made between
men of Yahweh's 'spirit' and men of 'flesh' (p. 105); and
we are forced to perceive that there are distinctions within
the realms of religion and spirit. Such distinctions are made
by Jesus (*e.g.*, Matt. vii. 15–23); and everywhere it is usual
for lines to be drawn between what may be regarded as
religious and spiritual and what, though seemingly on the
plane of religion, lies outside and is apt to be regarded as
the worst enemy of religion. Indeed in Religion, as in the
Arts, in Science and in Literature, there are criteria, however
imperfect, for distinguishing them from imitations. We
can *mentally* sever spirit and its embodiment, manifestation
or expression; it is not God who is variable, but the meaning
He has for men.

(2) Although there are times and occasions when a fresh
spiritual wave seems to sweep over an age, a people or an
individual, powerfully influencing the stage of growth each
has reached, we do not limit God's work either to these
occasions, or to those we call 'religious' or 'spiritual', or
even to man alone. God is creator and sustainer of man
and the world; 'creative activity', it has been well said,
'signifies more than the thing it creates'. We have to
recognize the creation of creators, the gift of spontaneity and
freedom—within limits. This in no way spells pantheism,
but an ultimate and fundamental theism, the rule of God:
even a wise parent enjoys giving his child freedom to
develop his personality, though he intervenes when he
believes it to be for the child's good.

Now, we can speak of the *esprit de corps*, or corporate
spirit, of any group or body united and animated by its
common principles; this 'spirit' is not an independent

[1] *E.g.*, Rom. xii. 3, 1 Cor. vii. 17, xii. 4–31; cf. 1 Pet. iv. 10 f.

entity, and its precise function depends upon the precise character of the group. Similarly we can speak of ' spirit ' throughout man and the world, although a more general term would be preferable, such as power, force or energy. And just as, for example, oxygen can be a constituent of a great variety of compounds, so this ' energy '—if we decide to use the term—takes an enormous variety of forms in man and the world, and these it is the task of progressive knowledge to distinguish and classify.

Consider the following pairs: the Bible and other sacred writings, man and the higher animals, the organic and the inorganic—how knowledge has progressed by emphasizing at one time the differences, at another the points of contact! In the latter case we are taking a wider view, building upon wider foundations; we are stressing the points of resemblance rather than those of difference. It goes without saying that many of us are unable to bridge the gap between the members of each pair; although, on the other hand, it is easy to obscure or forget the differences. Especially important here is the problem of Mind and Body, since it is only too common to treat Mind as an entity apart from Body, as the Soul, for example, and equally to treat Mind and the mental activities of man as quite distinct from physical ' energy '.

But our notions of ' mind ' are primarily based upon the *thinking* individual. Yet, at what stage of evolution or development, whether in the infant or in the history of the human race, does ' thinking ' begin? Among early peoples thinking is concrete; in their social life are practices which *we* treat as ' ideas '; the ideas may be said to be implicit, only in course of growth do they become explicit. What the gods require of men: the co-operation of men and their gods, holiness, regeneration—these are manifested in actions, not doctrines (p. 132 f.). Thought is the highest form of human energy, and to it we owe our knowledge of the world and of ourselves; mental activity is a normal part of man who, in turn, is part of the world of nature. One moment a man proposes to arise and fill his fountain pen, and he normally succeeds; the next moment he proposes to write a simple letter, and again he normally succeeds; the energy that is manifested in the former case cannot be severed from that in the latter. By mental analysis we contrast Mind and Body or Matter, whereas we have to deal primarily with the individual when he is thinking and with the manifestation or embodiment of his mental activities. Mental analysis reduces our thinking to concepts, categories, patterns and modes of thought. They are means of expression, and we must not confuse, so to say, the musician with his instruments, which may be imperfect or out of tune.

From the common-sense point of view we think of 'matter' as properly something extended in time and space. But, on the one hand, our conscious thinking is responsible to a greater or less degree for our higher physical and social activities in the every-day world; and, on the other, ordinary conceptions of 'matter' have had to be adjusted owing to the modern advances in science. Hence, at one end of the scale are beliefs, doctrines, theories, and all that is fundamentally conceptual, while, at the other end, ordinary notions of the reality of 'brute matter' have been found to be inadequate. Scientific research has found that at the limit of our analysis of our world we do not reach ultimate reality. We reach processes that cannot be represented in terms of space-time: they are scarcely imaginable. Between ourselves and reality are mathematical laws of nature, a mathematical description of nature: 'physical reality is reduced to a set of Hamiltonian equations'.[1] To quote Sir Arthur Eddington, 'I am convinced that if in physics we pursued to the bitter end our attempts to reach purely objective reality, we should simply undo the work of creation and present the world as we might conceive it to have been before the Spirit moved on the face of the waters'.[2] That is, mind is getting behind the *order* which it finds in the Universe, and which religion

[1] Sir W. C. Dampier, *History of Science* (3rd ed., 1942), p. 470; cf. E. T. Whittaker, *The Beginning and End of the World* (1942), p. 25: 'the mathematical laws of nature are the nexus between ourselves and external reality'.

[2] In *Science and Religion: A Symposium* (1931), p. 130. Cf. p. 122, the physical universe boils down into 'a scheme of symbols connected by mathematical equations'.

ascribes to a Divine Spirit or Logos (p. 129 f.). But we cannot get behind the processes of nature and of the mind that interprets nature. It is as though we found that $(a + b)^2 = a^2 + 2ab + b^2$, leaving it open what were the things of which there were a and b. The point is that analysis has reached its limits, but has not reached reality; although the mind has developed an invaluable instrument of thought. Words of Einstein have been quoted above (p. 188), and other quotations could be made from mathematical physicists and others who have been deeply impressed by the ultimate nature of their researches and the ' cosmic emotion ' these have evoked.

Now, when we turn to the testimony of religion and mysticism we notice the characteristic experience or conviction that the world as accessible to our senses is not all. Men get behind it, and find an overwhelming reality which has final and objective authority. In India, above all, this world of ours is felt to be *maya*, illusion (p. 17); and to a varying degree this consciousness of the actual impermanence of the world in contrast to the permanence of an unknown but overwhelming reality recurs in both East and West. But there is this essential difference, that typical mysticism tends to experiences of identity with or absorption into God or the Infinite Essence of the Universe, whereas typical religion expresses an actual or potential relationship or communion with God. And Religion reckons with this much more seriously than does mysticism. Brief life here may be our portion, men may be sojourners on earth, but this world is sufficiently actual and real to be a scene of soul-making.

There are, indeed, numerous variations of this fundamental experience. We need refer only to theosophy, spiritualism, occultism and black magic, or to the super-realists, logicians and others who would get ' behind ' language, our language not being moulded on reality. There are types of consciousness which cannot find adequate expression in our inherited forms of thought or canons of art and music. We have, then, (1) the consciousness of a vaster overwhelming and overpowering reality which transcends this world of space-time, and (2) the feeling of the inadequacy of our forms of thought and expression. But throughout it is men's subsequent attitude and behaviour that by and large affect the judgment we pass upon them, and not the experiences in themselves.

Thus, the world in which we live is as a veil between ourselves and an ultimate reality; or it is as a sea—not without its storms and dangers—over which we must pass to reach the goal, a goal of the actuality of which we are assured. And this veil or sea is one our description of which is being transformed as a result of modern research and knowledge. Now, our departments of knowledge and science can be arranged very broadly, but conveniently, in three ascending groups: (a) physics and chemistry, (b) biology and the science of living things, and (c) the ' sciences ' of man—if the word ' science ' be allowed—e.g., psychology, anthropology, sociology, history, etc. The ' lower ' go far to describe the ' higher ', but not far enough, whether we try to describe animate nature in terms of physics and chemistry, or history in terms of economics, or religion in terms of social custom and belief.[1] But instead of a scale or a hierarchy of classes or planes, each with its appropriate concepts, we can conceive a circle, since the highest of processes, the mental, is bound up with the analytical treatment of physics, our theory of knowledge and our description of the fundamentals.[2]

The upshot of the preceding paragraphs is that we seem to be—to use another figure—a sphere with ourselves as the centre and ultimate reality outside it. We seem to be gaining an immensely superior knowledge of this sphere, and it does favour materialistic views and methods. Yet the more we emphasize the actuality of this world of ours the more we enhance the actuality of the energy that operates in it, in nature and man, and notably in men when they

---

[1] Each subject has its appropriate terminology; thus in both physics and religion alike the necessary concepts are connected with one another, forming a closed circle. Such circular reasoning is as inevitable in science as in history or religion. In common-sense premises are read into our material: consequences are probable relatively to the premises, and premises are probable relatively to the consequences; ' there could hardly be a plainer case of circularity· than this ' (F. R. Tennant, *The Nature of Belief* [1943], p. 45).

[2] See *Rebirth*, pp. 170 n., 197.

think about it. Science has enhanced our conception of the energy which in religion—a subject which lies outside the sciences—we associate with a Divine Power. We may drive home to the utmost the significance of *this* world for us here and now, but we should not forget that the account we give of it is, so to say, printed on a white page without which our words would be in empty air, the ' grin ' of the Cheshire Cat.

The mind does not ' construct ' the Universe out of its inner consciousness, nor does it ' find ' it; there is a combination of the individual and the objects of his attention. Imagery, symbols and myths must be employed; and from time to time these are overhauled and must be changed. But there is no room for any thoroughgoing scepticism; this would destroy our belief in ourselves, it would cut away the bough upon which we are sitting: our ' religious ' and our ' non-religious ' modes of thought are inextricably interwoven. Looking back on the past we might sometimes believe that man was free to ' construct ' any Universe he liked, but the deeper our scrutiny the more secure is our assurance that the Universe is not what anyone might choose to fancy. Although the world seems to dissolve away the deeper we probe into our minds, we feel that we are none the less a real part of something that is real. And the function of religion is to evoke, develop and guide that fundamental consciousness or awareness which is reached in so many different ways and expresses itself so varyingly. In religion we have a particular way of evoking and expressing what is otherwise expressed in ways that are often regarded —and rightly—by a living religion as entirely unrelated to it, or as a rival or enemy to be rejected.

What do we learn from the Bible's view of man and the world? God, or God in Christ Who has all the fullness of God, is in and over the world and man. Christ is the Logos, the principle of order, law, reason and truth. Christ, the Son of God, is actually operating in the Universe, He is immanent in it, and in actual contact with all creation.[1] But God, the Father, is transcendent. This conception of

[1] See *Rebirth*, pp. 81 f., 196.

' transcendence ', which often occasions difficulty, can be reached in various ways. In everyday life we may be wholeheartedly attracted by a person, a pursuit or a topic; it is sufficiently well known to us, otherwise there would be no attraction, but it is still beyond us. 'A man's reach must exceed his grasp or what's a heaven for?' It is beyond our horizon but it is to be striven for. So, the ' transcendence ' of God is a concept with a meaning for us, because He is immanent. He seeks us to search after Him, and our souls are restless till they find rest in Him. A wholly transcendent God—or ' object '—would be meaningless for us; a wholly immanent God—or ' object '—would lose its meaning. Again, when we formulate our ideas, everywhere the ' object ' upon which we focus attention is part of a larger field, and we have to allow for a fuller knowledge. Every ' unit ' topic has outside it that which can contribute to our intellectual or personal growth. Hence, the ideal ' whole ' consists of what we already know and what will make for fuller knowledge. Thus, ' transcendence ' on the spiritual or religious plane has certain analogies in ordinary personal relationships of a deeper kind and in normal mental development.

In the Bible Christ becomes the Way, the Truth and the Life, the ideal ' whole ', incarnating the highest ideals and values of life, the goal of a complete human personality. Already in the O.T. we observe the heightening of conceptions of Yahweh, the God of Israel. The little girl in the story, hearing of some of the old cruder ideas of God in the O.T., exclaimed, ' Hasn't God improved since then, Mother! ' But it is not God who changes, it is men's conceptions of God. And so, too, when we go farther afield, we can note diverse and developing conceptions of Buddha, or the growth of higher ideas of the Indian Krishna. In the old Oriental religions are many fine ideas, and when we turn to the O.T. we can say with the late Archbishop of Canterbury : ' The One God of Heaven and Earth used the figure of Yahweh, the God of Sinai, as the means of revealing Himself to a particular nation '.[1] No one who believes in a God can deny that elsewhere He used

[1] Dr. William Temple, *Mens Creatrix* (1917), p. 304.

figures of contemporary belief as the medium for his
revelation of Himself. Only in this way do we come to
realize how men's knowledge is limited by their capacity
and readiness to respond to His call.

Philosophers speak of the *philosophia perennis*; the
system of thought which, due in the first instance to the
Greeks, represents the natural human mind, and is therefore an enduring system. Similarly, we may speak of
the *religio perennis*; it is not confined to the Bible and
Christianity, and no less represents human nature. For
man normally recognizes the reality of what we may call the
supernatural, the ' beyond '. Here we may think of cosmic
emotion, and all else that points to a reality other than that
of this world of space-time, the impulse that moves men—
workers and thinkers—to toil for that which is beyond the
here-and-now, and the deep feeling of the incompleteness
of life and the longing for what is less imperfect and fleeting
(p. 29 f.). Throughout there is an instinctive trait which it
is the function of a living religion to guide and organize.
And this organizing or integrating process works upon both
heart and head, and moves the whole personality to come to
terms with the great mysteries of God, Man and the Universe. Every religion will no doubt be relative to the
conditions of life and thought amid which it arose; but there
is a constant striving after an ideal completeness which
embraces, not religion alone, but the whole cultural environment. The fact that religion has a *history*, and that change,
development and progress are to be found, can only mean
that it is not static, and that one's best aim is to recognize
its dynamism. And this is attained when the transcendence
of the God who is immanent in His creation is recognized.

The Bible has a world-view and a place in world-history.
Although the history in it is that of its age, it can be placed
within the new framework of the past which the knowledge
of our race is giving us, and we can participate in the Spirit
which informs its contents. Hence the critical treatment
of the history is indispensable; it gives us a dynamic conception of the Bible and of the changes that affected its
growth. And forthwith it must be emphasized that,

however much our views of its contents may require modi-
fication and adjustment, the essence or spirit of the Bible is
but little disturbed: it is not the true religious and devotional
value of the Bible that is affected, it is the fuller body in
which it is enshrined, the shell of the kernel, that needs
adjustment. The ordinary 'critical' statement of the
sources J, E, D, P (p. 153) does not give us any real ' evolu-
tionary ' view of the O.T., though it is a valuable starting-
point. Nor is it any longer finally helpful on the ordinary
' critical ' view to frame a ' biography ' of Yahweh from a
tribal God to the God of Israel, and ultimately the One and
Only God of the Universe. We have, rather, the religious
development in Palestine from pre-Israelite to Israelite
times, from the post-exilic reorganization to the influence of
Hellenism, and ultimately the rise of Christianity and its
severance from Judaism.[1] Only by recognizing this can we
grasp the profoundly impressive advances in the growth of
ideas of the interrelation between God, Man and the
Universe.

We mark the ethical and spiritual advances; the inaugurating periods with subsequent adjustments, compromises and decline.[2] We note the tension between the
more individualist and the more social, national and
institutional types of religion (p. 111 f.). We see something of
the stage from a nation or people to a Church, and—not the
least interesting—the predominance of the ancient city of
Jerusalem (ch. vii). The development is neither a simple
one, nor along a single straight line; for the ' Judaean ' and
' Jerusalem ' treatment of the history in the O.T. obscures
the part played by non-Israelites, by the northern tribes
(North Israel), and by Galilee (pp. 166 ff.).[3]

Inaugurating periods can be recognized, fresh starting
points, but not actual beginnings. The latter lie outside
our experience and knowledge. We are ignorant of the
beginning of the Universe; and the notion of creation from

[1] See pp. 135 ff., and cf. 35, 38, 52 f., 72 f., 124 f., 159 f.
[2] The account of the decline of Israel after her entry in the fine poem
Deut. xxxii is classic.
[3] On the other hand, Jerusalem, its temple and sacrificial system,
in fact, its whole ideology, shaped post-exilic Israelite religion and
Christianity; see p. 113.

formless matter, or *ex nihilo*, is intellectually meaningless.[1]
We know only of the present ' cosmic epoch ', the Universe
of our sciences; we know of no absolutely simple or
undifferentiated primal matter. We know how a state of
relative chaos can become a state of relative cosmos or
order; but what preceded the beginning of our Universe
lies outside speculation. But we do know of fresh inaugurating steps in nature, history, and in ourselves. ' God ',
as creator and sustainer of all things, is not merely a concept; the concept is one that unifies both religious experience and intellectual enquiry, and on the spiritual plane it is
intelligible and reasonable. No doubt we are left with
questions of ' sub-creators '—if the word be allowed—to
account for the creativity and spontaneity in a God-given
Universe. But such questions, whether we agree with the
answers given by ' religion ' or not, are severely ignored on
principle by ' science '.[2]

The significance of biblical history for us lies not merely
in the chronological succession of events, but in those events
that changed history or gave it a new turn. The great
inaugurating occasions to which we have referred find their
significance for us in their wider and more sweeping influence.
Moreover, when we place the history within the modern
framework of world-history, and consider the course of
events from the Bible to Christianity, and to our own age,
we do not stop at the N.T.: to-day a fresh inaugurating
period is surely dawning, and what Christ and Christianity
have meant for the last nineteen centuries must be restated
with new conviction and power.

Now, a book on biblical history, or the history of biblical
study, or indeed of any branch of knowledge, would be concerned with the order of events; it would point to times of
stagnation and decline, or of fresh and new impetus. But
an exposition of the present stage of any study written for
current purposes would naturally be different. It would
ignore what proved to be irrelevant or erroneous, it would
not expound the discoveries or advances of the past in their
contemporary context, but place them in their present

[1] Cf. Wisdom xi. 17, 2 Macc. vii. 28.
[2] See *Rebirth*, pp. 69 n., 73, 81, 158, 193.

setting. Repeatedly, of course, one could give the date when such-and-such a novelty first appeared; but the exposition would have in mind the present and the future, it would not be a history of the subject. There is, then, a difference between a chronological and historical treatment of biblical religion and an exposition for modern needs, which would, in fact, be more in the nature of a ' theology '. Not what was believed in the past, but what was now to be believed would guide the writer.

Again, consider such figures as Moses, David, Amos, Isaiah, Jesus and Paul. We have by no means a full knowledge of all they said and did; we cannot understand all that was in their minds, and not all that is ascribed to them is authentic. We can endeavour to grasp their spirit and that of their followers; and frequently we are not disturbed by the question whether such-and-such a teaching comes from the figure in question, or from a follower of his who gives what we feel to be a true interpretation of his mind. The Fourth Gospel is a case in point.[1] We are, indeed, wont to pick and choose, and to superimpose our own interpretation upon passages; and some, for example, sincerely accept snippets of the Gospels, or of the teaching of Jesus, but reject or are indifferent to doctrinal teaching. On the other hand, the implications of even isolated passages may be extremely valuable; and whatever may satisfy one or the other of us, the fundamental need is for a structure, a body of thought, rather than miscellaneous separate links of a chain, isolated members so to speak. ' Righteous ' relations between a man and his fellows and between man and God cannot be held separate: the objective value of a religion lies in its social effects.

On the one hand, the purely historical treatment runs the risk of becoming antiquarian; it has its limits. What precisely did Moses, or Isaiah, or Jesus, or Paul say and do many centuries ago? But, on the other hand, there is the danger of seeing saplings and oaks in acorns; the N.T. is read into the O.T.—and today one reads one's own interpretation into the N.T.; the several parts of the O.T. or of the N.T.

[1] See p. 71. Cf. also the words of Mohammed, ' Whatever good saying has been said, I myself have said it '.

are often fused into one mass, and one loses sight of the real progressive development of religion. There are these two extremes, the one becomes antiquarianism, the other an uncritical and misleading confusion, and while each line of thought requires the other, the tendency is to form a conglomeration of what was believed and what we may believe —a premature synthesis that does due justice neither to criticism nor to progressive religion.

Sooner or later it is found that the religion and theology of the O.T. and that of the New cannot be rigidly held apart. But when we consider modern needs, we cannot ignore the Apocrypha, nor can we neglect other related literature.[1] Moreover, what shall be said of the fine ethical and spiritual conceptions outside the biblical field? The implications of great religious or spiritual convictions can in no case be overlooked; and what we may call the ' Theory of Religion' is of immense significance for our conceptions of God, Man and the Universe (p. 188 n. 3). These conceptions, it is true, take us outside religion, they involve scientific and other researches into Nature and Man. But a religion, if it is to live, must have a real cultural value. No doubt this does not make the question of the future of the Bible and Christianity any simpler; but we should have a false conception of the task before us if we proposed to ignore anything that might seem to make it more difficult. After all, if Christianity is to claim—as it should claim—a real and objective superiority, though it must do so only with a deep sense of responsibility and a spirit of sincerest humility, may it not be said that ' the right to a position is no more than the power to maintain it '?

The need for a theology is self-evident. It makes articulate the inarticulate knowledge and experience of individuals; it enunciates the broad principles which organize religious experience; and, as it has in view the normal wide variety of temperament and training among men, it seeks a common unifying basis. There never was a complete system or synthesis, but rather an effective and pregnant one, aiming at unity of truth and unity of personality. This is the aim, and it might be added that

[1] See pp. 35 f., 60, 120.

perhaps the best teaching is preaching—the preaching of trained and well-equipped men. For the appeal is from personality to personality, and the pattern set before men is the complete and final ideal of the Person of Christ. Even if a writer has the necessary erudition and competence, it is the personal appeal that has always been effective. Indeed, from what has been said above on the religious and related types of experience innate in human nature, it is ' vision ' that not only inspires the ordinary individual, but gives that deeper and wider grasp of things which is so necessary for deeper and wider intellectual work. The fear of the Lord—reverence and worship—is, indeed, the beginning of wisdom (Prov. ix. 10).

The ideal ' Christian world ' is a cultural one. God was always in the Universe He created ; but we have to remember the steps which have led to our vaster and more developed knowledge. It is this development which counts. Most religions have their special value, even as in the animal world there are creatures stronger, or fleeter, or of keener sight than men, or that can live undergound or in water in a way that man cannot. None the less we are persuaded that man is the most highly developed of all creatures. We cannot ignore or belittle this evolution ; and since God is the God of this evolving Universe, evolution in nature and His revelation to man of Himself and His Universe are more intimately associated than we think.[1] Hence the world for Christianity is not solely a religious or theological one.

Doubtless we tend to shift our ground and alter our focus when we pass from our view of the Universe of positive knowledge and the sciences to a specifically Christian view culminating in the Incarnation and Redemption nineteen centuries ago. But in the measure that our construction or conception of the Universe becomes more unified, the gulf between our ' non-religious ' and our ' religious ' ways of viewing the Universe is bridged. This gulf does not disappear, but the key to the bridge lies in our knowledge of human personality, modes of consciousness, mental processes and patterns of thought ; it lies in our analysis of the individual, now moving in this world of space-time, and

[1] Cf. *Rebirth*, pp. 155, 173 and 209 (last sentence).

now profoundly conscious of some more ultimate reality that inspires his whole self.[1]

The Bible takes us to great epoch-making occasions that have changed the world. A Divine Spirit moves through it; and it has made our history what it has been. And the future of that history will rest upon that Spirit and our response to it: this is what we mean when we say that the Spirit of the Bible is the Spirit of History (p. 170).

The Bible turns upon two great sweeping changes: the earlier, round about the Exile, when Israel underwent reconstruction. A new Israel was being born amid the decline or death of neighbouring powers, and were it not for this there would have been no O.T., no Christianity. The later was at the rise of Christianity, when this Israel was unable to advance further, and the line of development left the Middle East and passed to the West. At the earlier period Israel had witnessed the destruction of her Holy City and Temple; yet, exiles away from their native land did not feel that they were removed from their God. And at the later, the Jews despite their tragedies did not lose their faith. So, while the O.T. turns upon the reconstruction or rebirth of Israel and the N.T. upon the birth of another Israel, may one not believe that, whatever the present age may bring, when modern conditions of life and thought may seem to exile the Christian and destroy the integrity of his Bible, he may yet take courage and know that the very history of the Word of God in the past is the guarantee that it will not fail him in the future?

More than any other book, the Bible has led man to understand the Universe and himself; it has directed him along the road to a Truth and a Reality which no religion outside Christianity has ever conceived. In the Bible men have found that which answered their deepest needs; it has something for every crisis. In it there is a depth of feeling; the greatest figures were those whose consciousness of the reality of the Universe has not been surpassed. To an age of crisis such as this it comes with a compelling force, though not without a warning. If a people or its religion claim superiority, Amos (iii. 2), without denying it, utters his

[1] Cf. *Rebirth*, pp. 119, 198.

warning (p. 174). Should a Church pay too much heed to institutional requirements, it may be neglecting the weightier matters (Matt. xxiii. 23 f.). For Paul, the transition from the old Israel to the new, the Israel of God, was not to be taken as final (Rom. xi. 17–24); of supreme significance though the step was from the secular point of view, and one that on the religious plane could only be interpreted as due to the direct intervention of God, revealing himself afresh to a distressed and unstable world. During the growth and history of the Bible nations and states have risen and fallen; but 'the Word of the Lord abideth for ever' (1 Pet. i. 25, cf. Matt. xxiv. 35). The value of the Bible is not exhausted, 'Slowly the Bible of the race is writ'. To Jesus, as to the great prophets, there were the occasions when first things must come first; and of what these were, he and they had no doubt. It was Jesus who said, 'Lo, I am with you alway, even unto the end of the world' (Matt. xxviii. 20). He would come again; and one may surely believe that, were there a true spiritual revival, a 'rebirth of Christianity', subsequent ages would look back and interpret it as a 'Second Coming' after all.

EPILOGUE

THE preceding chapters, giving a very general introduction to the Bible, included the contents of the Bible itself and what was immediately relevant or illustrative, viz. the apocryphal and apocalyptic writings, archæology and the monuments. But besides the *object* of our attention and the light in which the Bible is to be viewed, not less important is the approach of the *subject*, viz. our approach to it.

The Bible is a book of unique spiritual and devotional value, but it raises many intellectual or academic questions, some of them affecting its religious significance, whereas others concern ancient history, archæology and anthropology. In a word, religion and scholarship cannot be severed. Nor can we sever the Bible from science. At the greatest turning-points in the history of the growth of the Bible men's ideas of God, man and the universe were involved. But the ' scientific ' and other knowledge of the past was vastly inferior to that which has accumulated since the Renaissance and Reformation, and we have to aim at an adjustment of ideas as reasonable for our day as were the earlier adjustments for their respective ages.

Scientific research has led to the recognition of the fundamental energy manifested in the multipicity of forms that are the subject-matter of science. Religion, in its turn, recognizes the direct or indirect operation of a Divine Power or Holy Spirit in God's universe. Energy is manifested in the outside world, in nature, and also in man when acting and thinking, and even when thinking on the religious plane. But energy takes many forms that are destructive and harmful to man, and progressive religion in its turn is often confronted by wrong ideas of God, misguided ideals and false idealism. And while we find order and law in nature—else we could not live and exploit it as we do—so the function of religion is to inspire and order ways of life and thought in harmony with its basic convictions which it can ascribe only to the ultimate Energy or Spirit—the Supreme God of the Universe.

Man has 'constructed' his knowledge of this universe (see pp. 188 f., 200). These constructions have not been everywhere or always identical. Our own derive from the Bible and the Christianity based upon it, and are now found to need 'reconstruction'. In the 'Kingdom of God' and the 'Body of Christ' are two great pregnant conceptions which have not yet been given concrete reality by the world —or by Christianity itself.[1] Yet the conception of Christ as the ultimate unifying principle of reason, order and truth surely demands the effort to co-ordinate afresh our ideas touching God, man and the universe. As it is, amid the ebb and flow of thought some ideas have become emasculated, notably those of life and death, and man's destiny. Specific conceptions of the hereafter and of heaven and hell no longer prevail, although the underlying experiences and convictions which evoked them remain untouched and cannot be ignored with impunity.[2] Whatever the 'other world' may mean for us severally, we cannot be indifferent to the reality of that Divine Power or Energy which embraces us, and in which we live and move and have our being (pp. 188, 198, 201).

Only too obvious in our age are the effects of the destructive, fanatical, intolerant and irrational schemes of men. Minds are devoted with untiring zeal to destructive plans, to scientific, social, political and other activities, but the efforts to embody the fundamental principles of life in religion, theology and philosophy are meanwhile as narrow in their foundations as they are restricted in their scope. Difficult times lie ahead with controversial questions that cannot be settled rationally by force or by might. The simple fact is that the world has not recognized the reality of the Divine Power in the universe. To understand what it has been in the past we must turn to the Bible as interpreted in the light of modern knowledge (p. 208 f.).

[1] See p. 128, and *Rebirth of Christianity*, pp. 24 f., 184, 196.
[2] See *Rebirth of Christianity*, pp. 138, 178.

CHRONOLOGICAL NOTES

Biblical chronology bristles with difficulties. Our sources are: (1) The Bible, where its own evidence is at times inconsistent, or that of the ancient Greek version conflicts with it; (2) the 'external' evidence, that of the monuments, which is invaluable, but at times inconclusive, and must always be treated critically, and (3) the archaeological evidence, whose date depends upon (1) and (2). Furthermore, we have to distinguish between (*a*) the chronological system, or rather systems, which were evidently, or apparently, used by one or other of the biblical writers, and (*b*) an absolute system of dates which can be accepted. Remarks on biblical chronology are to be found in most of the various books referred to below (pp. 216 ff.), and it may be observed, in passing, that the familiar ' Usher's chronology ' in the A.V. (first printed in 1701) is untenable, although as it approaches the fall of Jerusalem, which it dates at 588 B.C., it is pretty near the mark.[1]

The history of Palestine goes back to remote times. By the twentieth century B.C. the ' Bible lands ' are in close contact and a very general cultural similarity can be traced through South-west Asia and Egypt. A convenient starting-point is afforded by the contemporary Twelfth Dynasty of Egypt and the First Babylonian Dynasty. Jerusalem was already known to Egypt (p. 134), and it is probable that the famous Babylonian law-giver Hammurabi of the First Dynasty (p. 24) was supposed to be the Amraphel of Gen. xiv. 1. The biblical chronologists had some sort of material upon which to work (note Num. xiii. 22), and they probably associated the age of their great ancestor Abraham with what was a Golden Age in Babylonia and Egypt. But it does not follow that we can agree with them. The date of Hammurabi has gradually been lowered by specialists, even to round about 1800 B.C.; and if Amraphel's ally Tidal may be identified with a Hittite king of the seventeenth century B.C., the date of Abraham must be lowered correspondingly.

No less open to dispute are the dates of the Exodus and the Conquest of Palestine. It is at least certain that the age illustrated by the Amarna Letters (pp. 28, 134), the Ras Shamra tablets (p. 24), and numerous Hittite and other monuments was one of outstanding importance; it can fairly be called—

---

[1] See the *Cambridge Ancient History*, Vol. i, ch. 4, and the synchronistic tables at the end of the several volumes, also the writer's ' *Truth* ' *of the Bible*, pp. 329 ff., Oesterley and Robinson, *History of Israel*, i. 454 ff., ii. 19 ff., 466 ff., Miss Hippisley in *The Teacher's Commentary* (ed. Hugh Martin), pp. 386–405, and T. W. Manson, *Companion to the Bible*, pp. 492 ff.

popularly—the 'Mosaic Age'. Land-movements by Aramaeans, the activity of Philistines and other peoples of the Levant, and the occupation of Palestine by the tribes of Israel make the whole period about 1400–1200 B.C. a crucial one. On purely *a priori* grounds one might assume a sweeping conquest under Joshua, a religious movement like the rise of Mohammed, and the rapid conquests of Islam (A.D. 634–644), and replacing the old deities of Palestine by Yahweh (p. 155 f.). But what of the biblical evidence and an absolute dating? The descent into Egypt may have been associated with the Hyksos invasion, and the Exodus with their expulsion (about 1600 B.C.). Or the descent may have been in the time of the Amarna Letters, in the reign of Amenhotep IV (Ikhnaton), whose accession is placed at 1380 or 1375 B.C. The O.T. narratives point to (*a*) a twofold entry into Palestine (from the south and from the east), and (*b*) a gradual settlement and not the sweeping conquests of Joshua. Of this twofold entry, the earlier has been placed in Ikhnaton's day, the later in the reign of Merneptah, his predecessor Ramses II (1235 or 1225) being the Pharaoh of the oppression. Great importance has been attached to the independent archaeological evidence for the destruction of Jericho by Joshua (ch. vi); but experts differ as to the date, the suggestions being 1450–1385, or 1375–1300, or 1250–1200, or a double fall, about 1370 and 1187.[1]

The dates for the three kings of united Israel, Saul, David and Solomon, may be given as 1025–937, though a recent authority (Mowinckel) argues for 995–929. Rehoboam and Jeroboam I stand at the head of the two kingdoms of Judah and Israel respectively. The dates for the campaigns of Assyria in the west are fairly certain. Ahab was a member of an anti-Assyrian league defeated by Shalmaneser at the battle of Karkar in 853 B.C., and Jehu paid tribute to him in 841 B.C. This is a starting-point for the chronology of a period with which are associated the prophets Elijah and Elisha (1 Kings xvii–2 Kings x), though Elisha appears nearly fifty years later, in the reign of Joash (2 Kings xiii. 14–19), as an aged man, but apparently as one who had played a part in the Aramaean–Israelite wars after the accession of Jehu.

The middle of the eighth century B.C. is the age of the two powerful contemporary kings, Jeroboam II of Israel and Uzziah (Azariah) of Judah. It is the age of Amos, Hosea and Micah (p. 56), and in Greece of Hesiod (p. 21). The Assyrian campaigns lead to the fall of Samaria (722–721 B.C.) and Sennacherib's unsuccessful siege of Jerusalem (701). Contemporary with the latter is the prophet Isaiah and his writings, Isa. i–xxxiii (with the omission of xxiv–xxvii and various passages).

---

[1] See, *e.g.*, on the whole question, Rowley, *Israel's Sojourn in Egypt* (Rylands Bulletin, 1938), and *Journal of Near Eastern Studies*, April, 1944.

We approach an age of sweeping changes over a wide area. These include the astonishingly rapid decline of Assyria (Nineveh fell in 612 B.C.), the rise of the Neo-Babylonian Empire (from 605), and the Persian conquests with the capture of Babylon by Cyrus, 539 B.C. During these years the leading biblical events are the reforms ascribed to Josiah (621 B.C.) following the ' discovery' of Deuteronomy (p. 35), the capture of Jerusalem and the first deportation (597 B.C.), the destruction of the city and temple and the second deportation (586), the return of exiles and the building of the second temple (520–16). To this period belong the prophets (a) Zephaniah, Habakkuk and Nahum, (b) Jeremiah, Ezekiel and Lamentations, (c) the Second Isaiah, which marks a turning-point (p. 163), and (d) Haggai and Zechariah i–viii, the prophets of the restoration. How much more belongs to the period is disputed.

Important developments are associated with the activities of Nehemiah, who visited Jerusalem (in 444 and 432 B.C.), and of Ezra. There is a growing tendency to place the latter some years after Nehemiah, namely, in the reign of Artaxerxes II (397 B.C.). The general trend of criticism is to ascribe more and more of the O.T. *in its present form* to the exilic and especially the post-exilic periods; but for the many questions herein involved—and which lie quite outside the scope of this book—the various handbooks must be consulted.

During the seventh–fifth centuries B.C. we pass from an old Oriental epoch to the increasing prominence of Persia and Greece —and subsequently Rome. A new stage in human history is being set, not only in secular history but in the realm of religious, ethical and other thought. It is enough to refer to the Orphic movements in the west, Zoroaster (about 600 B.C.) and Buddha (560–480), and in China, Lao-tse and Confucius (551–484). These, together with the Second Isaiah and the Greek tragedians and thinkers (p. 21 f.) gave a new direction to all subsequent spiritual and intellectual life.

Among the dates for the late post-exilic period may be noted the fall of the Persian Empire to Alexander the Great in 332 B.C., the probable date of *Daniel*, 166 B.C., followed by the Maccabaean and Hasmonaean activities, and the beginning of Roman supremacy after Pompey's entry into Jerusalem, 63 B.C.

For the chronology of the New Testament the references to Roman names and events are, of course, the guide. But here, too, there is unfortunately much uncertainty, the date of the Crucifixion being placed varyingly from 29 to 31 A.D., though some accept 33 A.D. as the most probable.[1] The following dates may be given: Tiberius, A.D. 14–37 (John the Baptist,

[1] Streeter (*Cambridge Ancient History*, Vol. x. 649 n.) and Manson, following Fotheringham. A full discussion of the dates in *Acts* is contributed by Lake in *Beginnings of Christianity* (below, p. 217), v. 445–74.

about A.D. 28, Luke iii. 1); Pontius Pilate, Procurator of Judaea, 26; the famine in Judaea (Acts xi. 28), and the Council of Jerusalem, 45–6; banishment of the Jews from Rome by Claudius (Acts xviii. 2), 49; Gallio (Acts xviii. 12), 51–2; persecution of Christians by Nero, 64; fall of Jerusalem, 70; destruction of Jerusalem, 135. Josephus (born c. 37) wrote his *War, c.* 75–79, and *Jewish Antiquities, c.* 93–4. The Hebrew Old Testament canon and text were fixed about A.D. 100, and to the latter decades of the first century are ascribed the books of the New Testament, the dates ranging from A.D. 65 (or earlier, according to Torrey) onwards.

BIBLIOGRAPHICAL NOTES

So extensive is the literature on the Bible that it is impossible to do more than offer a few miscellaneous suggestions. Most books contain bibliographical information; a ' Scripture Bibliography for Teachers in Secondary Schools and Bible Students ' is published by Nisbet, and a bibliography is also issued by the Central Society of Sacred Study (Cambridge University Press).

An edition of the Bible and Apocrypha in the Revised Version with references and marginal notes is strongly recommended. It is difficult to suggest a course of reading. No reader should ignore *Amos*, the *Second Isaiah* (chh. xl–lv), and especially the Psalms, of which it has been said, ' You may fitly call the Psalter a Bible in miniature '. For the New Testament one might suggest, to start with, *Luke*, the Fourth Gospel and *Ephesians*. But every reader will have his own preferences, and some account of the contents of the Bible and Apocrypha is given in chh. iv and v. There are also anthologies (with notes) by W. R. Inge, *Every Man's Bible* (1931), *A Short Bible* by V. J. Brook and others (1933), and *A Bedside Bible* by A. Stanley (1942).

Among general books may be named, P. C. Sands, *The Literary Genius of the Old Testament* (1924); N. S. Talbot, *A Biblical Thoroughfare* (' an endeavour to share the main results of biblical scholarship with the general public ', 1928); S. C. Carpenter, *The Bible View of Life* (1937); H. E. Fosdick, *A Guide To Understanding the Bible* (on the development of ideas, 1938), and C. Ryder Smith, *The Bible Doctrine of Salvation* (1941).

For the English and other versions, see J. Baikie, *The English Bible and its History* (1928); the essays edited by H. W. Robinson in *Our Bible in its Ancient and English Versions* (1940), and Sir Frederic Kenyon, *The Story of the Bible* (' a popular account of how it came to us ', 1936), *Our Bible and the Ancient MSS.* (4th ed., 1939), also *The Reading of the Bible as History, Literature and Religion* (1944).

Among the dictionaries are the *Encyclopedia Biblica* and the Hastings *Bible Dictionary*, and the relevant articles in the *Encyclopaedia Britannica* (14th ed., fuller in the 11th ed.), and Chambers's *Encyclopedia*. There are several one-volume commentaries: Dummelow (1909), A. S. Peake (1920, with supplement by A. J. Grieve, 1936), Gore, Goudge and Guillaume (1923), the Abingdon (1929), the simpler *Teacher's Commentary* by Hugh Martin (2nd ed., 1935), to which may be added the handy *Companion to the Bible*, ed. by T. W. Manson (1939). Of the special commentaries, the *International Critical Com-*

mentary series is for students; more general are the *Cambridge Bible*, the *Century Bible*, the *Westminster* series, and the *Moffatt New Testament Commentary* series. Particular mention must be made of the admirable *Clarendon Bible* series.

For the Old Testament in general, see the essays edited by A. S. Peake (*The People and the Book*, 1925), E. Bevan and C. Singer (*The Legacy of Israel*, 1927), and H. W. Robinson (*Record and Revelation*, 1938). Invaluable are the works by W. O. E. Oesterley and T. H. Robinson: *Hebrew Religion* (1930, revised and enlarged, 1937), *History of Israel* (2 vols., 1932), and *Introduction to the Books of the Old Testament* (1934). See also J. N. Schofield, *The Historical Background of the Bible* (1938), and the interesting account by R. H. Kennett, *Ancient Hebrew Social Life and Custom* (1933).

For the apocryphal and apocalyptical literature, see the elaborate work edited by R. H. Charles, *Apocrypha and Pseudepigrapha of the Old Testament* (2 vols. 1913), his *Eschatology* (1913), and the concise account in *Religious Development between the Old and New Testaments* (Home University Library). There is a handy introduction to the Apocrypha by Oesterley (1935) and a general account by H. H. Rowley, *The Relevance of Apocalyptic* ('a study of Jewish and Christian Apocalypse from Daniel to the Revelation', 1944).

For the New Testament, see the *Reader's Guide*, by C. A. Alington (1938), the Introductions by F. B. Clogg (1937), K. V. S. Lake (1938) and Maurice Jones, *The New Testament in the Twentieth Century* (3rd ed., 1934); also Hoskyns and Davey, *The Riddle of the New Testament* (1931), and, for students, Foakes Jackson and Lake's valuable work (by several writers), *The Beginnings of Christianity: the Acts of the Apostles* (5 vols., 1920–33). For the background, see G. H. C. Macgregor and Purdy, *Jew and Greek: Tutors unto Christ* (1936), and the essays edited by Oesterley in *Judaism and Christianity*, Vol. I, *The Age of Transition* (1937). There are 'harmonies' of the Gospels (see p. 70), by C. C. James (1909) and J. M. Thompson (1910).

For chh. ii and vii, reference may be made to Sir G. A. Smith, *The Historical Geography of the Holy Land* (26th ed.), and *Jerusalem* (2 vols. 1907); the essays edited by D. S. Simpson, *The Psalmists* (1926), and by S. H. Hooke, *Myth and Ritual* (1933) and *The Labyrinth* (1935); E. O. James, *Christian Myth and Ritual*, chh. i, xi (1933); W. C. Graham and H. May, *Culture and Conscience* ('an archaeological study of the new religious past in Ancient Palestine', 1936); S. L. Caiger, *Bible and Spade* (1936) and *The Old Testament and Modern Discovery* (1938); Sir F. Kenyon, *The Bible and Archaeology* (1940), and W. F. Albright, *The Archaeology of Palestine and the Bible; from the Stone Age to Christianity* (1940), with his other writings. Attention may also be drawn to the volumes in the *Schweich Lectures on Biblical Archaeology*, and to the relevant chapters in the

Cambridge Ancient History (with full bibliographies), vols: i, chh. 4 f., ii. 13 f., iii. 3–5, 16–20, iv. 1, 7, vi. 7, vii. 5, 22, viii. 16, ix. 9, x. 11, xi. 7, and, for the immediate post-N.T. period, xii. 13–15.[1]

Finally, the following compilations may be mentioned: *The Bible of the World* by R. O. Ballou (1940), *The Eleven Religions* by S. A. Champion (1944), and—not seen—*Tongues of Fire* ('a Bible of Sacred Scriptures of the Pagan World') by Grace H. Turnbull (U.S.A., 1929).[2]

[1] Besides *The Rebirth of Christianity*, chh. ii, ix–xi (see also Index, *s*. Bible, Christ), and the works mentioned there on p. 212, the present writer may refer to his *Religion of Ancient Palestine in the Light of Archaeology* (1930).

[2] Mention should be made of the following books which have appeared since the above was written. R. L. Arundale, *Religious Education in the Senior School*; N. H. Snaith, *The Distinctive Ideas of the Old Testament*; and especially J. N. Schofield, *The Religious Background of the Bible*.

INDEX

The index includes the usual abbreviations of the books of the Bible, and references are sometimes made to the biblical and other footnotes in order to indicate more closely the part of the page in question.

219